'*Out of Control* is a call to action challenging and profoundly dis............ must-read for every church leader.'

Kate Coleman, founder and co-director of Next Leadership

'When I first began to review books, two decades ago, I was a jobbing pastor, and took a vow that I would never write 'every pastor should read this book' – the life is too busy, and too varied, for that ever to be true. Or so I thought. Today I repent: every pastor should read Natalie Collins's book, and should give it to their leaders to read as well. Domestic violence is an enormous hidden plague that infects every community, and every congregation, in the land, and Natalie exposes the reality of this, and points to practical steps we can all take to help.

Even better, Natalie communicates out of deep expertise, but simply, even colloquially. And all her passion, all her hope, all her joy, all her humour, are present in this book. It is a magnificent achievement, and it matters. Read it!'

Dr Stephen Holmes, Senior Lecturer in Systematic Theology,
University of St Andrews

'No one who has met Natalie Collins will be surprised at this book. It is authentically hers, full of energy, insight, quirks and personal narrative. Few people can pepper a serious, even scholarly, book on domestic abuse with comments that leave you laughing out loud! But finding humour in tragedy is Natalie's great gift, as is her refusal to be cowed by what she has gone through. This book is both realistic and hopeful, opening a window on abusers and abused, not least by Natalie's personification of the "tactics of torture". The profiles of abusing partners, and the struggles of those who suffer, will be soberly familiar to many. Written with Christian wisdom and vigour, Natalie's up-to-date, well-researched and "must-read" book challenges us all to work ever harder towards the eradication of violence against women.'

Elaine Storkey, broadcaster, philosopher, theologian and author of Scars Across Humanity: Understanding and overcoming violence against women

Natalie Collins is a gender justice specialist and set up Spark to enable individuals and organizations to prevent and respond to male violence against women. She is the creator and director of the DAY Programme, an innovative youth domestic abuse and exploitation education programme, and she seeks to improve the representation of women within Christian culture through organizing Project 3:28. She is a co-founder of the UK Christian Feminist Network, founded the Fifty Shades Is Domestic Abuse campaign, and has written the Own My Life course for women who have been subjected to male violence. She blogs and tweets as God Loves Women, and she speaks and writes nationally and internationally about understanding and ending gender injustice. She has written a Grove book on gender-aware youth practice, has contributed to various other publications, and is working towards an MA in Integrative Theology. She is a northerner living in Essex with her awesome husband, excellent children and adorable dog.

OUT OF CONTROL

Couples, conflict and
the capacity for change

Natalie Collins

First published in Great Britain in 2019

Society for Promoting Christian Knowledge
36 Causton Street
London SW1P 4ST
www.spck.org.uk

British Library Cataloguing-in-Publication Data
A catalogue record for this book is available from the British Library

ISBN 978–0–281–07890–5
eBook ISBN 978–0–281–07891–2

Typeset in 10.5/15 pt Bembo by Falcon Oast Graphic Art Ltd
First printed in Great Britain by Ashford Colour Press
Subsequently digitally reprinted in Great Britain

eBook by Falcon Oast Graphic Art Ltd

Produced on paper from sustainable forests

This book is dedicated to my dear friend Susan King,
whose knowledge, love and compassion
inspire me and teach me so much

Contents

Acknowledgements

There are lots of people I am grateful to for their support and wisdom in making this book a reality:

Nicola, Irene, Lauren, Anna and Alex, for reading through the book and sharing their wisdom and ideas with me; Paula Gooder and Steve Holmes, who responded to my theological questions with great wisdom, and my brother Danjo, who was on hand to help with legal stuff; Dave and Charlotte Walker, who invited me round to discuss book names, and Vicky Walker and Hannah Mudge, who have been on hand to offer their thoughts; Thomas Creedy, who was super-encouraging in getting me to consider writing the book, and Juliet, my editor, who has been lovely, encouraging and supportive; the team at SPCK, who are all part of making the book happen; the many women who have shared their lives with me, and I with them, whose tenacity and courage are the reason I continue to believe that change must be possible; the foremothers whose shoulders I gratefully stand upon, Elaine Storkey, Catherine Clark Kroeger and many others; the women working tirelessly to run women's services across the UK – support workers, counsellors, managers, children's workers, IDVAs, ISVAs – who continue to provide safe spaces for women, while their budgets shrink and the political demands on them increase; the feminists who've become my friends even though I'm a weirdo who loves Jesus; the generous people who support my work financially and through prayer, and those over the years who have worked with me and championed me; my husband Baggy, whose dedication to me and our family enables me to do all of the things I do, and our children, who make life excellent. Finally, to God be the glory in all that I do, for it is in him that I live and move and have my being.

1 Pretending I'm a traffic warden (What is this book about?)

The words 'domestic violence' provoke within each person a different story, feeling or mental image. They might involve a previous relationship, an ex-partner who harmed them in ways they have never shared or images they've seen in online articles of a bruised woman cowering in a corner. Some will envisage a large brutish council-estate resident swearing at strangers and being generally unpleasant. Others will feel the terror of a childhood lived in fear creeping into their hearts. The term 'domestic violence' is not value-neutral. We all bring our own perceptions, prejudices and personal stories to its meaning.

I am more keenly aware of this than most people. During social gatherings, hairdressing appointments and when passing the time of day with strangers, I find the topic of employment often comes up. 'What do you do for work?' asks the hairdresser. As I'm balancing an array of bring-and-share produce (including a large helping of quiche) on a paper plate at a friend's church, the vicar, head nonchalantly tipped to one side, asks: 'So, Natalie, what is it that you *do*?' The nice older woman in the café notices I'm working on my laptop: 'You look busy. What are you working on?'

Sometimes I'm tempted to give an answer that will cause less discomfort: pest control specialist, chiropodist, bailiff, even traffic warden. But no, as a good Christian I tell them the truth, explaining that I'm a specialist in addressing domestic abuse issues. In more recent years I have begun describing myself with the more generic term 'Gender Justice Specialist', which inevitably requires further explanation; I still have to utter those destabilizing words, 'domestic abuse'.

Let us take a short diversion away from my career disclosure over a plate of quiche. The eagle-eyed among you may have noticed that I switched from using the term 'domestic violence' to 'domestic abuse'. O eagle-eyed reader, let me tell you more about that shift in terminology. First used in 1787, the term 'domestic violence' referred to civil unrest but by the 1970s it was commonly understood as violence within the home.[1] In 1973, MP John Ashley was the first to raise the modern usage of the term in the UK parliament when he declared, 'Thousands of men in this country are subjecting their wives to physical brutality.'[2] As understanding grew, 'domestic violence' was understood to include brutality perpetrated within any intimate relationship. Unlike in North America, in the UK the terms 'battery' and 'battered woman' are rarely used to describe violence in relationships, particularly as the British verb 'to batter' refers to the coating of fish with a fried flour-and-egg mixture.

As understanding about domestic violence perpetration grew, it became apparent the terminology was limiting societal understanding. Although those working to address the issues saw brutality enacted within a relationship as being far wider than physical violence, media outlets, medical professionals, social workers, family members, friends and those subjected to domestic violence themselves viewed domestic violence as solely physical violence. Where abusers used mental torture, emotional manipulation, coercion or threats, many didn't consider that to be domestic *violence*. As such, there was a move to relabel it 'domestic abuse'. From the early 1990s we see the frequency of 'domestic abuse' growing within common usage.[3] These are not *different* issues; domestic abuse is recognized to be an inclusive term which more effectively represents the reality.

Let us now return to my hairdresser, the nice older woman

in the café and the bring-and-share vicar. After I utter the words 'domestic abuse', there are generally four responses. The person:

1 says, 'Oh, that must be rewarding. I bet you hear some *terrible* stories';
2 looks hot and flustered and rushes to exit the conversation;
3 smiles knowingly and explains own job role, which involves work around domestic abuse issues;
4 shares own or a friend's story of being subjected to abuse by a partner.

We all have our own reasons for wanting to know more about domestic abuse issues. For some it is a grim fascination with the horrors in the world. This is why so many 'misery memoirs' exist, which describe in graphic and unrelenting detail the terrible ways the author has been treated. Some are comforted to know their personal horror is not unique, while others read such books out of voyeuristic self-interest. Yet others want to know more about domestic abuse because their professional or voluntary role has brought them into contact with people who have been subjected to abuse, or with those who have chosen to abuse. They want to build their knowledge and skillset to offer better care. While there are people who abandon me mid-quiche – to avoid having to hear more about an issue that they think either has no relevance to their life or is all too relevant, with the idea of knowing any more filling them with such dread that all social niceties are lost – many have grown up with a parent who was harmful and unkind, while others have been damaged by a current or former partner. Some have a teenage or adult child who is being gradually decimated by a partner, or a close friendship that has been eroded by a friend's abusive partner. They may feel totally overwhelmed and confused, oscillating between wanting to rescue their friend or family member and feeling as though they have nothing left to give, tempted to abandon the person because of the exhaustion and never-endingness of it all.

Whatever your reason for picking up this book, I'm hoping it will be helpful to you. Most people avoid the subject of domestic abuse. I want to applaud your bravery in purchasing this book and committing to learn more (unless you're currently flicking through it at a bookstall, in which case I shall applaud you later . . .). In fact, take a moment to applaud yourself for choosing to read this book. Except *you*, book peruser, who will look silly clapping yourself in the bookshop and must purchase this book immediately and delay the self-applause until you are alone.

I have delivered training, talks and keynote speeches about domestic abuse issues to thousands of people including professionals working within medicine, social care, probation and youth offending, youth workers, teachers, those in the housing sector, the women's sector, the corporate sector and more. My work includes years of programme provision for women who have been subjected to abuse, alongside work with young people and youth practitioners in my role as Director of the DAY Programme, which is a domestic abuse and exploitation education programme for young people.[4] I have delivered programmes to male perpetrators of domestic abuse and have written national resources on child sexual exploitation, domestic abuse and young people, understanding pornography, gender-aware youth practice (I even wrote a Grove Booklet on this) and materials for working with women who have been subjected to abuse. I am a Christian and love Jesus a lot.

Throughout the last decade I have worked with many different denominations and Christians, and have variously found myself writing for national newspapers, speaking on national television, attending a Catholic bishops' conference, writing chapters for people's books, voicing lots of opinions on social media (mainly Twitter) and sharing a platform with a few bishops (apparently the name for a group of bishops is a psalter: a psalter of bishops, a school of fish, a gaggle of geese and a superfluity of nuns[5] – yes, really!).

Delivering domestic abuse awareness training in a church, I

began discussing with the participants what their training expectations were. I stated that I expected us to have fun. One participant vehemently disagreed with such a sentiment and had no qualms about telling me so. She felt that fun would be highly inappropriate, making light of a topic that should always be serious. Domestic abuse is the primary topic of much of my life. This participant might choose to approach the issue in misery; however, I want to bring life and hope to a subject that is inevitably distressing and painful. The subject must be approached with a suitable degree of seriousness. Never should someone's experiences be laughed at. But to bring humour, fun and, dare I say, *joy* to the issue of domestic abuse can prevent it having too much power over us. As Salman Rushdie has said, 'Those who do not have power over the story that dominates their lives, power to retell it, rethink it, deconstruct it, joke about it, and change it as times change, truly are powerless, because they cannot think new thoughts.'[6]

Charlie Chaplin is quoted as saying, 'I believe in the power of laughter and tears as an antidote to hatred and terror.' In Genesis 21.6, Isaac was so named because Sarah laughed at the ridiculousness of having a child in old age. Science has found that laughter relaxes your body, boosts your immune system, triggers the release of endorphins, can protect you against a heart attack and may even help you live longer.[7] My attempts to lighten the darkness of domestic abuse may not achieve all these, but laughter is proven to help. My tone may be light in places and might feel at odds with the seriousness of the topic; however, I hope you will humour me (pun intended!). Laughter can help us break some of the power of abuse in the world. Cancer survivor Scott Burton explains,

> The other reactions; anger, depression, suppression, denial, took a little piece of me with them. Each made me feel just a little less human. Yet laughter made me more open to ideas, more inviting to others, and even a little stronger inside. It proved to me that, even as my body was devastated and my spirit challenged, I was still a vital human.[8]

I was born into Christianity. My mum didn't give birth to me on to a church pew, but I was born on a Sunday. (According to the nursery rhyme this makes me bonnie, blithe, happy, wise, good and gay.) My dad rushed to their Elim church's evening service and ran down the aisle announcing, 'It's a girl! She's called Natalie Joy!' That was 1984. Within two years we had moved to our local family-friendly Anglican church. The 1980s and 1990s were of course the most awesome decades for Christian culture (along with fashion, music and television shows, obviously). This may be the rose-tinted lenses of childhood, but I don't think so. I grew up loving church. We had Psalty the Singing Songbook (you can Google him to find out more; other search engines are available), amazing action songs, marching for Jesus, Maranatha Praise parties and Ishmael concerts. What a time to be alive and loving Jesus!

At the start of the new millennium, I was a naive 17-year-old armed with all the information Christian culture had deemed necessary for me to form romantic relationships. I knew the potential suitor must be a self-proclaimed Christian. As long as he was washed in the blood of the Lamb, he was a goer. No questions need be asked of his character: his stated belief in Jesus as his Saviour was enough. That was Part 1 of Christian Relationship Education 101. Part 2 was about *not* having sex. Variously this involved not touching things you don't have (the ubiquity of nipples and bottoms clearly going unnoticed), limiting alone time with the must-be-Christian romantic interest and taking every thought captive. That was it, the focus quickly shifting to more important topics: forgiveness, evangelism and mission. Many Christians (including those who are still young people today) will be nodding at my experiences. This is still the norm for Christian culture.

As a teenager, I viewed sex before marriage as the ultimate betrayal of Jesus, the modern-day Judas kiss. Seventeen-year-old me met a handsome young man – let's call him Craig (his name is not really Craig). Craig told me he was a Christian, making him acceptable boyfriend material. When he coerced and manipulated me into sexual activity, the parts of me that felt uncomfortable, fearful and degraded I explained away as 'What It Feels Like to Betray Jesus'. This was the beginning of a four-year relationship in which Craig utterly decimated me. He made me hate myself. He made me think that I was worth nothing, that I was ugly and fat and that everything he did wrong was my fault. I stayed with him, first because his sexual coercion meant I had betrayed Jesus, then because within six months I was pregnant. At 18 I married him, thinking that I was honouring God.

Throughout this book I will share my experiences of Craig's abuse and of my recovery. I'll bring composite stories that encompass the realities of hundreds of women I've had the privilege of journeying with. Rather than being individual women's stories, they will contain elements of many stories. None will be exaggerations and all will resonate with the experiences of women that you, dear reader, may already know: women in your church, community, family or friendship group. Maybe they include the woman you see at the school gate when you pick up your children, your boss at work or the woman who comes to read your electricity meter. Or maybe, dear reader, the stories will resonate with you.

I can approach this topic with humour because it is my own story. I know the pain and damage abusive behaviour can cause, but I also know the power of liberation; when we are 'clothed with strength and dignity; [and] can laugh at the days to come'.[9]

You may be curious about my focus on women here. When I deliver training, 'Men can be subjected to abuse and violence too!' is the most commonly raised comment. There are a number of motivations for such a comment. They generally fit into three categories that shall henceforth be known as Bob, Valerie and Rodger. Bob knows a man who has been subjected to abuse or has himself had an abusive partner. Valerie has heard from somewhere (perhaps a Facebook meme) that men are subjected to violence at the same rates as women. She feels that my focus on women is unjust. She thinks my reverse sexism should be challenged. Valerie might have heard a statistic that one in three victims of domestic abuse is male or that men find it harder to report violence, thereby skewing the statistics. Rodger isn't interested in any of that. He is engaging in 'whataboutery' (i.e. what about the men?). His purpose is to derail me and undermine my credibility. I haven't done scientific research into Bob, Valerie and Rodger, but in a decade of delivering presentations I estimate that approximately 10 per cent are Bob; they are personally invested in their experiences being represented and feel that by focusing on women I am invalidating their story. About 70 per cent are Valerie, while 20 per cent are Rodger.

Men *can* be subjected to abuse. Abuse perpetrated against anybody is unjust and should be addressed and challenged. However, the one in three statistic that Valerie may have heard is incorrect. The figures below are for 2016, but they remain static for domestic abuse-related crime in England and Wales.

- Of defendants, 92.1 per cent were male, 7.9 per cent were female.
- Of victims, 83.3 per cent were female and 16.7 per cent were male.[10]

Valerie's suspicion that this disparity is underreporting from men is also incorrect. There are lots of communities that do not report domestic abuse-related crime, yet we know the rates are high. For instance, reporting from the Traveller community is incredibly low, yet one survey found that 61 per cent of English Gypsy women and 81 per cent of Irish Gypsy women have a partner who has abused them.[11] Research has found that women are three times more likely than men to be arrested when either is reported as a perpetrator of domestic abuse, which suggests that it is women and not men who are failed by the system.[12] Another indicator where underreporting does not account for statistical disparities is UK murder rates; of all victims of homicide, 44 per cent of women and 6 per cent of men are killed by a partner.[13] In 2002, it was found that around 93.9 per cent of adults who were convicted of murder were men. The British activist Karen Ingala-Smith, who has pioneered a femicide census, explains:

> [N]early always when a woman kills a man, the woman herself has been a victim of his violence or abuse. When men kill women they tend to have been perpetrators of violence against that woman and other women for years.[14]

Throughout this book I will refer to those subjected to abuse as female and those who perpetrate abuse as male. I am not seeking to invalidate or undermine the experiences of men, those not in heterosexual relationships or those who don't identify as either women or men. I refer to women as those who are abused, primarily because this has been the focus of my work and because it is the most likely situation you, dear reader, will be presented with. It is not a value judgement; I do not view all men as bad or all women as victims. It is a pragmatic decision based on the vast majority of situations where someone chooses to perpetrate domestic abuse. If you are Bob, or if you have been subjected to abuse within a same-sex relationship (or know someone who has), I hope you will still find this book helpful; Appendix 1 includes resources that may be useful for you. Many of the dynamics of abuse are universal, and hopefully you will be able to switch the pronouns around to make them appropriate for your circumstances. For me to attempt to generically address everyone in this book would dishonour the experiences and pain of men, gay and lesbian people and those who are trans★. The asterisk on trans★ 'makes special note in an effort to include all transgender, non-binary, and gender nonconforming identities'.[15] If you are Bob, or gay, lesbian or a trans★ person, and are passionate about addressing domestic abuse, maybe this is an opportunity. A decade ago God called me to address domestic abuse issues. Since then I have built up the expertise to write a book on the topic. Maybe this is the start of a similar decade for you! This is not the only book about Christians and domestic abuse that needs to be written (I hope my editor doesn't mind me saying this!). Take what you can from this book. Hopefully it will inspire you to ensure that books are written to represent other facets of domestic abuse.

For some people, Christian teaching has been so toxic that their faith was lost in their recovery; that is not the case for me. It is not hyperbole to say that I would be dead without Jesus. I am a full-on, sold-out Christian. Some view faith as a crutch for the weak to lean on. It's much more than that for me. It's the life support system that keeps me living and breathing. You may have already noticed this is a Christian book, but in case you hadn't, THIS IS A CHRISTIAN BOOK! If you're not a Christian and you've somehow picked this book up/accidentally ordered it online/had it thrust upon you by a well-meaning friend or colleague and you've managed to get all the way to page 10, then give yourself a pat on the back! This book will have lots of useful content for you as a non-Christian. It will be factually accurate and will not veer into such debates as whether Noah's ark was real or if creation took place in seven 24-hour days. It will, however, include content specific to the cultural and theological positions of Christian people. You are very welcome to skip straight past those sections. I hope that in spite of our differing faith positions, you will find this book useful. And perhaps, if you choose not to skip through the Christian bits, you might be better equipped in your friendships with Christian women. That's not just a way of convincing you to read *all of my words*, but because we Christian women are everywhere! We work and do shopping and even frequent such places as nightclubs. And if we've been brought up or enculturated in Christianity, there is a load of stuff we've learned about relationships, marriage, gender and life that it would be helpful for you to know.

I have written this book primarily to help those who are seeking to understand domestic abuse issues better so they are better able to support those subjected to abuse. As I write this book I am in the middle of a Master's in Integrative Theology, so a great big hello to any of you reading this book as part of your academic study! I hope, if you've picked this book up because it speaks to your own story, that it will also be of great value to you. You will know how best to safely read this book. If you are still in a relationship with someone who is harmful, you may need to keep this book hidden or sneak reads of it in your local bookshop. Maybe you can keep it at your workplace or ask a friend to look after it for you. You are the most qualified person to decide what will enable you to stay safe and you are awesome, even if you don't feel it right now.

Some of what I cover in this book will be painful, disturbing and difficult to read. For those with personal stories of trauma, either currently or in the past, it could trigger a physiological response or difficult feelings. I have found certain resources so overwhelming that I could only look at them in 30-second bursts. And that is OK! Whatever the reason, it's OK to find it difficult. Triggers feel awful, but they can be opportunities for addressing our pain. The important thing is that you feel in control of the process. Even if it takes you five years to read this book in 30-second sections every week (this is not a mathematical calculation), that's OK. This is *your* process and it belongs to you.

I attended a workshop a few years ago and the content triggered me into a traumatized state. For days afterwards my brain was foggy and my body felt as if it didn't belong to me. After I emailed the workshop facilitator to ask for help, he responded with a science-based explanation for how I was feeling and suggested I go for a run (the sciencey stuff about this is in Chapter 9). I'd done a bit of running years previously and thought that I'd have a go. It couldn't hurt (well, apart from the breathlessness, muscle aches and all that). I decided to go for a run and something amazing happened. My brain woke up. *I can go for a run!* I realized. I wasn't beholden to the feelings or zombie state. I realized it was *my* body and that I could take charge of it. I went for a run and immediately felt better.

At other times I've needed to access professional support. Deciding to go for a run isn't always going to fix it, and plenty of people have physical restrictions that prevent running from being an option. I thought it might be handy to provide you with self-care ideas to help you make it through this book in one piece, still at peace. It may or may not be helpful to you, but be aware that your body belongs to you and if it starts feeling out of sorts then you can take action to look after yourself. Here is Natalie's Self-care List.

- Make a cup of tea/coffee/hot chocolate.
- Drink water.
- Go outside. Get some fresh air.
- Go for a walk/run/gallop/bike ride.
- Write a list of things you are thankful for.
- Draw a picture.
- Write a poem.
- Have a pray.
- Place your hands on your knees and tap rhythmically. (There is actual science behind this. It stops your brain disconnecting from your body. In fact, anything that rhythmically uses both sides of the body can help: knitting, drumming, running, etc.)
- Do some colouring in.
- Take a moment to pause and become conscious of yourself.
- Play a song you love, and either sway gently to it or dance around your home frantically. Whatever works for you.
- Have a super-big cry. (Research shows that having a cry which ends with those big sighing sobs and the whimpering – where there's snot and tears everywhere – can help complete the stress cycle. Even if it is a bit messy!)[16]
- Ring someone you love for a chat.
- Eat cake.

At the start of this chapter, I mentioned how the term 'domestic violence' raises our preconceived ideas about what abuse is, who is subjected to it, who perpetrates it, why they perpetrate it and how we should respond. For some people those preconceived ideas may lead them to a response such as that of the aforementioned Rodger. They might feel so uncomfortable with the content that they simply discount it. If you find yourself feeling uncomfortable or disbelieving the content within this book, you could use that feeling as an opportunity to ask yourself why you feel that way. This book is well researched and founded on years of professional practice and personal experience, both mine and those of hundreds of other people.

Throughout the book I may move into talking in first-person plurals: 'we' and 'us'. When I am training practitioners to work with those who have been subjected to abuse I insist we all talk from I/we/us to enable us to remain non-judgemental and inclusive. For example, saying 'When you are abused, you might have reduced self-esteem' might imply that if *I* were abused, *I wouldn't* have reduced self-esteem. The only way we can ensure that our language doesn't appear judgemental, or doesn't negatively set those who have been subjected to abuse apart from those who haven't, is if we speak with first-person pronouns. This is a huge linguistic shift and can feel very uncomfortable, particularly if we presume that abuse happens to people unlike us.

Let us finish this chapter by pausing. Stop for a moment and reflect on what you've read so far. What thoughts and feelings has it raised for you?

If you are a Christian you could now take a moment to pray (if you are not, feel free to take extra time to pause, or move on to the next chapter). For the more charismatic among you, freestyle prayer may feel most appropriate. For those who prefer a written prayer to read and repeat, I hope this may be helpful:

God, please be with me as I continue reading. Give me an open heart and an open mind to hear you as I learn more about this issue of domestic abuse. Please enable me to know you more and be known by you more as I read and learn. Amen.

> We have an anchor that keeps the soul
> Steadfast and sure while the billows roll,
> Fastened to the Rock which cannot move,
> Grounded firm and deep in the Saviour's love.

> Priscilla J. Owens (1882)[17]

2 Bulldozing safety (Understanding harmful behaviour in relationships)

The UK government's definition of domestic abuse is comprehensive (and inevitably rather long):

> Any incident or pattern of incidents of controlling, coercive, threatening behaviour, violence or abuse between those aged 16 or over who are, or have been, intimate partners or family members regardless of gender or sexuality. The abuse can encompass, but is not limited to: psychological, physical, sexual, financial, emotional.
>
> *Controlling behaviour:* Controlling behaviour is a range of acts designed to make a person subordinate and/or dependent by isolating them from sources of support, exploiting their resources and capacities for personal gain, depriving them of the means needed for independence, resistance and escape and regulating their everyday behaviour.
>
> *Coercive behaviour:* Coercive behaviour is an act or a pattern of acts of assault, threats, humiliation and intimidation or other abuse that is used to harm, punish, or frighten their victim.[1]

This definition is not used within Scotland, where domestic abuse is recognized as 'one aspect of a range of forms of violence against women'.[2]

Although this is not a legal definition, the Serious Crime Act of 2015 created a new offence of controlling or coercive behaviour in an intimate or family relationship.[3] This book will focus primarily on domestic abuse perpetrated by men within heterosexual intimate relationships but, as this definition makes clear, there are other types of relationship in which someone can perpetrate domestic abuse, including wider family relationships, parent-to-adult-child and vice versa, adult siblings and wider family relationships (e.g. in-laws and stepfamily). Not included within this definition, but commonly understood to be an aspect of domestic abuse, is child-to-parent abuse. Although these situations are not the focus of this book, further resources are provided in Appendix 1 for those who would like additional support or information on wider forms of domestic abuse.

The UK definition delineates abuse into five categories: psychological, physical, sexual, financial and emotional. It also specifies two types of abusive behaviour: control and coercion. Although the five categories are widely used, I find they reduce the issues to clinical words that prevent us from fully envisaging what perpetrators actually *do*.

Sitting in a café, drinking a frappalapachino-type thing, I heard a woman's slightly raised voice, 'You've hit me once; you won't do it again.' Subtly turning, I saw a man with his back to me and a woman opposite. I began eavesdropping in a hopefully non-rude or at least non-obvious way. The woman's voice grew quieter as she asserted her feelings and the man awkwardly mumbled responses. I scribbled a list of helpful domestic abuse resources on scrap paper, awaiting a safe opportunity. She left the café alone. Quickly following her, I waited until we were away from her partner. I tapped her on the shoulder (hopefully in a non-weird way). Telling her I had overheard some of her conversation I handed her the note. She looked at me aghast. 'Oh no!' she said. 'It's not *abuse*. We're just going through a rough time at the minute.' She rushed off.

Rarely does anybody self-identify as being subjected to abuse. Whether there is physical violence or not, most of us find ways to avoid or deny labelling our partner as *abusive*. Either to other people or to ourselves, we will say things like:

- 'I know he can be unkind, but he doesn't mean it.'
- 'My ex-husband wasn't exactly abusive. He only held me against a wall by my throat once.'
- 'I make him so mad. He wouldn't do that if I didn't wind him up.'
- 'It's not abuse because he's a good man and I'm a strong woman.'

Throughout my relationship with Craig he was abusive. Constantly demeaning me (his pet name for me was C*ntface), he refused to share responsibility for any household tasks (he once hid a collection of teaspoons that he had washed; why should I benefit from his work?). He consistently lied to me, coerced me into sex, mocked me in front of his family and friends, physically harmed himself when I said I needed to separate from him, and made me 'let' him strangle me (so he would know how quickly I would pass out). I never identified his behaviour as abusive. Far too invested in the relationship, I was convinced that he was simply damaged and that my love and Jesus' love could fix him.

Craig regularly had affairs. Within 18 months of our relationship beginning, when he was 19, he was convicted of sexual offences relating to a teenage girl. After considering leaving, I stayed because I thought he would change, if only he could choose God. I had a huge fear about becoming a young single parent (I was 19 and the mother of a toddler) and convinced myself that being a married young mother (even with a sex-offender husband) was a better option. I wanted to make the relationship work and I believed that if I just forgave Craig and prayed enough, he *would* change.

After he was convicted, a childcare worker referred me to the local Women's Aid service. Five months pregnant with my second child, I sat opposite a well-meaning woman who kindly informed me that there was a space in a refuge if I wanted it. My face remained fixed while horror rose inside me. I didn't need to go into a refuge. I didn't need *Women's* Aid. I wasn't even a woman. I was still a girl!

My husband wasn't *abusive*, he was just having a difficult time. I left the meeting incensed: why would anyone think I needed that sort of help?! Soon after this meeting, Craig raped me and a week later my son was born, three months premature.

Nobody wants to identify that their partner is abusive. The psychological and emotional barriers can be insurmountable. It feels safer to live in denial:

- 'If it's not abuse then I am safe.'
- 'If it's not abuse then he will change.'
- 'If it's not abuse then my children are living in a lovely family, with only occasional difficulties.'
- 'If it's not abuse then no one can think of me as one of *those women* who are abused – *those women* who are weak and stupid for staying with an abuser.'

We're too far into denial to realize that there's no such thing as *those women*, only 'us women'.

Rarely do I divide abuse into the clinical terms of psychological, physical, sexual, financial, emotional; instead, I focus on the way abuse looks. The way it feels. The way it hurts. I do this using a model that was not originally developed for talking about abuse, entitled *Communist Attempts to Elicit False Confessions from Air Force Prisoners of War* and written by Albert D. Biderman.[4] Published in 1957, this work describes the ways prisoners of war are tortured, and although the context of domestic abuse is different, the tactics used to control or damage other human beings are finite, whether in personal relationships or in a Chinese prison. As a result, many use Albert Biderman's work to understand domestic abuse perpetration.

Biderman identifies eight tactics of torture: isolation, monopolization of perception, exhaustion, threats, occasional indulgences, demonstrating omnipotence, degradation and enforcing trivial demands. I have personified these tactics:

- isolation: the Isolator
- monopolization of perception: the Brainwasher
- threats: the Threatener
- demonstrating omnipotence: the All-Mighty
- exhaustion: the Exhauster
- occasional indulgences: the Nice One
- degradation: the Humiliator
- enforcing trivial demands: the Demander.

This personification, as illustrated in Figure 1, enables us to visualize the abusive tactics and can make them easier to identify. A potential pitfall of this is that people can assume an abuser uses just one of the aspects, when all abusers use multiple types of abusive behaviour. We're going to look in more depth at the ways an abuser might use these facets, using examples from either my own experiences or the general experiences of women. Given the ubiquity of digital culture, I will specify how an abuser might use technology and/or social media to further abuse his partner. (Now might be a good time for a quick self-care break. This stuff is not pleasant to read – or write about – but it is absolutely necessary.)

THE ISOLATOR

The intention of the Isolator is to isolate his partner. He wants to undermine her relationships with family, friends, work colleagues and her church community. By doing this he ensures that his perspective is the only one she has. He removes people from her life who give her strength. He might accuse her of having affairs, causing her to modify her behaviour in order to prove that she is faithful. If he is unfaithful, this may cause her to no longer socialize so she can keep tabs on him and ensure he doesn't start another affair. By putting doubts into her mind about whether she can trust others, he may gradually erode her relationships with friends or family. He could

The Humiliator

Makes us feel dirty and ashamed
Abuses us sexually
Makes us shrivel up inside

The Threatener

Makes us scared for our own or other people's safety
Makes us feel we can't trust anybody
Makes us feel trapped

The Isolator

Stops us seeing family and friends
Prevents us from having any perspective other than his
Manipulates or forces us to stay at home

The Exhauster

Goes on and on and on
Keeps us up late
Makes us do all the household tasks
Wakes us up at night

The Nice One

Confuses us by being nice
Makes us feel as if things are getting better
Makes us feel as if all the awfulness is worth it

The Brainwasher

Keeps us focused on him
Doesn't give us time or space to think
Minimizes, denies, blames

The All-Mighty

Uses acts of extreme power (e.g. violence or aggression) to convince he has all the power

The Demander

Forces or manipulates us into doing trivial or pointless tasks
Makes constant demands of us

Figure 1 The personification of Biderman tactics

create social awkwardness with visitors, his rudeness stopping them coming. Telling her that she needs only him and no one else, he might stop her speaking to friends or family. He might get aggressive if she tries to communicate with them. He might encourage her to move away from her support networks, and if they have any children he may use them to isolate her, refusing to care for them so that she has no time or energy for friendships. He could convince her to leave her job or take action that leads to her being fired. He may use finances to isolate her, limiting how much money she is allowed to spend so she cannot socialize. He may interfere with her access to transport: hiding her bus pass, denying her money for a train fare or letting the air out of her tyres so she can't go out. Locking her in, he may prevent her leaving the house, or he may 'accidentally' leave the baby's pram in the car so she can't go out. Using technology to check up on her, he might track her through location software, listening in to her phone calls or viewing her messages remotely using spyware. He may demand she give him her device passwords or use itemized billing to obsessively check up on her. He might use social media to isolate her, posing as her and sending her friends or family members offensive messages.

THE BRAINWASHER

The intentions of the Brainwasher are to devalue his partner and make her take on his perspective. He might gradually erode her confidence and self-esteem. There's a misconception that a woman with an abusive partner lacks self-esteem. Sometimes self-esteem courses are run for girls to try and prevent them being subjected to abuse. However, rather than seeking out those with low self-esteem, many abusers *create* low self-esteem by systematically devaluing their partner.

Author and counsellor Leslie Vernick explains, 'The opposite of love isn't hate, it is indifference.'[5] Indifference is a tool the

Brainwasher may use to harm his partner by simply having no interest in her feelings or needs. He may mock his partner and, when she objects, mock her further for 'not being able to take a joke'. Making her feel as though she's going mad, he may move things, hide things or lie about things he has said or done. She might assume she's getting particularly forgetful because she keeps misplacing her keys when in reality he keeps moving them. Continuously telling her that she is going mad or that she's 'not right in the head', he may leave her doubting her own sanity. He might publicly point out things about her that he knows make her feel uncomfortable, and enlist their children to mock her or call her names. Insisting she is incompetent with finances, the Brainwasher may take full control of the money. He may falsely accuse his partner of spending money, and when she denies it he will use it as evidence that she's going mad or losing her memory.

A significant element in the way the Brainwasher operates is using strategies of minimization, denial and blame. The purpose of this is to avoid responsibility and monopolize perceptions.

- **Minimization** This involves using words like 'just' and 'only'. 'It was *just* a little love strangle,' says Brian. 'I *only* broke one of your arms,' scoffs Albert. Minimization seeks to reduce the impact: 'I hardly touched you; it's just that you bruise so easily.'
- **Denial** The abuser will refuse to acknowledge he has done anything wrong. 'I didn't touch you – you fell.' 'I don't remember hitting you, but if you say I did then I must have.' This was the defence utilized by actor Kevin Spacey in response to accusations he had sexually assaulted a 14-year-old boy.[6]
- **Blame** To shift responsibility for his behaviour there is a plethora of things an abuser will blame: it's because of his diabetes/high blood pressure/low blood pressure/Asperger's/childhood trauma/stress levels/financial difficulties/depression/tiredness/hunger/drunkenness/horniness/being high/being overworked/being unemployed. Most of his blame will be placed on his partner. She

made him mad, wound him up, answered him back, didn't give him what he wanted, looked at him the wrong way, didn't stop the kids crying, didn't want sex, did want sex, didn't cook the dinner right, wasn't wearing the correct clothing, used too much washing-up liquid, went to the doctor's, talked to her mother, made eye-contact with a stranger, wore make-up, didn't wear make-up, left the house, didn't answer her phone quickly enough, didn't wear slippers in the house.

These tactics of the Brainwasher are often so effective that his partner fully internalizes the blame. She may say or think things like:

- 'It's my fault he hurt me. I wound him up.'
- 'He can't help it; it's because of his awful childhood.'
- 'I know if he just gets help for his alcohol issues, he'll stop hurting me.'

The Brainwasher's behaviour is often described as 'Gaslighting'. The term originated with the 1938 play *Gas Light*, in which a man manipulates his wife into thinking she is insane.[7] The Brainwasher may use technology to do this. By setting up fake profiles on social media sites or sending her messages from a number she doesn't know, he can confuse his partner or accuse her of cheating on him. He might send messages from his partner's social media accounts to other people and then deny sending them, or leave comments on her profile mocking her, posting photos or information about her without her permission. 'Greg', a self-confessed Gaslighter, explains his tactics to a journalist:

> 'I was leaving traces of infidelity in the digital world, on social media,' says Greg. He said he made jokes over a period of time pointing to [his partner's] 'obsession' with social media, making her feel that she was suspicious in an unhealthy, even 'crazy' way. 'I deliberately used demeaning language to make her lose confidence in her reading of the situation, of my infidelity. She

was "paranoid", she was "crazy", she was "full of drama". I'd say this all as jokes. But they would build over time, and she then started to believe.'[8]

THE THREATENER

Threats are a significant aspect of an abuser's behaviour. Sometimes women will repeat the abuser's minimization: 'It wasn't abuse; he was *only* violent once.' One incident of violence is enough for the abuser's threats to be taken seriously. The Threatener may be overt and callous, or may use humour and a light tone which leaves his partner feeling fearful but unsure of why. Rob lay next to Lynda one morning. The topic of their relationship ending came up. Rob began to tenderly stroke her neck. 'You can't ever leave me,' he said gently. 'Because if you did, I'd have to slit your throat.' His tone of voice and the context did not match the message Rob was giving and Lynda was left confused as to why she felt highly anxious.

Non-violent threats can be equally effective. An abuser may threaten to share his partner's secrets or coerce her into illegal activities that he can use against her. He may threaten others – the children, the wider family, pets – or threaten to destroy precious belongings: photographs, jewellery, ornaments, memorabilia. Beyond threatening harm, he may intimate that he is considering having an affair or that he will leave his partner unless she does what he wants. He may threaten suicide or self-harm. If his partner is considering leaving him, the Threatener may assert that he will gain full custody of the children; that he will leave his partner destitute and destroy her reputation. The Threatener may have a tone of voice or signal that his partner knows is a precursor to physical violence; his doing this at social gatherings may leave her frozen with fear. Using his whole body, the Threatener may block exits, use unexpected movements to startle her or punch walls. The marks he leaves in their home become permanent reminders of the threat he poses. Through play-fighting with his partner or children he can display how strong he is while plausibly denying that he's being serious. Recently a London police officer tweeted a photograph of a stairway with 21 knives embedded on either side of the wooden steps.[9] A man in the house had forced the inhabitants to walk up and down the stairs with the constant threat of severe violence.

Even if an abuser is given a custodial sentence, he may use letters to continue to threaten his partner. Technology may be a tool for threats to release sexually explicit images (a woman might have consented to appearing in sexually explicit photos or videos; her partner may have coerced or forced her, or someone may have digitally modified non-sexual images, such as placing her photograph on a pornographic image). The legal term for this is 'revenge pornography', but I view this as a highly problematic term. Just as it is inappropriate to call images of children being abused 'child pornography' and the official term is 'child sexual abuse images', so sexual images shared without consent should be called 'partner sexual abuse images'. Defined as 'the public sharing of sexually explicit media without the consent of the pictured individual',[10] revenge pornography became a criminal offence in England and Wales in 2015. Within six months there had been 1,160 reported incidents of revenge pornography.[11] The abuser may threaten to share private or libellous information online. If he carries out the threat, this could result in his partner losing her job, personal relationships or possibly even custody of her children. He may post ambiguous (or overt) statuses on social media which intimidate his partner. Telling her he has placed spyware on her phone and can track her, he listens in to her calls and reads her messages. He may insist that she video-call him (or send photographs of herself) so he can check her location.

Several women and I were sitting around a large table. They had previously lived in a women's refuge after separating from abusive partners. The conversation turned to a local scheme where, on being rehomed, they were surprised with a large parcel containing a gift of toys for their children. They were not warned about this surprise. Each woman shared how fearful the delivery had left her; all of them were horrified, assuming that their ex-partner had found them. One woman said, 'I thought there was going to be a severed head in it.' Another nodded: 'I didn't let my kids go near it for days. I thought he'd posted me a bomb.' Yet another said, 'I was petrified when I opened it. Even when I saw the toys in it, I thought they were from him and he'd put a listening device in the toys.' The Threatener's impact continues long after the relationship has ended.

THE ALL-MIGHTY

The All-Mighty works in partnership with the Threatener. Occasional acts of extreme power will prove to his partner that any threats will be carried out. For some abusers, the All-Mighty is constantly utilized. His violence may be physical or sexual. The purpose of the All-Mighty is to ensure his partner complies with him and he gets whatever he wants. Violence may include him slapping/punching/biting/burning/scalding/kicking/stamping on/ strangling/suffocating his partner. He may pull her hair, force-feed her, deny her food, smash objects, drive dangerously or prevent her taking prescription medication. Using weapons, he will injure her more severely. Weapons may include knives, hammers or guns, but could include other objects. Women have shared with me how they have been beaten with a milk carton, a chair, a beer bottle, a child's toy, a Christmas tree, a food tin, a spoon their partner had heated up and other implements. Such violence might not only be perpetrated against his partner: he may also harm family pets, children or other family members. Sexual violence is a significant tactic of the All-Mighty. Penetrating his partner against her will is often the ultimate act of violence. We will explore this horrific subject in more detail in Chapter 7, but it is important to locate sexual violence as a tactic of the All-Mighty.

The All-Mighty may not use violence at all; instead, he will become the Brainwasher, the Exhauster and the Threatener (along with other tactics) to create a context where his partner will do whatever he wants. Early in our relationship, Craig used to make me call him god. He would start off jokingly, gradually becoming more insistent, badgering me and telling me if I really loved him I would. While he was living four hours away he told me that if I really loved him I would romantically kiss one of my male friends. After I kept refusing he pestered me until I did. He then became aggressive and told me I was a terrible person; that I had betrayed him.

The All-Mighty may force his partner to do things that she doesn't want to, particularly if this causes her to lose her integrity or betray her values. He may badger her, shame her, threaten her or bribe her to do what he wants. This may include signing her up for credit cards, loans or other financial commitments. A debt counsellor I spoke with acknowledged that nearly every female client she worked with had been forced into debt by a previous partner's abusive or controlling behaviour. The All-Mighty may invoke God as his trump card, using distorted theology to force his wife to do what he wants. This is clear in the practice of Christian Domestic Discipline, where the main website states that Christian men should physically discipline their wives:

> A sound lashing is five to ten strokes with your hand, or three to five strokes with a strap; some wives need more. To avoid brusing (*sic*) do not strike the same area in repetition. Gauge your decision to proceed based on your wife's readiness to repent.[12]

It is often assumed that when abusers use violence they are angry and out of control. This is inaccurate. After speaking at a Christian men's conference I was approached by a man who recognized his own behaviour in the descriptions of abuse I had given. He described a situation with his wife and son in which he had thrown a chair. I asked him whether he had thrown the chair at his wife or child.

He looked horrified: 'No, I would never throw anything at them!' I suggested that if he had been able to choose where to throw the chair, then perhaps he could have chosen not to throw the chair at all.

Sarah told me, 'Every time my partner kicked off he would smash my phone, then later he would get annoyed because he couldn't keep tabs on me by checking my phone. This one time he kicked off and went for my phone, then stopped himself and smashed something else. I realized then that he knew exactly what he was doing.' Abusers may appear out of control when they use violence, but they're not. We presume a lack of control in part because we don't want to believe such violence is calculated.

THE EXHAUSTER

The Exhauster wants to exhaust his partner in order to keep her compliant. Sleep deprivation is a form of torture, but the subtle tactics of the Exhauster prevent his partner identifying it. He might talk about his feelings late into the night, especially if his partner has to get up early for work, study or with children. When I was pregnant with my daughter, Craig refused to work. I was doing three jobs, leaving home at 7.30 a.m. most mornings. We lived in a bedsit and he would insist on watching TV loudly until 3 a.m. each day. I repeatedly ended up in hospital with illnesses that were related to lack of sleep and rest. The Exhauster may refuse to do household tasks (or deliberately do them badly) or refuse to share childcare responsibilities so his partner has to do everything. His refusal to be an equal partner with the finances and house can be exhausting for her. He might even deliberately create mess (and encourage the children to do so) so that his partner has even more work to do. He might regularly wake her up in the middle of the night for sex. Going on and on and on, he might use pester power to badger his partner into giving him what he wants. The Exhauster may leave his partner so scared through his physical or verbal violence that she is in a perpetual state of high anxiety and adrenaline, unable to sleep. If the Exhauster has a night job, he may demand that his partner be awake and available for phone calls or text messages. He might constantly change the 'goal posts' and 'rules' of the relationship, leaving his partner feeling she is always walking on eggshells trying to second-guess what he wants. If his partner has phobias, he might 'jokingly' bring these up just before bedtime. Waking his partner forcefully, the Exhauster may begin interrogating her, accusing her of having an affair or of not adhering to his rules. Some abusers sleep with a weapon, leaving their partner terrified, while others use physical violence, awakening their partner with punches, kicks or bites. He might use drugs to keep his partner drowsy and compliant or tamper with her prescription medication. Living with an abuser is generally exhausting and saps energy and motivation. The Exhauster will expect his partner to stay awake during the day, even if he himself then sleeps to recover from being awake during the night. Using technology, the Exhauster might covertly set alarms on his partner's phone to wake her up in the middle of the night, or he could have a rule that his partner must call him every hour, even through the night. He could insist that his partner always answers his calls within a certain number of rings or that messages are answered within a specified time period. 'I just want to check that you're safe. I worry about you so much.'

Sleep deprivation is a rarely recognized tactic of abusers, yet almost all abusers utilize it. The impact of this aspect of abuse is far-reaching. An article from *Psychology Today* gives this overview of the physical damage caused:

> The first signs of sleep deprivation are unpleasant feelings of fatigue, irritability, and difficulties concentrating. Then come problems with reading and speaking clearly, poor judgment, lower body temperature, and a considerable increase in appetite. If the deprivation continues, the worsening effects include disorientation, visual misperceptions, apathy, severe lethargy, and social withdrawal . . . Various behavioral impairments accu-

mulate along the way as the deprivation continues, but if the experiment is pushed far enough the final result is always a widespread physiological failure leading to death.[13]

THE NICE ONE

Abusers do not start off a relationship with knives on the stairs, sleep deprivation tactics or constant put-downs. They'd never make it past the first date if they did. Instead, abusers use a variety of tactics to groom a potential partner into a relationship; this is collectively known as 'love bombing'. First used to describe the tactics of the religious group the Moonies in the 1970s, the term has been used in both negative and positive ways. Psychology professor Margaret Singer popularized it in 1996 in describing how cults groom potential victims.[14] Clinical psychologist Dale Archer explains:

> Love bombers are manipulators who seek and pursue targets. They're like emotional vampires, because they use attention and affection to build trust, as a means to maintain control, and end up sucking the emotion and joy for life right out of their partners.[15]

Love bombing is the first stage of the Nice One. His intention is to overwhelm a potential partner with positive experiences that prevent her having space to analyse the reality of the relationship, including the following tactics.

- **Constant communication** He will bombard her, in person and/ or through online communications, messages and voice and video calls.
- **Extreme flattery** He will idealize his victim, seeing her as perfect and showering her with compliments.
- **Inappropriate gifts** Gifts from him will be excessive in either quantity or cost.
- **High vulnerability** He will rapidly share his inmost feelings, worst traumas and deepest hopes, needs and dreams, which may

seem very attractive, particularly when men are stereotyped as unemotional and closed. He will expect his openness and vulnerability to be reciprocated. 'Lovingly' interrogating his victim, he will want to know everything about her. Feeling positive, her defences may come down and she will share deeply personal information, including her secrets and deepest thoughts and feelings.

- **'For ever' love** Quickly talking about the relationship being 'for ever', he will present the relationship as immediately long-term, swiftly suggesting cohabitation, engagement, marriage or a baby. He tells her that no one understands him as much as she does and that he has never felt so close to anybody. Sadly, these messages are normalized by popular culture in songs and films that portray love as highly intense and all-consuming.

The Nice One's tactics leave his partner overwhelmed and overstimulated. She will have no capacity left to rationally assess the relationship or the love bomber. Her time and energy will be so monopolized by the Nice One that she is unable to maintain other relationships with family and friends, leaving her isolated, with little outside support to help her recognize the toxicity of the Nice One. If friends or family members raise concerns, the love bomber will discount them: 'They're trying to split us up because they're jealous of what we have.'

Once the relationship is established, the Nice One will develop the other tactics, becoming the Brainwasher and withdrawing affection when he doesn't get what he wants, calling his partner names and belittling her. Using information gained through love bombing to coerce or manipulate her, he will become the Threatener, intimidating her but quickly making it into a joke. After spending hours on the phone to her, it is easy for him to shift into the Exhauster, expecting her to always answer the phone and talk late into the night. The love bombing effectively draws her into the relationship, and the Nice One keeps her believing that the relationship isn't all bad. He will occasionally demonstrate loving behaviours which give her hope that things can change. Sometimes the Nice One remains fixed until the wedding night, when abuse begins. This is understandably very shocking to his new wife and reveals a particular belief held by the man which delineates between the role of a wife and that of a girlfriend or fiancée.

The Nice One's behaviours do not appear abusive. Often when I speak to women they want to prove their partner isn't *all* bad. Their examples are almost always the Nice One's tactics. When someone is living with brutality, unkindness and oppression, even the smallest reprieve can feel like a huge act of love. Marilynn explains, 'I know it sounds like everything is terrible, but we do have some good times together.' Freya clarifies, 'He can be so caring. He took the kids to the park a couple of weeks ago which was really great!' Maya tells me, 'He was so upset last time he smashed up the house, he cried for hours. I knew he was sorry.'

An expert in fake remorse, the Nice One will cry, plead and promise to change. After being the All-Mighty, he will convince his partner that he is sorry, assuring her that this time he will change, this time everything is different. He will enlist others to help him: his family, her family, their marriage counsellor, church leader or wider church community. Christian culture often naively accepts an abuser's false remorse. Our faith is rooted in redemption, so we are primed to hope for changed hearts, minds and lives. As wonderful as this can be, it can create a context of collusion with abusers. The Nice One takes advantage of this. Well-meaning friends, family and clergy may unwittingly convince his partner she should give him another chance, or provide sympathy which encourages his toxic behaviour.

The Nice One may use technology both in the love-bombing stage and beyond. Rarely perceived as 'harassment', the constant text messages, phone calls or social media updates are full of loving compliments and positivity, but operate in a similar way, wearing the recipient down and overwhelming her into doing what the Nice One wants. Encroaching on his partner's online communities, the Nice One might take over conversations with his excessive compliments and can alienate others within the group. Before the relationship has been confirmed, the Nice One might announce it online, putting his potential partner in an awkward position. His positivity makes it hard for her to assert her discomfort. The work of US psychologist Dana Crowley Jack has found that women generally 'learn to censor themselves, to devalue their experience, to repress anger, to be silent'.[16] The Nice One takes advantage of this.

THE HUMILIATOR

Within the love-bombing stage of abuse, the Humiliator may desensitize his partner from her own discomfort with sexual activity. In the first few days of our relationship Craig wanted us to have baths together. When I objected, he pointed out that baths were not sexual; it was just about spending time together and getting to know each other better. On her first visit to his house, Olivia's new boyfriend asked her to retrieve something from a drawer. As she did so, she found that the drawer was filled with pornography DVDs. Her boyfriend noticed her discomfort and mocked her. In most sexual exploitation cases girls describe how their 'boyfriend' bought them sexy lingerie they were then expected to model, or played pornographic films during social gatherings. This tactic desensitized them from their own legitimate embarrassment with sexual activity and they felt less able to assert their right not to be sexual. Escalating from desensitization, the Humiliator's tactics may include forcing his partner to do sexual acts she doesn't want to, mocking her body or sexual performance and sharing intimate details of their sex life with friends and family members.

Much of an abuser's humiliation will be non-sexual; seeking out her diary or other private thoughts, he might make them public or mock her for them. Regularly making jokes at his partner's expense, he laughs at her and encourages others to do the same. Either publicly or privately he might spit on his partner or put food, waste or even faeces on her face or body, telling her how disgusting she is. Food can be used in a lot of ways to humiliate, ranging from taking issue with the way his partner eats, or telling her she's fat whenever she eats, to forcing her to eat. He might insist on going to the toilet with her or remove locks from bathroom doors. Driving his partner to tears with insults, he may laugh at her crying or make a mess and force her to clear it up, all the while telling her how disgusting and useless she is. He may describe her as dirty or sexually bad, telling her she smells or is dirty, possibly with a particular focus on her genitals and using sexualized words: 'whore', 'slut', 'c★nt', 'dyke', 'frigid', 'skank'. Early in our relationship, Craig began a job 260 miles away. I went to visit him for a week. He refused to let me go to the toilet alone. I felt hugely uncomfortable but my protests were met by his assertion that he loved me so much that he couldn't let me out of his sight, even to go to the toilet.

The Humiliator might compare his partner unfavourably to other women, sexually or otherwise, pointing out how other women are better wives, lovers, mothers. He tells her they are prettier, sexier, kinder, thinner, more intellectual, less annoying. His financial control leaves her humiliated as she begs him for money, and she is ashamed when he refuses her money to pay for their children's school trip or uniforms, or for sanitary products. He makes her beg for his love or forgiveness, possibly using Bible passages to justify himself. Calling her a Jezebel, he tells her she is sinful like Eve. He may insist that she has been created as his helper[17] and therefore must do whatever he asks. He tells her she is inferior, coming from man's rib, that women's subordination to men is evidence that God thinks women are despicable. The Humiliator will degrade and violate his partner using technology. Uploading her photo to websites that rate women's appearance or sexual performance, he may also make comments that humiliate her on social media sites. After forcing or coercing her into sexually explicit photos or videos, he may share them, or insist she join group sex sites with him, or sign her up to escort sites without her knowledge.

THE DEMANDER

The Demander may be explicitly demanding or may manipulate or coerce his partner to get what he wants. Expecting his partner to provide evidence of where she's been, he demands proof, including receipts. Timing her when she leaves the house, he berates her if she is a minute late, accusing her of having an affair or trying to leave him. 'He accused me of having sex with someone in the frozen food aisle in Tesco. I knew it was ridiculous, but I still started shopping at Asda to prove I wasn't.'

Craig insisted that I take responsibility for all the finances. However, he would demand money to purchase expensive computer parts (building computers was a hobby of his). I may have been responsible for the finances but I had no power over them.

Constant messages or phone calls may be used to make demands. These demands are designed to increase and maintain obedience. An abuser might use biblical passages about submission and headship to prove that his behaviour is *God's will* for their marriage. The Demander may demand that his partner wear certain types of clothing. Preventing her from working, he might demand that she do all the household tasks and childcare. Some abusers take a different approach, stating that she must work full time and provide for his needs, demanding she have no contact with the children. I am regularly asked for a definitive 'how to spot abuse' list. One abuser may force his partner to work, while another may prevent her working. In these two scenarios, the signs of abuse are opposing; the abuse is the man controlling his partner.

Fundamentally the Demander expects his partner to meet all of his needs, with little reciprocity when it comes to her needs. He demands that she wake up for him, have sex whenever he wants it, cook, clean and care for him. Expecting her to put aside her own needs, he consistently totally disregards them. No matter how much she does, he will always demand more. He will occasionally become the Nice One to assuage her fears that she is in a game she can't win, but even that will be just a small respite designed to prevent her from seeing how demanding he is being.

In a situation of domestic abuse, only the abuser's needs will be consistently met. Not only does the abuser devalue, undermine and ignore his partner's needs, he forces her to ignore her own needs and isolates her from other people who might be able to meet her needs. Academic and forensic social worker Evan Stark has described domestic abuse as domestic terrorism:

> [W]hat we're really dealing with, although the analogy [is] by no means perfect, is a kind of domestic terrorism. A kind of domestic hostage taking in which the victim has no outside to escape to, because the supposed safe place, the relationship, the home, the family network, has been identified as the point of imprisonment and entrapment.[18]

For those of you who are new to the subject of abuse, the abuser's tactics are likely to be deeply disturbing. Some abusers use all the behaviours listed; others use only some of them. Anyone who has had an abusive partner will read this chapter and recognize the different tactics. You may think the abusive behaviour listed here is extreme, something that few women are subjected to. Sadly, that is not the case. The Office for National Statistics found that 30 per cent of women have been subjected to this type of abuse.[19] Furthermore, research by the National Society for the Prevention of Cruelty to Children (NSPCC) found that for girls aged 13–17:

- 25 per cent had been subjected to physical violence;
- 72 per cent had been subjected to emotional violence;
- 31 per cent had been subjected to sexual violence.[20]

The research for all these statistics is very robust and was gathered by asking questions related to the aspects of abuse detailed within this chapter.[21]

Pause for a moment. Visualize four girls you know, perhaps girls who attend your church or your daughter/sister/niece and her friends. Three of them will be subjected to emotional abuse by a boyfriend by the time they are 17 years old. Or if you're at home and live near other houses, take a moment to step outside your home and look at three other houses on your street or cul-de-sac. Behind one of those three doors will be a woman who has been, is being or will be subjected to abuse. It's horrifying. The pervasiveness can be overwhelming. We attempt to construct lives where we (and those we love) are safe. Becoming aware of how ubiquitous abuse is can feel as though our carefully constructed safety is being bulldozed.

Some of you may be thinking, 'Hang on a second, she hasn't given any statistics for Christians. Surely it's not that bad in the Church?!' Sadly, it is. Research has found that 'the incidence [of domestic abuse] in the Methodist Church reflected the incidence in society as a whole'.[22] The Church of England's 2017 *Responding Well to Domestic Abuse: Policy and Practice Guidance* acknowledged that this is reflective of the wider Church.[23] Christian communities are not immune from abusive behaviour and, as has already been shown, some abusers will use theological justifications for their behaviour. Christians have a tendency to see problems as 'out in the world' and the Church as a haven from those problems (like the organizers of the Christian youth event who informed me they were going to work to end sexual violence in the UK, but were ambivalent about whether their event was promoting messages that could be harmful to young people who had been subjected to sexual abuse). Yet we need only read a few of the New Testament letters to discover the Church's issues have always mirrored those of the wider world. As the old saying goes, 'If you find the perfect church, don't join it or you'll ruin it.' Churches are filled with human beings, and every human flaw and failing will be present within our midst. The difference is that our community is supposed to have recognized our failings and chosen to die to ourselves in order to be raised with Christ.

Believing abuse to be a distant horror may enable a façade of safety, but as Jesus said, 'The truth will set you free.'[24] Recognizing that abuse is perpetrated by those within our church communities and wider family and friendship groups may be painful, but only through a willingness to see this brutal and horrifying truth can we begin challenging abuse and building safe spaces for those who are being subjected to abuse.

This chapter has been very full on! Let's take a few moments to pause. Concentrate on your breathing. Become conscious of your body. What feelings are going on for you? Are you doing OK? Do you need to take a break? You can choose to stop reading for a bit if you need to. Please use this prayer if it is useful:

God, there is so much brutality, so much pain. Please enable me to keep my heart open to the reality of abuse. Be with those who are being or have been subjected to abuse; bring them freedom, healing and justice. Amen.

> Then that little man in black there, he says women can't have as much rights as men, 'cause Christ wasn't a woman! Where did your Christ come from? Where did your Christ come from? From God and a woman! Man had nothing to do with Him.
>
> If the first woman God ever made was strong enough to turn the world upside down all alone, these women together ought to be able to turn it back, and get it right side up again! And now they is asking to do it, the men better let them.
>
> Sojourner Truth (1851)[25]

3 It's not his diabetes (Why does he behave like that?)

When I was chatting to another stallholder at an event where I was womanning a stall (yes, I did use the word 'womanning'), he explained that he knew nothing about abuse. This older man was taken aback as I began to tell him about Craig. His eyes widened. 'You?' he exclaimed. 'Some small shrivelled-up thing I could imagine being abused, but not someone like *you*.'

Heading from the car park into a conference where I was due to speak, I began chatting with a group of conference participants. One woman remarked, 'I'm really looking forward to hearing the victim perspective.' I nodded. 'Yes. It will be interesting.' At the end of the day, when I had shared my story, that same woman sought me out. 'I will never think about victims in the same way again. In the car park I had no idea that you would be the "victim perspective" and it's shown me that we can't know from looking at someone what their story is.' After another conference, the organizer told me how one of the conference attendees was extremely surprised about my personal story. 'I would never have expected that to be Natalie's story. She's so young. And pretty!' By telling me that I don't look like the sort of person who would be abused, they reveal a presumption that only a certain sort of person is subjected to abuse. The above comments would suggest those subjected to abuse are small, shrivelled up, old and ugly.

During my keynote address I asked the audience to shout out

reasons why abuse happens. One person suggested it was due to the low self-esteem of the person being subjected to abuse. Isn't that interesting? To assert that the *cause* of abuse is the self-esteem of the person who is being abused? This position leads many to conclude that addressing low self-esteem among women and girls will prevent abuse. A Christian youth organization began working with vulnerable girls, to prevent adult men sexually exploiting them. Their programme primarily aimed to raise the girls' self-esteem. When I asked what they were doing with boys in their project, the boys who were exploiting girls, they looked at me blankly. They were working with the girls to make them 'unabusable'. They were not working to stop the boys being abusive. Isn't it extraordinary that people (either consciously or subconsciously) see abuse as the fault of those who are abused? If we think back to the abusive tactics detailed in Chapter 2, we could see society as 'the Brainwasher', blaming women for the abuse their partner is inflicting on them. Research has found that, far from being small, shrivelled up, old and ugly, it is well-educated and highly paid women who are much more likely to be subjected to abuse, particularly if they earn significantly more than their partner.[1]

Abuse does not happen because those subjected to it have low self-esteem. Having a relationship with an abuser inevitably causes someone to develop low self-esteem; when someone is demeaning towards us, lying to us, isolating and degrading us, hurting and exhausting us, we will be miserable. When people blame abuse on the victim's low self-esteem they mix up cause and effect. The abuser is causing her low self-esteem; her low self-esteem is not causing the abuse.

'Abusive relationship' is a widely used term among domestic abuse services and the general public. Seen as less alienating than the term 'domestic abuse', it wasn't a formal rhetorical decision. The term has simply slipped into common usage. As understandable as it is for services to want terminology that does not alienate, it is hugely problematic to imply that abuse is a relationship issue. The phrase

'It takes two to tango' and stating that a relationship is 'a two-way street' suggest that relationship issues are caused by both parties in the relationship. If we treat domestic abuse as a relationship issue, it could be logical to presume that relationship support (e.g. marriage counselling, communication skills or conflict resolution strategies) might stop the abuse. Abuse expert Lundy Bancroft explains:

> Attempting to address abuse through couples therapy is like wrenching a nut the wrong way round; it just gets even harder to undo than it was before. Couples therapy is designed to tackle issues that are *mutual*. It can be effective in overcoming barriers to communication, for untangling childhood issues . . . or for building intimacy. But you can't accomplish any of these goals in the context of abuse. There can be no positive communication when one person doesn't respect the other and strives to avoid equality.[2]

Relationship solutions will not resolve abuse because domestic abuse is not a relationship issue. It is the issue of an abusive person within the *context* of a relationship. The term 'abusive relationship' implies that if the relationship ends then the abuse will end. This is not the case. Although separation is the best way for women (and their children) to gain safety, for many women the abuser's behaviour continues post-separation. A study found that 37 per cent of women subjected to abuse reported that the violence continued after separation,[3] while a review of domestic violence homicides in London found that 76 per cent of women who were killed by a partner had already separated from him when they were killed.[4]

It is really important for Christian culture to grasp that domestic abuse is not a relationship issue. Christianity values marriage highly and has a plethora of relationship resources: pre-marital counselling, the Marriage Course™, marriage enrichment weekends, books on marriage, dating, singleness, being equally yoked, praying for your future spouse (and children and pets – OK, so not pets), avoiding sex, having good sex . . . Rarely do these resources offer caveats about abusive behaviour or acknowledge that abuse is *not* a relationship issue. We have a Saviour who brings us abundant life,[5] yet by ignoring or misunderstanding the nature of abuse we prevent those subjected to abuse from finding freedom and may even collude with abusers.

If abuse is not a result of women's low self-esteem or is not a relationship issue, why does abuse happen? Fundamentally the answer is that *abusers choose to be abusive*. This statement raises significant discomfort for a lot of people. Nobody wants to live in a world where a significant number of men choose to harm women, and we have developed false cultural narratives about why men abuse. Across society there are five main false cultural narratives:

- health and well-being
- other people
- substances
- lack of emotional literacy
- circumstances.

As we explore these, there may be elements that you recognize in your own thinking. That's OK! It may be an obvious statement but we don't know what we don't know, and if you're feeling uncomfortable or disagree with me, then see it as an opportunity to learn more. Take your time and please do be open to the uncomfortable thoughts and feelings that might occur as we go through this together.

HEALTH AND WELL-BEING

PHYSICAL HEALTH

Sarah told me her husband's diabetes caused him to be abusive. She admitted she had never seen abuse as a symptom of diabetes on any official guidance, but he had told her his low blood sugar made him hurt her. Physical health problems like epilepsy, heart disease or a stroke may be invoked to justify abusive behaviour, while testosterone levels are blamed for sexually violent behaviour. There is no physical health problem that causes abusive behaviour, and testosterone doesn't make men rape. (All men and women have testosterone. We're not all rapists.)

MENTAL HEALTH

Stress may be used to justify abusive behaviour, but although violent incidents may escalate during times of stress, the wider abusive behaviours generally remain stable. An issue with identifying abusive behaviour as only physical violence is that it prevents us understanding the bigger picture: isolation, humiliation, brainwashing, exhaustion, demands, threats and love bombing and seemingly nice behaviours, which are the norm of an abuser.

Abusive behaviour appears volatile and unstable, leading to conclusions that the abuser is mentally unwell. An abuser's tactics are intended to create certain outcomes: the All-Mighty is seeking to gain total power; the Brainwasher twists reality; the Exhauster wants his partner to be exhausted and unable to think straight; the Isolator wants to undermine his partner's relationships. When we have a clear framework for analysing an abuser's behaviours, we see that, rather than evidencing instability, he shows an intention to control or harm. Someone with mental ill health is much more likely to be a victim than a perpetrator of abuse,[6] and there is no mental ill health diagnosis that guarantees someone will behave abusively. Many of those involved in treating mental ill health do not understand abusive behaviour and may collude with the abuser, providing additional justifications instead of holding him accountable. As Lundy Bancroft explains, it is an abuser's '*value system* [that] is unhealthy, not their psychology'.

OTHER PEOPLE

HIS MOTHER

As valuable as attachment theory is, it often leaves women blamed for their adult children's choices, particularly those of their sons. The theory was developed (some would say malevolently) during the Second World War, when women had taken up roles traditionally only available to men. At the end of the war women were encouraged to give up their new-found skills and independence; men needed their jobs back. John Bowlby's theory of attachment supposedly showed that children who were not in the full-time care of their mothers would become delinquents.[7] These post-war efforts to resocialize men and women into traditional roles have led to the blaming of mothers for many and varied social problems, including bed-wetting, schizophrenia, homosexuality, colour blindness, aggressive behaviour, learning problems and even 'homicidal transsexualism'.[8] Researchers Dr Anita Garey and Dr Terry Arendell have said that 'when we contribute to the processes of mother-blame, we uncritically accept and even add to the oppression of a group that is already subordinate'.[9]

Few counsellors are trained in fully understanding the dynamics of domestic abuse. They may see attachment theory as a legitimate lens through which to understand abusive behaviour. The counsellor may unintentionally collude with an abuser by identifying the problem as attachment rather than encouraging him to take responsibility. An abuser may use this information to further harm his partner.

HIS CHILDHOOD

They say that 'Hurt people hurt people', yet when it comes to domestic abuse, the statistics suggest that hurt men hurt women but that hurt women don't seem to hurt men. In fact, the research suggests that 'men who are violent toward other *men* are often victims of child abuse – but the connection is much less clear for men who assault women'.[10] Most people who are abused as children do not go on to become abusive adults. The so-called 'cycle of abuse' from childhood abuse to adult abuser perpetuates damaging myths that victimization leads to perpetration. It doesn't have to. During counselling, an abuser will seek to keep the focus away from his current abuse towards his partner and children. With all empathy and care directed towards the abuser, there is none left for his partner or children. Some abusers become therapists themselves; to avoid responsibility, they use psychological language, which their partners may be unskilled in arguing against.

HIS EX

Some abusers blame their controlling behaviour on a previous partner, claiming that their ex-partner has caused them to be untrusting. A previous partner could have damaged them, but to blame current abusive behaviour on an ex is simply another way of avoiding responsibility. Plenty of people are wounded through previous relationships; most are not abusive. Given that the majority of those subjected to abuse are female, if an ex were to blame then surely there would be a proliferation of women abusing subsequent partners? Negativity about an ex-partner can sometimes be an early warning sign that somebody is abusive. Setting up a scenario where his ex is responsible for all negative aspects of the previous relationship may show an inability to take responsibility. If his ex-partner subsequently discloses abuse, he has already undermined her credibility to his new partner. Where someone has children from a previous relationship and communicates with them about their mother in negative ways, this can be a form of domestic abuse known as maternal alienation, which causes significant continuing trauma to children and their mother (this is also known as parental alienation, but the degendered nature of this language is used by abusive men to describe the ways mothers may seek to safeguard their children).

HIS BOSS/WORKPLACE

Some presume men are abusive because they feel powerless in other areas of their life (their work, friendship group or other relationships). The reasoning is: a man feels powerless at work so he goes home and assaults his wife to feel powerful. But this is not logical. If it was natural human behaviour, surely women would be as likely (if not more likely) to do this? Women are much less likely than men to hold positions of power in the workplace, yet women are not the majority of those abusing a partner.

Abusers are found in all occupations (one US report found that domestic abuse is perpetrated in at least 40 per cent of police officer families).[11] Where abusers have significant power in their workplace, they may utilize that to further abuse their partner. If an abuser is a soldier, police officer, church leader, high court judge, politician or CEO, it may be even harder for his partner to seek help. The abuser may use his power, privilege and influence to avoid arrest, destroy his partner's reputation or perpetrate abuse with impunity. Powerlessness is not a cause of abuse.

HIS PARTNER

A church leader asked advice about a member of his congregation. Her husband had tried to kill her, strangling her until their children had dragged him off. The words he used to describe the woman were 'difficult', 'feisty' and 'able to stand her ground'.

Dave sat in a semi-circle with the other men at the perpetrator programme I was co-facilitating. As they talked about their week, Dave mentioned arguing with his girlfriend. When asked to elaborate, he stated that his girlfriend was spending the evening having a meal with her family and he hadn't wanted her to go. According to him she was 'irrational' because he'd physically assaulted her a couple of weeks previously. When asked why it was irrational for her to want to go out with her family, he simply repeated that she was irrational. I repeated my question, 'Why is it irrational for her to want to go out with her family?' He restated that she was irrational. We went back and forth like this until suddenly it dawned on him. It wasn't irrational for her to want to go out with her family. It was irrational for him to try to stop her spending time with her family.

In 2014, the public discovered that an estimated 1,400 children (mainly girls) in Rotherham were sexually abused and exploited between 1997 and 2013. An investigation found that 11-year-old girls were raped by large numbers of male perpetrators.[12] Refusing to arrest the perpetrators, police and social services viewed many of the victims as making life choices to sell sex for money.

Whether it is police officers blaming 11-year-old girls for men raping them, a man blaming his 'irrational' girlfriend or a church leader characterizing a brutalized woman as difficult and feisty, the ways women and girls are blamed for abusers' choices and behaviours are infinite. Nobody can make another person abusive. And any messages, whether these are within the media, from abusive men or within our own minds, which blame the victimized for the abuse they are subjected to must be challenged.

SUBSTANCES

Alcohol consumption and drug use are regularly blamed as the cause of abusive behaviour. The majority of research providing evidence for this focuses solely on physical violence and not wider control and coercion. Alcohol or drug use may increase the incidences of physical violence but the wider control, isolation, humiliation, brain-washing and demeaning that an abuser inflicts on his partner are not substance-induced. Lundy Bancroft has said, 'Alcohol cannot create an abuser, and sobriety cannot cure one.'[13] As a professional who has worked with thousands of perpetrators, Bancroft would know.

Though technically not 'substances', both gambling and pornography can have an addictive quality that may be used to explain abusive men's behaviour. Attending Gamblers Anonymous or accessing sex addiction therapy will not stop abusive behaviour. In fact, both of these support mechanisms may give an abuser further ammunition for abuse. Using his recovery to further control his partner, he insists that she must do what he wants in order to help him get better. Rarely are those offering sex therapy or support around gambling, sex, drug or alcohol addictions equipped to understand the dynamics of domestic abuse.

LACK OF EMOTIONAL LITERACY

ANGER

It is assumed that men who are violent cannot control their anger. This would seem quite logical; why else would someone aggressively harm another person or their property? The vast majority of abusers restrict their violence to their partner (and children). They are not violent towards their boss, friends, colleagues or those they go to church with. They manage to control their anger in other situations. And once the wider control, isolation, humiliation and brainwashing is considered, it is clear that much of it is not done in anger. Domestic abuse is about control, not anger. Respect, the UK organization that accredits perpetrator work, has stated, 'There does not appear to be any evidence that a generic anger management programme, in and of itself, is capable of ending violence in intimate relationships.'[14] Respect has found that abusive men may utilize anger management strategies to further abuse their partner.

INSECURITY

Insecurity and fear of intimacy or abandonment have been suggested as the root causes of an abuser's behaviour, yet many people struggle with these issues and manage not to terrorize their partner. The abuser's controlling behaviour and possessiveness may be 'repackaged' by well-meaning people (or the abuser himself) as jealousy or insecurity. The abuser's *possessiveness* stems from him viewing his partner as a *possession*. It is not insecurity or fear of abandonment. By giving this framework to an abuser, we collude with his narrative of being the one who is hurt, wounded and in need. This shifts our concern, support and care from the person being harmed to the person who is causing the harm.

CRIME OF PASSION

News reports about men who murder women often create a picture of a man who couldn't live without the woman who had recently separated from him. They focus on his partner having had an affair or having been involved in some other betrayal which led him to kill her in a fit of 'passion'. In 2009, the UK Labour Party's Minister for Women, Harriet Harman, sought to abolish the 'crime of passion' defence for murder.[15] Dawn Clinton's estranged husband killed her in a 'savage attack'. He strangled her and filled the house with gas fumes, threatening to take his own life and requiring nearby properties to be evacuated. An appeal court ruled that his 'crime of passion' defence could be allowed and ordered a retrial. Dawn's new relationship had been discovered when her husband hacked into her Facebook account. Evidence of infidelity remains a legally sanctioned justification for murder.

Women whose partners have been the All-Mighty will identify how he would smash up the house, often breaking things that were precious to them. When I ask them how many of his own items he smashed, they were often astonished to realize he had only ever smashed things that were not his own. When I was about 12, my family and I visited an ostrich farm owned by close friends. They kindly gave me an empty ostrich egg as a keepsake. It was about 15 centimetres tall and I loved it, displaying it proudly in my and Craig's home. One day I came home to find fragments of white shell embedded within the textured wallpaper and strewn across the carpet. He had smashed my precious ostrich egg against the wall. I asked him why and he just shrugged and said he'd wanted to. It didn't occur to me he would deliberately destroy something precious to me for his own ends. I concluded he must have been really angry. But he wasn't. Not at all.

Google tells me that passion is a 'strong and barely controllable emotion'. In a similar way to anger, 'passion' implies that the man is out of control, consumed by something he has no power over. As we have already seen, this might seem logical if we only considered an abuser's physical violence, yet makes no sense when placed in the wider context of his control, manipulation, degradation, brainwashing and isolation. This idea of him being 'out of control' leaves people assuming that an abuser's behaviour is fixed and static. He can do nothing about it and has no control over it. The conclusion then is that his partner must take action. A friend said to me, 'Well, an abuser is just mad so there's nothing you can do about him. His partner must be the one to take action.' When we see men's violence as static and out of their control, this leads us to blame their partner. She becomes 'responsible' for the abuse because she has not left. However, men's violence is not fixed; it is a mechanism for control. The abuser has control; his partner does not.

NEURODIVERSITY

Australian sociologist Judy Singer coined the term 'neurodiversity' in 1998.[16] Originally referring to those on the autistic spectrum, it now encompasses other neurological differences including dyspraxia, dyslexia, attention deficit (and/or hyperactivity) disorder (ADD/ADHD), dyscalculia and Tourette's. In recent years increasing numbers of women have blamed their partner's abuse on him having Asperger's syndrome, also known as autistic spectrum disorder (ASD). The most recent edition of the *Diagnostic and Statistical Manual of Mental Disorders*, the standard work on psychiatric illness, does not include 'being abusive to a partner' under the criteria for any autism-based diagnosis and there is no evidence that autism causes someone to be abusive. Someone with ASD may cope better when able to control *his environment*, but that is different from controlling his partner. As Fiona explains, 'My husband has Asperger's and he might say that he doesn't want to go to a party, but he would never seek to prevent me from going to a party.' Unlike Fiona's husband, an abuser would seek to stop his partner socializing.

COMMUNICATION ISSUES

It could be assumed that if an abuser learned to 'use his words', he would stop hurting his partner. Most abusers are extremely skilled communicators, which is why a man's partner finds it so hard to leave him. His manipulation and coercion are predicated on his ability to communicate effectively. He can usually communicate appropriately with his boss, his family, his friends, colleagues and church community, often using these skills to manipulate them into supporting his abuse. He simply chooses to use his communication skills to harm others.

LOVE MAKES US DO CRAZY THINGS

Luke Howard set up a piano in the UK city of Bristol, vowing to play continuously until he won back his ex-girlfriend; they had been together only four months when she broke up with him. He lasted less than 48 hours after there was a public outcry at the creepiness of his supposedly romantic gesture.[17] In the Osmaniye province of southern Turkey, 22-year-old Erdogan Ceren used Facebook live video-streaming to film his suicide. Producing a shotgun, he explained to the camera that his girlfriend had recently broken up with him, stated 'No one believed when I said I will kill myself, so watch this,' and shot himself.[18] Zoe Morgan and her partner Lee Simmons were stabbed to death outside their shared workplace by Zoe's ex-partner after he had researched the easiest way to kill someone.[19] Men who kill women are often described as 'heartbroken'. Whether someone is refusing to accept the end of a relationship, attempting suicide unless he gets what he wants or threatening to harm his ex-partner or others, these are tactics of abuse and are not loving actions. They stem from a belief that only he has a right to end the relationship, and from a lack of respect and value for his partner's autonomy and free choice.

DOMINEERING PERSONALITY

An abuser may have a domineering personality, but he is choosing to cultivate parts of himself that harm others. In recent years, narcissistic personality disorder has gained prominence in conversations about domestic abuse, alongside antisocial, avoidant, borderline and histrionic personality disorders. Dr Kate Middleton, a Christian psychologist, explains:

> Personality 'disorders' stem from an acceptance that there is a 'normal' – i.e. the more common, central patterns along certain traits. Beyond a point therefore we start to call some personality patterns (behaviour, feelings or emotions) 'abnormal'. Personality disorders in a clinical sense describe patterns which are problematic – generally because they either trigger difficult and painful emotions for the individual, or because they lead to people acting towards others in very unpleasant or upsetting ways. However the concept hangs on the acceptance of 'normal' versus 'abnormal', and of course where exactly you draw the line . . . [and] the treatment of personality disorders is notoriously difficult and it is difficult to define 'success'.[20]

Within the growing acceptance that personality disorders cause people to have interpersonal difficulties, we must be careful that a personality disorder diagnosis does not diminish an abuser's responsibility. The abuser's behaviour must not be pathologized. Our priority should be the person (or people) he is harming, enabling her to access the treatment she needs. If someone's personality leads him to steal cars or punch strangers, then he will be held accountable; he doesn't get a free pass because of his personality.

You may be wondering why we are more likely to offer

excuses to an abuser than a car thief. Well, dear reader, that is a great question. And one I am greatly obliged to answer! It stems from the much larger issue of the way we organize society into two separate spheres, something which can be traced back to the ancient Greeks but which formally emerged in Europe and America during the Industrial Revolution. The public sphere is defined as 'the social space in which different opinions are expressed, problems of general concern are discussed, and collective solutions are developed communicatively'.[21] In comparison, the private sphere 'is a smaller, typically enclosed realm (like a home) that is only open to those who have permission to enter it'.[22] For many generations the public sphere belonged to men, while the private was female. In the sixteenth century 'a London law forbade wife beating after 9.00 p.m., but only because the noise disturbed people's sleep'.[23] The public interest in such a law was to do with the noise disturbance, not the woman being harmed. Until very recently domestic abuse was seen as a private matter, irrelevant to the public sphere. Although Western laws have changed dramatically, human socialization doesn't move very quickly and many would still view domestic abuse as a private matter, for instance viewing car theft as a public issue while viewing an abuser's behaviour as a private issue. There are 20 countries across the globe that have no laws against domestic violence,[24] while in the last few years Russia has decriminalized some forms of domestic violence – this in a country where 40 women are killed every day by a partner or ex.[25] We still have a long way to go.

CIRCUMSTANCES

UNEMPLOYMENT

Unemployment is often linked to the idea that abuse is perpetrated because of powerlessness in other areas of life. Unemployment or poverty does not cause someone to be abusive. When an abuser is unemployed, he has *more time* to harm his partner; his lack of employment does not cause him to be abusive, it simply provides him with greater opportunity to be abusive. Many abusers are employed and/or wealthy.

FINANCIAL ISSUES

The lunchtime radio show began. A man had stabbed his children to death and the presenter announced that the phone-in discussion would focus on debt. Apparently the man's debt had driven him to stab his children to death. People called in to say that they understood what the man had done because they themselves had been in debt and it was terrible and made people do awful things. Except, it seemed, none of them had actually stabbed two small children to death. Calling the radio show, I complained that the obvious domestic violence elements of the case were being ignored in favour of a narrative around debt. The researcher on the other end of the call was incredulous: 'What do you mean, domestic violence? We know nothing about his relationship.' My sardonic response, 'Do you not think stabbing someone's children to death is a form of domestic violence?' did not get me an opportunity to offer my views on air.

Debt can be a terrible burden, but it does not cause someone to stab his children to death. It does not cause someone to become violent. And it certainly does not cause an abuser to isolate, degrade, brainwash, coerce and control his partner. As we noted in Chapter 2, many perpetrators use finances to further control their partner, spending money irresponsibly or taking full control of the finances. Many women find themselves manipulated into debt, coerced or tricked into signing contracts or having loans taken out in their name. If they do manage to escape the abuser, they will often be left with large debts. Despite the prevalence of this, there are no cases (that I have been able to find) of women stabbing their children (or the abuser) to death because of the debt they are in.

CHRISTMAS

Days after Christmas I was invited to do a series of BBC radio interviews across the UK, focusing on reports of increased domestic abuse perpetration over the Christmas period. The presenters wanted to concentrate on the increased consumption of alcohol and the stress of Christmas. Just as Craig destroyed my precious ostrich egg, abusers seek to destroy what is precious to their partner. His partner's hope that Christmas, birthdays and anniversaries will be special gives the abuser an opportunity to more easily destroy her, with her being less likely to resist him in the hope that the special day can be salvaged. Many women can recount memories of the knocked-over Christmas tree, their children's new toys smashed or broken by their father.

Sophie tried to adhere to every rule and demand made by her partner Colin over Christmas, desperately trying to placate him so the children could have a nice day. It never worked. The façade of control he allowed her to feel was never real, and all her hard work would be fruitless as he screamed at the children and smashed their toys. He poured scalding hot gravy over her and mocked her efforts, encouraging the children to say how disgusting the Christmas dinner was. His promises to behave if she had sex with him on Christmas morning led to a day of mocking her sexual performance and ruining the day anyway. Christmas is a time of greater opportunity for the abuser. There are prolonged periods where he will be in the house with his partner (and children). Christmas does not cause abuse. Christmas creates opportunities for an abuser.

Those who rarely attend church may cross the hallowed threshold for midnight Mass, carol services, children's nativities or Christingle services. (For those unaware of the Christingle service, it involves holding an orange wrapped with a red ribbon, which has a candle and cocktail sticks with sweets poking out of it. This may not have made the situation any clearer for you, but do Google it if you'd like to know more.) It is important that church leaders and congregations grasp the reality of what Christmas means for those subjected to abuse. The tendency of Christian culture to avoid difficult topics and idolize the nuclear family can make the Church an extremely unsafe place for women and children subjected to abuse.

FOOTBALL

At a Christian event I raised the issue of domestic abuse with a well-known Christian speaker (I can always be counted on to bring up awkward topics in polite company!). I began saying, 'The reason domestic abuse happens is . . .' and he cut me off, finishing my sentence, '. . . football! Domestic abuse happens because of football!' It is likely that this well-known Christian man had read about research entitled 'Can the FIFA World Cup Football (Soccer) Tournament be associated with an increase in domestic abuse?' This small study found that domestically violent incidents rose by 26 per cent when the English national team won (or drew) and by 38 per cent when the national team lost. Does this mean that watching football tournaments causes men to be violent? No. It does not. The research concluded that football tournaments are 'intensifying the concepts of masculinity, rivalry and aggression'.[26] The research did not find that football causes violence, but rather the concepts of masculinity, rivalry and aggression, which *cause* men to choose violence, are *intensified* by watching football. The researchers found that men's violence increased *regardless* of whether their team won, drew or lost. What a terrifying prospect for women and children! Just as the Christmas season may be dreaded for the way it is utilized by an abuser to harm those he is supposed to love, so the football season becomes another time in which women and children are left fearing for their safety and possibly even their lives.

CULTURE

There can be a perception that male violence towards women is a non-Western issue. In my work I suggest that every culture has a set of 'Unlesses' regarding abuse; these are the cultural justifications for violence or abuse that reduce or erase the culpability of the abuser. Within Western cultures these usually include anger, unfaithfulness and/or his partner ending the relationship. Although not explicitly stated, there is a subconscious perception that a partner should not use violence *unless* he's angry or *unless* she's been unfaithful (or ended the relationship). Newspaper reports about men who kill their partners describe them as 'jilted',[27] 'broken-hearted'[28] or 'pained by . . . separation'.[29] The men have 'lost it',[30] 'flown into a rage'[31] or 'freaked out',[32] while she is referred to as the 'cheating wife'.[33] Cultural Unlesses are rarely visible. Westerners will not see that their justifications collude with abusers, yet regard another culture's Unlesses as barbaric. Western Unlesses may be anger, unfaithfulness and ending the relationship. Other cultures have Unlesses that include lack of female servitude (it's not OK to abuse a woman *unless* she cooks the dinner badly) or accusations of witchcraft (*unless* she is controlling her husband). Within some cultures, anger is not a cultural Unless and so Westerners may judge the violence as more brutal. Focusing on non-Western Unlesses enables Westerners to feel superior, while absolving us of having to become aware of or challenge our own Unlesses.

Aside from the five alternative narrative categories about abuse, there has been a tendency within some academic and popular writing to use evolutionary biology to explain abusive behaviour. Theologian Dr Elaine Storkey spends chapter 10 of her book *Scars Across Humanity* explaining and then unpicking the idea that men's violence towards women is biological or rooted in evolution. She explains that some experts in evolutionary biology have suggested rape is part of men maximizing 'their genetic potential', that 'paternity uncertainty' underlies a male abuser's control of his partner and that when men kill their partners it is an 'evolved [mechanism] associated with weighing the cost and benefits of homicide'.[34] To contest this Elaine persuasively argues that such ideas involve a 'lack of evidence and the stretch of imagination', that they have 'logical and methodological problems', resulting in a 'loss of moral responsibility', and cause 'the disappearance of the self'.[35]

You must be wondering by now, dear reader, why exactly someone would *choose* to be abusive. You must be very keen for me to move on to the actual reasons. That time has now come upon us! If you would like a small break, please take one. If you would like to build the tension by producing a drum roll with your hands, please do. For the truth will now be revealed!

It is crucial that an abuser's *choice* to abuse remains front and centre within our minds whenever we try to understand abuse. Abusive behaviour is a choice. So much of society avoids accepting this by creating false cultural narratives, layers of justification that mitigate for or deny the choices of abusers. Who wants to live in a society where a significant proportion of men are choosing to be abusive? It is much less unsettling to live in a society where alcohol, drug use, stress, mental illness – US research has found that only 4 per cent of violent crime is linked to mental illness, but that news reports discuss mental illness in relation to violent crime 55 per cent of the time[36] – or uncontrollable anger acts upon men and causes them to do something that they would not otherwise choose to do. But we must be willing to be unsettled.

An abuser's choice to abuse is based on his beliefs and values. He believes he owns his partner (and children) and that he has the right to do whatever he wants within the relationship. As Lundy Bancroft has said, 'Abuse grows from attitudes and values not feelings. The roots are ownership, the trunk is entitlement, and the branches are control'.[37] (See Figure 2.)

It is an abuser's beliefs of ownership and entitlement that drive his need to control his partner (and children). Addressing any issue other than his beliefs of ownership and entitlement is not going to stop his abusive behaviour.

When considering abusive behaviour we generally focus on

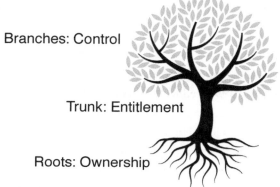

Branches: Control

Trunk: Entitlement

Roots: Ownership

Figure 2 The tree of death

impact rather than intention. We are perplexed as to why someone would go to the efforts of decimating his partner's confidence through insults, mocking retorts and exhausting her. We look at the impact on her and at his inability to have a positive relationship, and are puzzled as to why anyone would do such a thing. However, if we look at his intention in decimating his partner's confidence, we find that it enables him to maintain his beliefs of owning her and being entitled to get whatever he wants from her. It keeps her controlled and unable to assert her needs and wishes.

When we look at every type of abusive behaviour – the All-Mighty, the Isolator, the Exhauster, the Humiliator, the Threatener, the Demander, the Brainwasher and the Nice One – we can see that the intention of each is to gain power over his partner and control her. Work with perpetrators that is proven to be effective has this analysis of abuse and works with men to challenge their beliefs of ownership and entitlement and the intentions behind the behaviour, and to enable abusers to build empathy for their partner and children.

As academics, both Dr Liz Kelly and Dr Nicola Westmorland were sceptical about the effectiveness of perpetrator programmes. Yet, after five years working on Project Mirabal, a major project researching UK perpetrator programmes, they changed their minds. They found that:

- 30 per cent of women had a partner who had made them do something sexual they did not want to; a year after men had started the programme, this was reduced to 0 per cent;
- 29 per cent of women had a partner who had used a weapon; this was also reduced to 0 per cent within a year;
- 87 per cent of women had a partner who had slapped or punched them or had had something thrown at them; after the programme this was reduced to 7 per cent;
- 'Far fewer women reported being physically injured after the programme (61 per cent before compared to 2 per cent after), and the extent to which children saw or overheard violence also dropped substantially, from 80 per cent to 8 per cent.'[38]

Kelly and Westmorland write:

> Can a leopard change its spots? No, because a leopard is born with spots, it does not make the choice to continue to have them. Men are not born violent, they derive benefits from not being held accountable for their use of violence and abuse, and just as they make decisions about other areas of their lives, they can choose to stop being violent and abusive. Perpetrator programmes can help them make those changes.[39]

Is all of an abuser's behaviour done on purpose? To understand the answer to this question, we need to reflect on the benefits of abusive behaviour. It may seem incomprehensible that anyone would choose to hurt another human being in such awful ways. But laying aside moral and ethical restraints, we find that being abusive gives us everything we want. We never have to take responsibility, we get sex whenever we want it and have a permanent servant who meets our every need. We never have to consider her needs at all. We get to feel superior and justify every complaint she has as irrational, stupid and ridiculous.

We have the status of being in a relationship, of being a parent, and the world treats us as a good person, but we don't have to put in any of the effort. This could be a seriously attractive proposition, except that we can't ever put aside those moral and ethical restraints. The cost to our partner and children is immeasurable. And we never get to have an authentic relationship characterized by equality, respect and love.

Although many abusers will be deeply calculating and every action they take will be considered and deliberate, for others their behaviour stems from the benefits gained. When Dave chooses to motivate his girlfriend Dawn's weight loss by stating that if she doesn't lose weight she has to let him have anal sex with her, he is possibly not thinking about the full impact of that threat on Dawn. He's thinking about the anal sex he's finally going to get, and the fact she'll stop 'bitching and moaning' about her struggle with weight loss. When Mervin punches a hole in the wall, he's thinking about how it will make his wife Miracle shut up and get him what he wants. He's not thinking about how frightened Miracle will be or how she will spend the next ten years avoiding challenging him because she's so scared. Fundamentally, the abuser is not thinking about his partner (or children). He's not thinking about her feelings and needs, or about the way his children's lives are being damaged. All he is thinking about is himself and what he is going to gain from his actions.

There can be great resistance to the idea that abuse cannot be fixed through counselling, conflict resolution skills, marriage enrichment courses, psychotherapy, cognitive behavioural therapy (CBT), rehab, non-violent communication (NVC), neuro linguistic programming (NLP), addiction treatment programmes, anger management, antidepressants or women's empowerment courses. The resistance to this is because people assume I am demeaning or undervaluing the importance of these tools. I am not. I personally have benefited from psychotherapy and marriage counselling (this was in my current relationship, with my extraordinarily brilliant second husband or, as I often refer to him, 'the good one') and know many who have benefited from the other resources listed. The issue is not with the treatments, it is with the diagnosis.

When we have a physical health problem, there will be various symptoms. Tests will be done to ascertain the diagnosis and then treatment can be offered. If someone has skin cancer and it is diagnosed as a verruca, no matter how effective the verruca treatment is it will not cure the cancer. From the 'symptoms' of abuse, we may diagnose the abuser as having mental health difficulties, emotional issues or relationship troubles. That diagnosis will lead to us offering treatments that are absolutely effective for his diagnosis. But the diagnosis is wrong. The treatments might be excellent, but they will not enable an abuser to change. That is not an indictment of the treatment but takes issue with wrong diagnoses. None of the treatments mentioned above have been developed by experts in domestic abuse issues. They are designed to be used with people who have specific needs. The fact that the treatments are not appropriate for perpetrators does not undermine either the treatment or the pioneers who developed them. It is simply that those treatments will not be effective for an issue they were not designed to deal with.

We've come to the end of this chapter. You may be feeling overwhelmed by the amount of information I've packed into it. Maybe you realize you have accepted some of the false cultural narratives. At some point we have all done so because they are the wallpaper of our lives. They are the messages we receive through all forms of media and within the justice system. They are both deeply historical and absolutely current.

It may be that reading this chapter has been exceedingly difficult for you. Like me, you may have had (or currently have) a partner who is extremely hurtful. Discovering that it is his choice to behave in those ways can be devastating. While I was with Craig I really believed he could change, either through my love or by Jesus' saving power. I explained away his behaviour as resulting from mental health issues and a bad childhood. I was shattered by the realization that it was a choice; that someone would *choose* to hurt me in all those ways was too much to bear. And yet I return to what will become a familiar theme throughout this book: it is the truth that sets us free. And no matter how unbearable that truth feels, accepting it plants a seed in our soul which can grow into liberation, hope and new life. At the minute it might feel totally incomprehensible, but I am living proof that things can get better.

If you are struggling with this chapter, do take some time out to reflect. You could write your thoughts in a journal, go for a long walk or just take a bit of time to sit quietly and focus on your breathing. The process of reading this book belongs to you. You get to decide how to do it, how long to take and whether to finish it at all. Your experience of reading this book belongs to you and nobody else.

Let us pause for a minute. If prayer is helpful to you, feel free to offer some up to God now. And here is a prayer, if you'd prefer one to read and repeat:

God, it is hard to believe that abuse is a choice. Please would you open my heart and mind to your truths, help me to make sense of all I've read and guide me into more of your truth and freedom. Amen.

I ask no favors for my sex. I surrender not our claim to equality. All I ask of our brethren is, that they will take their feet from off our necks, and permit us to stand upright on that ground which God designed us to occupy.

Sarah Grimké (1837)[40]

4 What in the world is going on? (This is not only about individuals and their relationships)

> [I]t cannot be an accident that everywhere on the globe one sex harms the other so massively that one questions the sanity of those waging the campaign: can a species survive when half of it systematically preys on the other?
>
> Marilyn French[1]

This quote may leave people uncomfortable. Reception of my work often comes with a suspicious undercurrent that I am advocating man-hating. On various occasions this rises to outright hostility, with one seething man approaching me angrily: 'You are harming people. What you're saying is harming people and you're going to continue harming people.' Berating me for a few more minutes without pause, he walked away and left the building without giving me time to respond.

It is uncomfortable to notice that the vast majority of violence is perpetrated by men, whether it is violence mainly directed at women and girls (domestic violence, rape, forced marriage, trafficking) or violence across society (war, terrorism, school shootings, gang violence). Our discomfort at naming men as the majority perpetrators of violence both in the UK and globally is not because we are unaware of the facts, but because we all know men who are not violent. We feel uncomfortable with a portrayal of *all men* as bad. They say the last thing a fish notices is water; we are oblivious to the ubiquity of men's violence. Yet if we want to respond effectively we must not remain oblivious.

Men reading this (if you've stuck with me this long), you may be feeling angry or uncomfortable about my articulation of male violence. You may not be hostile enough to shout at me, but regardless I direct you to the words of American academic Andrea Dworkin,

> Men come to me or to other feminists and say: 'What you're saying about men isn't true. It isn't true of me. I don't feel that way. I'm opposed to all of this.' And I say: Don't tell me. Tell the pornographers. Tell the pimps. Tell the warmakers. Tell the rape apologists and the rape celebrationists and the pro-rape ideal-ogues. Tell the novelists who think rape is wonderful. Tell Larry Flynt [Larry Flynt is a pornographer who published *Hustler* magazine]. Tell Hugh Heffner. There's no point in telling me. I'm only a woman. There's nothing I can do about it. These men presume to speak for you. They are in the public arena saying they represent you. If they don't, then you had better let them know.[2]

We've looked at *what* domestic abuse is and *why* abusers choose to perpetrate abuse. This chapter is all about *how* abusers develop beliefs of ownership and entitlement. If the majority of abusers are male and the majority of violence globally is perpetrated by men, does that mean that men are inherently bad? Does being born male create a propensity to violence? Absolutely not! No matter what the evolutionary biologists try to say!

The dominance of men is known as patriarchy and its prevalence across human history is indisputable, but it wasn't always that way. Anthropologist Mark Dybbe explains: 'There is still this wider perception that hunter–gatherers are more macho or male-dominated. [Yet] it was only with the emergence of agriculture, when people could start to accumulate resources, that inequality emerged.'[3] It was the accruing of resources that caused men to dominate women. Men wanted to ensure their possessions were inherited only by those they had spawned. Women became counted among men's resources, no longer seen as human beings. Interestingly, we find that there is often a correlation between how patriarchal a society is and the levels of male violence towards women.

Recently, I had the privilege of travelling to South Africa to deliver training to a group of practitioners. Prior to my arrival, my materials had been piloted for a year with girls in a school for disadvantaged young people. I arrived in the beautiful city of Cape Town with great trepidation: was I, a white British woman, really able to speak into a culture extremely different from my own? Would it be more difficult to convince them that my analysis was right given that I had not walked in their shoes? As it turned out, that was not the case.

South Africa has the highest rates globally of men killing their partners; a woman is killed by a partner every eight hours. I arrived in Cape Town in the same week that South African athlete Oscar Pistorius had his sentence for killing his girlfriend Reeva Steenkamp increased from 6 years to 15 years. His conviction remains unusual in a country where only 38 per cent of intimate-partner femicides lead to a conviction in less than two years.[4] One in four men in South Africa admit they have raped a woman,[5] while one in every two women will be raped in her lifetime.[6] As Rape Crisis South Africa explains,

> Rape in South Africa has emerged as a crime of extreme violence. Commentators liken the types of rape they see in South Africa to those perpetrated during armed conflict, in terms of the degradation, ritual humiliation and the extent of injuries, such as mutilation, that are involved.[7]

Globally, South Africa has the highest rates of HIV and AIDS. This is not unconnected to the country's rates of sexual violence. Young women contract HIV at rates twice as high as young men, explained by the levels of sexual violence and exploitation men perpetrate towards girls and young women, particularly older men who are seen as 'blessers' and function as so-called 'sugar daddies'.[8] Alongside this, every week in South Africa ten lesbian women are raped by men, apparently to turn them heterosexual; this is known as 'corrective rape'.[9]

In delivering training in South Africa, I discovered that, when men's violence is so pronounced, there is much less resistance to the idea that domestic abuse perpetration is rooted in male socialization. Where I thought there would be resistance to me, there was only a deep sense of relief that someone was openly saying what the participants already knew to be true. When I presented the abusive behaviours described in Chapter 2 there was not incredulity, but knowing nods. The disturbing reality is that abusers across the globe use the same tactics. The dominance of patriarchal norms in South Africa leads to increased male violence. After Reeva Steenkamp's murder, South African politician Lulana Xingwana publicly stated, 'Young Afrikaner men are brought up in the Calvinist religion believing that they own a woman, they own a child, they own everything and therefore they can take that life because they own it.'[10] The more a culture or community believes that men own women, the more violence there will be. Sadly, there is no country in the world that is not historically rooted in the idea that men own women.

In prehistoric societies, it was assumed women produced babies without male involvement as sexual intercourse long preceded a woman's visible pregnancy. From 322 BC Aristotle's idea took hold that, in reproduction, 'all the child's characteristics lay complete in the male sperm. The woman was the soil, receiving and bringing forth the seed, whilst man was the "sower".'[11] This view of women as no more than a receptacle for male seed was accepted until 1677, when the Dutch scientist Antonie van Leeuwenhoek saw through a micro-scope sperm trying to fertilize an egg. For 1,500 years women were not seen as actively involved in the reproduction of humanity. They were seen as 'unfinished men',[12] had no rights and only had value in their relationship to their fathers, husbands and sons. Outrageously, this is still the case for women in much of the majority world: 603 million women live in countries where domestic violence is not yet considered a crime. (Rather than referring to the developing world, I describe this as the majority world, to remind us that we are in the minority.)[13]

Until very recently in the West, men owned women. Men were legally entitled to do what they wanted to the women (and children) they owned. The beliefs of ownership and entitlement that abusive men have are not an aberration, they are historically rooted facts from which we have had a century of legal reforms to distance ourselves. Over the last century women have gained the right to vote. This didn't happen until 1971 in Switzerland, with Saudi Arabian women only gaining voting rights in 2011. Voting rights for women of colour have been hard fought, with Australian Aboriginal people receiving the vote in 1962, 60 years after white women gained the vote. Similarly, African Americans gained the right to vote in 1965; white women gained the vote in 1920, although the suppression of black people's votes in the US continues.[14]

The UK's 1963 Equal Pay Act means women can now expect to be remunerated at the same rate as men. Women can no longer be asked to leave their job once they are married and they can get a loan without their husband's permission. They can drink full pints in the pub (in Ireland in the 1970s it was deemed unladylike for women to drink pints and this was therefore banned)[15] and are allowed to be members of golf clubs.[16] Women can expect that men who rape them, who are violent to them or who stalk them will be prosecuted (it wasn't until 1991 that it became illegal for a man to rape his wife).[17] Within the UK, Western Europe and the US at least, women are full citizens and have full rights with men. In theory.

The pay gap between women and men in the UK remains at 13.9 per cent.[18] Only 5.7 per cent of reported rape cases end in a conviction for the perpetrator,[19] while laws are only just being introduced that will prevent abusive men cross-examining their ex-partners in the family court. Recent House of Commons figures provide evidence that women are bearing 86 per cent of the burden of UK austerity measures.[20] Women's legal rights do not seem to protect them. With a female British prime minister and supposedly equal rights, it can be difficult for society to recognize the continuing injustices women face simply for being born female. These inequalities not only make women's lives difficult, they reinforce abusive men's views of ownership and entitlement.

There is also the media to contend with. Research suggests that adults today consume nearly ten hours of media per day (almost double the amount consumed in 1945).[21] Great harm is done through digital manipulation of images, the sexualization of women, targeted advertising on social media and aggressive consumerism. Add into the mix freely available graphic hardcore pornography and we find that all of our lives are permeated by images of women as objects, men as aggressors and human relationships that prioritize superficial montages of #couplegoals above human connection.

What messages does this send to abusive men? The objectification and sexualization of women encourages men to view women's value as solely sexual, enforcing the role of women as sexually serving men. Pornography shows all those who consume it (both adults and children) that women enjoy pain, like to be degraded and are aroused by aggression and violence.

Alongside this, children are socialized into strict gender roles. Parents tell their little boys not to cry while putting little girls in pretty dresses which restrict their movement. Children are bought toys that reinforce the idea of women as caretakers and men as violent: dolls, toy kitchens, guns and toy soldiers. Their books, TV programmes and education leave girls and boys socialized differently. In the seventeenth century, the French philosopher Nicolas Malebranche stated that women were 'incapable of penetrating truths that are slightly difficult to discover', while in Victorian society it was proposed that 'women's intellectual inferiority stems from their smaller and lighter brains'.[22] Even in 2003, clinical psychologist Simon Baron-Cohen (he is indeed the cousin of the Ali G actor Sacha Baron Cohen!) said: 'The female brain is predominantly hard-wired for empathy. The male brain is predominantly hard-wired for understanding and building systems.'[23] These scientific ideas are undermined by research which has found that the brain is not hard-wired and has 'neural plasticity'. Although this idea was understood by some as early as 1890, it is only in recent years that it has been widely accepted.[24] Research shows that the brain's neural pathways develop as humans interact with the world. These neural pathways can change and die off as new behaviours are enacted.

The significance of this for the way we parent children cannot be overstated. Children are socialized into gender roles, not born into them. As US writer Stan Goff has said, 'We humans are . . . biologically determined not to be biologically determined.'[25] From the moment a baby's sex is announced (whether *in utero* or after birth) the world relates to it according to its genitals. Tone of voice, choice of words, how it's held, its clothes, toys and expectations for its behaviour – every person the child interacts with will be placing it within a gender role of either 'girl' or 'boy'. Girls are told they are pretty or cute. They are given toy make-up and princess dresses and are rescued by princes. They are taught to be nice, kind and friendly, but by their teenage years are assumed to be bitchy and gossip-prone. Men are taught to see blood shed through violence as a symbol of bravery, but see women's monthly blood as shameful and disgusting. Women's lives are saturated with gossip columns telling them they need a man, but also urging them to be an independent woman. They are too fat and too thin and too tall and too short and a dick tease and a prude. As mothers they are not good enough, but without children they are failures. They can never win.

Boys are brought up into a strength that rejects tears, failure and kindness. Boys and girls have the same muscle mass until puberty, but boys are presumed to be stronger than girls. A recent BBC documentary found that seven-year-old boys didn't have words for any emotion except anger.[26] They are taught to reject anything that is girly and are alienated from all that is socially constructed as feminine. TV adverts and programmes mock men's ability to care properly for children or do housework, presenting these jobs as 'women's work'. Such messages are offensive to both men and women. Men build friendships over banter and brutality, and their camaraderie is often based on mocking those who don't conform to masculine stereotypes. They are taught to see women as something to conquer. Slang words used by teenage boys to describe sex include 'smash', 'destroy', 'bang', 'beast', 'hit' and 'pound'.[27] In the UK, the main cause of death for men between 20 and 49 is suicide, which has been linked to the lack of emotional literacy among men.[28] They are socialized to deny weakness and not acknowledge their feelings.

Gender Equity and Reconciliation International (GERI) is an organization working to bridge the huge gap between men and women, creating spaces where men and women can witness the pain caused by patriarchy. I have twice organized UK workshops for women and men. During one of the exercises, men and women sit in two concentric circles, the men witnessing the women's stories and conversations, then the women witnessing the men's. As a witness to men's experiences I found there was an overriding sense that men do not notice their socialization, that they couldn't pinpoint the moment when they began to feel they couldn't admit weakness or fail, that they had to be providers, strong, powerful. As women, we could all share explicit experiences of how patriarchy had damaged us; we all knew its cost. For the men, it was revelatory.

Men are not bad. They live within a system that defines masculinity as not-like-women. These ideas are reinforced by structures which disadvantage women and benefit some men (masculinity is a hierarchy and only the 'Alpha Males' are fully rewarded). Men have an entire system that socializes them into beliefs of ownership and entitlement, and then gives them greater *opportunity* to be abusive. If the structures had favoured women for as long as they've favoured men, the majority of abusers would be female.

Some may see a flaw in the position I am presenting. Surely all men would be abusive if the system worked like that? Why do most men choose not to abuse their partners? There are protective factors that can 'dilute' the impact of patriarchy on boys and men. These include, but are not limited to:

- being brought up within a family where men treat women and girls with respect and empathy;
- having a peer group who encourage them to develop non-patriarchal values;
- having access to strong, diverse female role models;
- their gifts and talents – if a boy is terrible at stereotypically masculine activities he will learn early that patriarchy doesn't benefit every male;
- their personality – some people are naturally gentler than others;
- experiencing serious consequences for harming others, e.g. not getting away with sexually harassing girls in school or bullying other boys and being charged for every offence committed against a woman;
- being encouraged to take responsibility for bad choices, e.g. not being able to lie his way out of consequences;
- being given opportunities to build emotional literacy;
- not being celebrated for abusive or damaging behaviour;
- having gender stereotypes challenged;
- seeing male role models who don't conform to patriarchal expectations;
- living in a society where girls and women are encouraged and able to challenge a male partner who is behaving badly;
- being taught empathy and having it modelled;
- being taught about the challenges women and girls face;
- being taught to be a critical consumer of media.

It is a Christian belief that God designed humanity with free will. Living within a system where we are taught inequality and where some face discrimination and pain does affect our free will, but it does not eradicate it. Ironically, where Christians suggest that gendered behaviour is God's plan, it seems they are suggesting God is limiting our free will based on our genitals. This seems neither logical nor loving. Christian theology is a framework that underpins most Western societies and the woman-hatred present in the writings of the church fathers has contributed to women's oppression. St Aquinas followed Aristotle's view that woman was an unfinished man and concluded that woman should not have been created.[29] St Clement stated: 'Every woman should be filled with shame at the thought that she is a woman.'[30] Tertullian called women 'the devil's gateway',[31] while St John Chrysostom said, 'For what is a woman but an enemy of friendship, an inescapable punishment, a necessary evil, a natural temptation, a domestic danger, delectable mischief, a fault in nature, painted with beautiful colours?'[32] Christian thinkers have much responsibility for the plight of women over the last 2,000 years. We'll look more at Christian theology and domestic abuse in the next chapter.

I was delivering training to church leaders. One participant asked, 'How do I ascertain what is and what isn't abuse? If you are a hammer, you see everything as a nail. I don't want to just assume that every man is abusive.' There is a concern about labelling or becoming excessively cynical and jaded. What could be worse than presuming that someone might be an abuser? Perhaps presuming someone is not an abuser, and him murdering his wife after we encouraged her to re-enter her marriage? What could be worse? Perhaps a significant proportion of abusers being colluded with because we are reluctant to consider that they could be abusive. The current situation is one in which we assume there are no nails. While abusive behaviour remains outside our frame of reference, we have no capacity to be part of the solution. We don't even recognize there is a problem in need of a solution. And while we remain concerned about seeing everything as a nail, 30 per cent of women continue to be subjected to abuse.

Jesus' instruction in Matthew 7.1, 'do not judge', is fundamental to the Christian faith. By suggesting that you identify abusers, is that not in direct contravention of the 'do not judge' rule? The following verse, Matthew 7.2, says, 'For in the same way as you judge others, you will be judged.' Judgements are an entirely necessary aspect of human life. We judge the weather before deciding whether we need a sun hat or an umbrella. We judge how much cake we should eat based on how hungry we are or how delicious it is. We judge whether we should leave our children with someone based on our experience of them as a responsible and safe adult. Life is based on being judgemental.

Jesus is telling us in Matthew 7 that we will be judged by God according to the way we have judged others. The problem comes, then, if we make judgements from a place of malicious or selfish intent – for instance, in a work or social situation, someone new arrives, making us feel threatened so that we judge everything the newcomer does negatively, based on how he or she, probably unintentionally, is triggering our insecurities. This is hilariously depicted in the US film *Bridesmaids*. Equally, prejudices may inform our decisions. Prejudice is about pre-judging, without substantial evidence:

- being outraged at someone who appears able-bodied parking in a disabled space until, two minutes later, he emerges from the shop with an elderly person in a wheelchair;
- presuming someone with a Birmingham accent is an unintelligent and unimaginative criminal, until she tells us she is an Anglican bishop (research has found that those with a Brummie (Birmingham) accent are viewed in this way);[33]
- assuming black girls are more sexually mature and less innocent than white girls of the same age (it has been found through research that this is a prevalent racist judgement made by white people);[34]
- presuming the woman who discloses her husband's abuse is exaggerating, because he is such a nice man.

When we view someone as 'not abusive', we are making a judgement. And when we don't believe women who tell us they have been raped or abused, we are making a judgement that they are liars and the men who harmed them are falsely accused. I am not advocating for an approach that assumes all men are abusers. I am suggesting that we reserve judgement. We should not assume either way. It is never out of the realms of possibility that someone could be abusive. Accepting that fact does not make us judgemental; it makes us realistic about the nature of human beings (this is well documented in the Bible).

If selfish attitudes, insecurities or prejudice are the dominant forces in our decision-making, we risk being judged very harshly by God. Do we really want to be judged in the same way we are judging others? If our judgements become based on reality and self-awareness, and are founded in the spiritual gifts of love, joy, peace, patience, kindness, generosity, faithfulness, gentleness and self-control – the gifts that Christians believe the Holy Spirit gives us to live out our lives as Christians – we will find that they will more closely align with how we would want God to judge us.[35] Interestingly, in a letter to Christian believers in Corinth, the Apostle Paul tells us that we should judge: 'What business is it of mine to judge outside the church? Are you not to judge those inside?'[36] Paul suggests that it is not our place to judge non-Christians, but that actually we should be judging other believers. Are they living according to Jesus' teaching? Certainly this provides a precedent for holding abusers who profess to be Christians to account within our church communities.

Some people view my analysis as 'too simple'. The idea that abusive behaviour is rooted in beliefs of ownership and entitlement seems too simple for such a huge problem. Particularly for those coming from a background in psychology, it seems I am reducing the complexity of human beings to a couple of basic beliefs. That is not what I am doing. Humans are extremely complex and are driven by innumerable agendas. I am not reducing all human activity to two beliefs. I am stating that a particular facet of human activity (men's abuse of women) is rooted in two beliefs that are propped up by a massive interconnected and complex web encompassing history, culture, law, media, religion and more. This web is formed of a thread made of male power over women (also known as patriarchy). The solutions are expansive and complex, not least because women's liberation is not a forward-facing trajectory. Women throughout history have done extraordinary things that have subsequently been ignored: Artemisia Gentileschi was a master painter, Rosalind Franklin discovered DNA, Queen Salome Alexandra had an extra-ordinary reign in Israel (my friend Lauren Jacobs has written a book about her),[37] the Apostle Junia was 'prominent among the apostles'.[38] These women, and many more, both those we know about and those we don't, have been ignored by history (or, in the case of Junia, rewritten as a man until 2011).[39] Writer and activist Bidisha calls this 'cultural femicide'.[40]

Currently, women's contributions are more likely to be recognized and we have more legal rights. Films like *Wonder Woman* present women as powerful but, as the #metoo social media pheno-menon demonstrated, this does not stop men in positions of authority systematically sexually harassing and abusing women. Family plan-ning resources and contraception have enabled women to control their fertility, but male sexual power continues to dominate intimate relationships. Women can work outside the home and can generally have financial independence, but men rarely do more work in the home. Women end up doing second, third and even fourth shifts in their personal lives. Women usually remain responsible for all the emotional labour[41] and most of the housekeeping and childcare. One of the many things I cannot abide is when men are described as 'babysitting' their own children. YOU CANNOT BABYSIT YOUR OWN CHILDREN. IT IS CALLED PARENTING.

As mentioned previously, rape within marriage became illegal in the UK in 1991;[42] although this did help women, we have seen a proliferation of other forms of sexual violence, including date rape and an increasingly uncritical acceptance of graphic sexual violence in pornography, television series and films. The now infamous song 'Blurred Lines' includes a lyric about a woman getting her 'ass' ripped in two. Although it has been over 20 years since UK judges had to warn juries in rape cases about the 'untruthfulness of women', disbelief of women who have been sexually abused continues.[43]

We have to stop somewhere when seeking to demonstrate the all-pervasive nature of patriarchy and its continued impact on our lives today. Knowing the cause of men's violence is not as simple as it might first seem. My wonderful friend Susan King likens patriarchy and male domination to gravity. When Isaac Newton identified gravity in 1687, it turned out to be relatively simple; what goes up must come down. However, overcoming gravity to become airborne in vehicles that were heavier than the air took until 1900, with the work of the Wright brothers. In the same way, identifying the cause of male violence may be relatively simple, but finding solutions is much more complex. Gravity is a static force that remains stable, unlike patriarchy and male domination, which morph and change shape in every culture and community. We've got a huge task on our hands if we want to change things! Thankfully, as Christians we know that we don't do this work alone: we have the God of all creation living inside us.

As we come to the end of this chapter, take some time for processing. Has it triggered any concerns for you? Do you agree with my analysis? If not, why not? What can you do to make sense of the bits that don't feel right for you? It can be really hard to become conscious of the many different influences that affect our lives and choices. We can resist understanding them. But denial is not a useful strategy for human flourishing (no matter how useful it can be in the short term). We need to be willing to face the reality with open hearts and minds if we hope to make the world a better, safer place. If you're the praying sort, take a few moments to consider this chapter. Bring to God your concerns and your feelings – he can handle them! If reading a prayer is helpful for you, here's one to read. If prayer isn't your thing, then feel free to ignore this bit!

God, there is so much that is wrong with the world. It is hard to become aware of inequality and the forces that are influencing my ideas and feelings. Please make visible to me your views on this. Help me to move forward into greater knowledge, understanding and freedom. Keep my mind and heart open according to your great love and grace. Amen.

> When I speak of an end to suffering, I don't mean anesthesia. I mean knowing the world, and my place in it, not in order to stare with bitterness and detachment, but as a womanly series of choices: and here I write the words, in their fullness: powerful; womanly.
>
> Adrienne Rich (1983)[44]

5 What would Jesus do? (All that theology stuff)

I was a teenager when Christian bookshops began selling 'What would Jesus do?' (WWJD) paraphernalia. I would dream of owning all the rainbow-coloured bouncy balls, magnets and plastic slide puzzles, yet would inevitably leave the bookshop with only one WWJD bracelet purchased by my mum. Since then we've had critiques of this phrase that range from 'Shouldn't we be asking "What is Jesus doing?"?' to it being an example of the 'absolutized "Conservative Self"'.[1] One writer explains: 'It is the very presence and indwelling of the resurrected Christ that gives vitality to the Christian faith and distinguishes it in essence from ethics-based religions. WWJD robs young believers of that essential vitality.'[2]

I thought WWJD bracelets were what all the cool (Christian) kids were wearing. Admittedly, I wasn't especially cool myself, but I did desperately want to gain God's approval (it took a few more years for me to discover that God's grace invalidates any need for his approval, hallelujah!). I had an impressive collection of bracelets, including various different-coloured WWJD wristbands and a FROG one (the acronym for Fully Rely On God)! I would wear all my bracelets on my left wrist to hide cuts I had inflicted on myself. The first time I self-harmed I made a cut in the shape of a cross. It was my way of mitigating the fact I felt I'd failed God by not treating my body as a temple. In an unintentional allegory, the badly thought-out Christian platitude covered the destruction I was wreaking on myself.

Much of Christian culture is filled with badly thought-out platitudes. We believe in a God who came to earth to make a way for us to relate with him directly, but we're often keener on listening to people telling us what God wants than on going directly to him. Which is a shame, given how much it cost Jesus for us to get direct access to God.

Within this chapter we will consider both Christian culture and Christian theology. If you're not a Christian, it might be worth approaching this chapter as a curious anthropologist delving into these strange Christian-shaped human beings, whose world seems quite different from your own. For those without a faith perspective, the implications for Christian women subjected to abuse can be difficult to grasp. However, if someone believes God (an almighty force she seeks to love and serve and who she believes loves her too) is telling her she has to stay with her partner, that will be the defining factor in her decisions. I've worked with women who felt that domestic abuse services expected them to leave their faith at the door of the refuge and were unable to understand that their faith was as important to them as their ethnicity, culture, sexuality or family (sometimes it will be more important than these other parts of their identity). This chapter may be full of alien concepts, but please stick with me as we consider Christian faith. And if you really can't endure it, you could always skip a couple of pages (not too many, though!). If you need some cake to make it bearable, please do cut yourself a *large* slice!

It's not easy to sum up Christian doctrine in a few points, but I shall try.

- God made humans perfect.
- Humans made bad choices and were no longer perfect (this is known as the fall).
- God left humans to deal with the consequences of their bad choices, but promised there was hope for redemption.
- A long time later, God chose to become a human baby in Jesus. His life and teaching modelled how humans should choose to live.

- After his 33 years on earth, the earthly authorities were threatened by Jesus' teaching. Jesus chose to die, taking upon himself the eternal consequences of human failure.

- Jesus rose from the dead, and his life, death and resurrection became the way of redemption for all of humanity. After he returned to heaven, the form of God found in the Holy Spirit became available to humanity.

- By accepting that we are messed up and make bad choices, and that we can't be perfect on our own, we can choose to follow Jesus. If we believe that Jesus' death and resurrection transform us and if we choose to follow his teachings we can be set free from the eternal consequences of our bad choices. After we have made this choice, the Holy Spirit will help us to make good choices and enable us to do supernatural stuff.

Regardless of how Christian history has tried to place greater blame on women than men for the fall, mainstream Christianity is now agreed (at least in theory) that men and women are both equally responsible for the fall and that both have 'sinned and fall short of the glory of God'.[3] Feminists fighting for women's liberation would not subscribe to this gospel narrative, but would argue that a view of women-as-perfect and men-as-evil dehumanizes both men and women and denies women the humanness of bad choices while men are denied the innate humanness of good choices. Alongside this, if men are evil, then their abuse is not a choice, it is an inevitability. Neither the gospel nor any of the women's movements allows for such an appallingly distorted view of humanity (a view that truly is man-hating). Women and men are human beings capable of great goodness and great evil. What does the Bible have to say about this?

For those reading this without a Christian worldview, there are different ways the Genesis account is understood by Christians. Some believe in a physical Adam and Eve, while others see the account as a myth filled with truth. In the original texts, the creation narrative is written as a poem. Genesis 3.16 comes soon after the fall, as God explains the consequences of human bad choices: 'To the woman he said, "I will greatly increase your pangs in childbearing; in pain you shall bring forth children, yet your desire shall be for your husband, and he shall rule over you."' There is little time for me to explore the first part of this verse, though biblical scholar Carol Meyers has suggested that the first part of the verse could be translated, 'I will greatly increase your work and pregnancies.'[4] Across biblical scholarship there are two ways of reading the second half of this verse, usually described as 'complementarian' and 'egalitarian'. The complementarian view is that this verse is God's plan for humanity: God decrees that men will rule over their wives and it is a good thing. The egalitarian view is that God's best plan for humanity happened before the fall, so this verse is God listing the consequences of their bad choices; husbands ruling over their wives is not God's plan, it is the reality of what happens in a post-fall society. You may (or may not) be surprised to learn that I hold an egalitarian view.

If a *consequence* of human bad choice is patriarchy (as mentioned previously, patriarchy is a system in which men dominate women), then Christians can respond to male violence as a consequence of the fall. After reading this far, you're probably beginning to see the harm abusers do, and it's important we locate that as part of the wider system of 'sin' that ravages our planet. And as Christians we can offer the gospel as hope for change. Jesus' life, death and resurrection give us a redemptive narrative that says, 'This isn't how it was meant to be.' The Holy Spirit can enable us to live redeemed lives free of 'sin and death',[5] including the death brought about by patriarchy. The theologian Walter Wink explains that when we think about spiritual powers, we should consider them as greater than individual demons inhabiting people. Racism and consumerism are two of the many spiritual principalities and powers that Wink suggests the Apostle Paul is urging us to wrestle against, 'For our struggle is not against flesh and blood but against the rulers, against the authorities, against the powers of this dark world and against the spiritual forces of evil in the heavenly realms.'[6] Wink views patriarchy as a principality and power. For egalitarians, the Christian call is to abolish patriarchy.[7]

Complementarians would generally view male violence as a distortion of God's good plan of patriarchy. Men are called to protect, love and lead women. Rather than challenging the power men have, complementarians would argue that men's power is to be used in service of women. The gospel does not eradicate patriarchy but redeems it to be as God intended. If you hold to a complementarian view of Scripture, I hope that you feel my characterization of your theology has been fair. We may disagree theologically, but I hope you will find significant benefit in reading this book. My expertise and knowledge is based on a decade of working on domestic abuse issues and I hope that my theological stance will not alienate you from utilizing this book. If you have never heard of complementarian or egalitarian theology and are feeling thoroughly confused, please don't stop reading! I hope my explanations give you food for thought rather than leaving you alienated or confused. You don't have to know what theology you hold to go forward, but these two positions are the framework for different Christian views of male violence.

For those of us who are Christians in the West, our understanding of the world is a conglomeration (what a word!) of our upbringing (which may or may not have been Christian), our experience of the world and our understanding of our faith. The ground we stand on has a layer of bedrock, which is Western civilization; the topsoil is our experiences of the world, and the surface layer is Christian culture.

Christian culture (I am generally referring to evangelical Christian culture) is full of gendered language, expectations and re-strictions. Male Christian leaders introduce themselves with anecdotes about their hot wives and beautiful daughters. Christian bookshops sell princess Bibles for girls, warrior Bibles for boys, books about how wives should pray, why men hate church and how to be wild at heart or captivating. Christian women's events are called things like

'Radiant Glow' (which disappointingly won't include actual women who glow) while Christian men's events are called 'Raw Meat for Jesus'. Women are asked to join the crèche and tea rota while men are asked to preach. Our entire culture is predicated on gender differences and the building of rapport through predictable tropes about women and men.

Alongside gender stereotyping in Christian culture, we must reckon with the culture's super-weird approach to sex. Christian culture teaches that women barely think about sex, unlike men who think about sex every seven seconds (this is a made-up statistic),[8] which means that women should not wear clothing that might make men think about sex because then men will only be able to think about sex, and 'civilization will crumble' (this is something Christian writer Dave Murrow actually states about the need to maintain toxic masculinity).[9] Christians are taught that they mustn't think about, look at or have sex until they are married. But once the marriage vows are exchanged, married Christians should have awesome, mind-blowing Christian sex that honours this amazing gift that God has given to his people. It is rather unrealistic for someone to immediately transition from avoiding thinking about sex to suddenly having mind-blowing sex.

Christian culture's approach to sex and to gender differences may reinforce an abuser's beliefs of ownership and entitlement and undermine the protective factors boys and men need in their lives to prevent them developing negative beliefs about a partner. Let's move beyond these implicit messages within Christian culture to look at the explicit messages about domestic abuse in churches.

One day, Sarah, a church leader, called me. Mark, Marion and their three children were a family in their church. Marion had disclosed that Mark had been physically violent to her. Sarah was unsure how to help. My first question: did Sarah feel able to advise Marion to leave Mark? 'Of course!' replied Sarah. 'We wouldn't want anybody to suffer abuse!' Twenty minutes into the conversation

Sarah said to me, 'Mark was going to leave Marion, so we felt we could support her.' I clarified with her: was Mark's instigation the only reason she felt able to support Marion's marriage ending? She hesitantly agreed that it was and, when I asked why, told me that the Bible insists divorce is wrong and that forgiveness is important. The majority of Christians think that they think abuse is wrong. But a more in-depth conversation about abuse often reveals that their beliefs about divorce, forgiveness, headship, submission, repentance, gender roles and relationships are subconsciously driving them in a different direction, pushing the woman towards the abuser. The pain many Christian women carry from their church's collusion with the man who abused them is heartbreaking. Although occasionally women will tell me of positive experiences, too often churches compound the abuse and further hurt the woman (and her children).

How should we approach the Bible? Some Christians identify as 'Bible-believing' and consider themselves as simply doing 'what the Bible says'. However, care must be taken not to reduce the Bible to a 'how to' book. The Bible is a collection of ancient literature. It was written in ancient languages and cultures. The geography, politics and translation of the text are all important aspects to understand. God is indeed big enough to reveal himself to us through the text, but he also created us with brains. For many Christians, there is an appreciation of the strangeness of the Bible. Its language, the cultures it describes, the historical and geographic locations and even people's names can feel strange to us, reading it in the twenty-first century. However, something we are often not very aware of is how oblivious we are to all that we bring to the biblical text. We always bring more to the Bible than we take away. There are a few questions we can ask ourselves when reading the Bible to consider what we are bringing to the text (the technical name for this is an 'in front of the text' matrix).

- Am I open to being transformed by the text? Or am I reading to prove that I am right?

- Where is the text coming from? Who was the original audience? What is the purpose of the text? What does Christian tradition tell us about the text? How do other books and passages in the biblical canon connect with this one? It's important not to read a Bible passage in isolation from the rest of the book it is in, the wider biblical canon or the context in which it was written.[10]
- Where am I coming from? What is my culture, language, social framework, experience? How might that influence the way I read?
- Why am I reading this text? What is my motivation? What am I hoping to get from it?
- Is this a universal thing, like loving my neighbour? Or is this a contextual thing, like not eating prawns?[11] (I do *love* a nice prawn cocktail.)
- In the time the text was written, how was the society ordered? Who has the power in this text?
- Does this text relate to Jesus' life, death and resurrection? Particularly with the New Testament, are we reading the text with an acknowledgement of Jesus' teaching and life?
- What can I imagine that has not been said in the text? Whose voice has been silenced? (It is often women's voices that are silent or women who are unnamed, e.g. Tamar, Bathsheba and the woman at the well.)

Having established that there's lots to take into account when we read the Bible, we find there are three elements to the subconscious beliefs underpinning the actions Christians take around abuse: power, gender and relationships.

POWER

What comes to mind when we think about power and the Bible? Is it God's mighty power? Is it the power of the Holy Spirit? Perhaps you haven't read the Bible much and nothing comes to mind. That's OK! There are two passages we're going to consider:

As Jesus himself said:

> You know that the rulers of the Gentiles lord it over them, and their high officials exercise authority over them. Not so with you. Instead, whoever wants to become great among you must be your servant, and whoever wants to be first must be your slave – just as the Son of Man did not come to be served, but to serve and to give his life as a ransom for many.[12]

As the Apostle Paul said in his letter to the Philippians:

> In your relationships with one another, have the same mindset as Christ Jesus: who, being in very nature God, did not consider equality with God something to be used to his own advantage [to gain power]; rather, he made himself nothing by taking the very nature of a servant, being made in human likeness. And being found in appearance as a man, he humbled himself by becoming obedient to death – even death on a cross![13]

Jesus' model, as explained by both Jesus and Paul, is that Christians are not to dominate or exercise power over others. We are called to make ourselves nothing and be willing to serve others. Is this the model we see used by churches? Perhaps not. There are mega-churches with huge congregations and multimillion-dollar budgets and small parish churches with power-hungry parishioners dominating PCC meetings. There is an entire Christian industrial complex centred on large numbers of people paying money to hear another person tell them what God is saying. When Christians do not use Jesus' model for power, it will spill over into the way domestic abuse issues are responded to. Jesus *made himself* nothing. He wasn't forced to become nothing. He chose it. When someone is subjected to abuse, she is being forced to become nothing by another human being. She is not choosing it. Power cannot be laid down by someone who has no power. When someone has been subjected to abuse we must seek to restore her agency and autonomy so she is in a position to make choices about *how* she uses her power. And where someone is seeking out power or abusing it, we have a responsibility to challenge him.

GENDER

There are many Bible passages that are used to perpetuate men's abuse of women. Whole books have been written on them.[14] We will explore only two Bible passages. We'll start with Genesis 2.18, which takes place in the Garden of Eden. God has made the world, the animals and Adam. Even though Adam has named all the animals, none of them are equal to him. Up until this verse, God has said that each thing is good, but now he explains that something is not good: 'The LORD God said, "It is not good for the man to be alone. I will make a helper suitable for him."'

Many books, websites and Christian events focus on the role of woman as man's 'helper' or 'help meet'. One of the bestselling of these is *Created to Be His Help Meet* by Debi Pearl. Within the book she explains, 'The only position where you will find real fulfilment as a woman is as a help meet to your husband.'[15] Although many Christians would dispute this statement, the view remains pervasive across Christian culture. This verse has been used to oppress women, but there are ways of understanding the original text that emphasize equality. As biblical scholar Phyllis Trible explains:

> In the Old Testament the word helper (*'ezer*) has many usages. It can be a proper name for a male. In our story it describes the animals and the woman. In some passages it characterizes Deity. God is the helper of Israel . . . By itself the word does not specify positions within relationships; more particularly, it does not imply inferiority . . . The word *neged*, which joins *'ezer*, connotes equality: a helper who is a counterpart . . . My translation

is this: God is the helper superior to man; the animals are helpers inferior to man; woman is the helper equal to man.[16]

With deeper analysis, we find that many biblical passages which have been used to justify the oppression of women can actually be a source of liberation. This is the case for Ephesians 5.21–25, the second passage we'll explore. This is an excerpt from a letter to a church at Ephesus (the people who lived there were known as the Ephesians). This passage comes towards the end of the letter and the author is instructing the Ephesians on how to live a holy life:[17]

> Submit to one another out of reverence for Christ. Wives, submit yourselves to your own husbands as you do to the Lord. For the husband is the head of the wife as Christ is the head of the church, his body, of which he is the Saviour. Now as the church submits to Christ, so also wives should submit to their husbands in everything. Husbands, love your wives, just as Christ loved the church and gave himself up for her.

This passage has been used to insist women submit to an abusive husband, indicating that if a woman submits well enough her husband will stop being abusive. Not only is this a toxic and incorrect application of the text, it also colludes with the abuser and enables him to keep sinning. Jesus' life shows us that we have a responsibility to challenge those making bad choices and not enable their behaviour. In this passage the original word for 'head' in Koine (or biblical) Greek is *kephalē*. Often assumed to imply a husband's authority over his wife, the word *kephalē* was never used to imply leadership or authority over others. It was frequently used to describe a physical human head and to mean 'source': the source of a river.[18] This led biblical scholars Letha Dawson Scanzoni and Nancy Hardesty to affirm a reading of verse 23 as 'the husband is the *source* of the wife', linking this to the creation narrative in which Adam's rib was the source of Eve's creation.

When this passage is not hijacked by readings that assume headship as 'authority over', we find that verse 21 exhorts us all to submit to one another, rather than just women submitting to men. In verses 22–24, Paul illustrates this *mutual* submission by providing an example of women submitting to their husbands, explaining that the man is the source of the woman. In verse 25 he insists that men love their wives as Christ loved the church; husbands should be willing to 'give themselves up for' their wives. The woman is told to submit to her husband; the man is told to love and be willing to die for his wife. This is mutuality, not unequal authority. As theologian Elaine Storkey has said, 'We assume that because the Bible doesn't ask men to submit to their wives, that they should not. Nowhere in the Bible does it ask women to love their husbands and we don't assume that they shouldn't.'[19]

RELATIONSHIPS

All aspects of relationships are relevant to the support (or lack of it) offered by churches to women who have been subjected to abuse. For the sake of brevity, there are only five relationship themes that we shall consider: forgiveness, repentance, divorce, suffering and prayer.

FORGIVENESS

Christian writer Max Lucado famously said: 'Forgiveness is unlocking the door to set someone free and realising you were the prisoner!' Jesus' teaching states that forgiveness is a Christian imperative. In the books of Matthew and Mark, Jesus explains that God will not forgive us unless we are willing to forgive others.[20] When I was with Craig, I thought I had to forgive whatever he did and try to forget it – then God would fix everything. If I showed Craig Jesus' love through my forgiveness then he would become a Christian and everything would be wonderful. But it turns out forgiveness does not mean nullifying the consequences of someone's behaviour.

Joseph without his technicolour dream coat is a helpful biblical character when we are thinking about forgiveness. Along with his stint in an Andrew Lloyd Webber musical, Joseph takes up more space in the Bible book of Genesis than his great-grandad Abraham. Thanks to Joseph being super-annoying, his older brothers sell him into Egyptian slavery. His rich mistress attempts to rape him; because he is a man she doesn't manage to, but because he is a slave he is thrown into prison. His supernatural skill of interpreting dreams leads to him becoming Pharaoh's second-in-command. While he's in control of famine rationing, Joseph's awful-but-now-starving brothers come and beg Pharaoh's second-in-command for food. They don't realize he is their brother because he is important and has a snake hat. He tests them to see if they can be honest: will they care for their youngest brother or betray him to save themselves? When they pass both tests they have an emotional reunion befitting the *Long Lost Family* TV show.

Joseph's reconciliation with his brothers is delayed until they prove they have changed. Can they be honest? Can they be caring? He avoids vulnerability, hiding behind his snake hat until he is confident they aren't going to hurt him again. Unless an abuser proves he has changed, forgiveness should never require the people he has abused (his partner and children) to be vulnerable to him. Even where change is evident, forgiveness is primarily an attitude of the heart. The damage an abuser does may never be healed, but forgiveness can be a choice to no longer wish an abuser be castrated without anaesthetic.

In Matthew 18.15–17, Jesus teaches on accountability, saying that if another believer sins, we should hold him or her to account. If someone refuses to listen, that person should be rejected from the community. After this he speaks about forgiving someone 77 times (or 70 times 7, depending on the translation you look at). It often goes unacknowledged that the forgiveness passage in Matthew comes within a context of accountability for those who refuse to stop making bad choices. My attempts at forgiveness while with Craig were actually a form of denial that left me highly traumatized. I could never really forget what he did to me, yet I thought forgiveness meant wiping the slate clean. It is only God's forgiveness that 'washes us whiter than snow';[21] we cannot offer such forgiveness to other human beings. My life was the slate of Craig's abuse and I can't forget or wipe away the suffering he has caused me.

Before we can forgive we must begin by counting the cost of what has been done to us. If we are unable or unwilling to face what someone has done to us, if we minimize or deny the full impact of what he has done (it was just a slap/I'm OK really/it could have been worse), then we are not truly counting the cost of his actions. Similarly, if we justify his behaviour in order to forgive him (he didn't mean it/ couldn't help it/was drunk, etc.) we are reducing the cost to make it bearable. My experience is that forgiveness is a lifelong journey. Craig has damaged me in ways that will never be repaired. The joy of my children's early years will always be overshadowed by Craig's abuse. If he had cut off my leg, I would be forever physically disabled by his actions. As it is, I am forever emotionally and psychologically disabled. I have forgiven him and feel no anger towards him but I needed time to be angry with him, to truly feel the pain and own it, before 'releasing him from prison'. I needed to gain understanding about what abuse does and stop blaming myself. It was only once I had regained ownership of my life that I was able to forgive Craig.

REPENTANCE

Christianity is based on repentance and the understanding that people are able to change. Becoming a Christian is about accepting that we are messed up and choosing to live differently, helped by the Holy Spirit. As brilliant as this is, it can make it much harder to break free from an abuser. A repentant person will apologize, but not everyone who apologizes is repentant. When I was with Craig, I thought that every time he said he was sorry it meant he had repented. Desperate for God to change him, I would cling to an apology as proof of change, even when his apology was, 'I don't remember hurting you, but if you say I did, then I'm sorry.'

'Sorry' might be the hardest word for Elton John but, for an abuser, 'sorry' is often the easiest word. It is taking full responsibility that is hard for an abuser, choosing not to minimize, deny or justify his behaviour. Most abusers say sorry. Most do not change. Without negative consequences, an abuser's behaviour may escalate. Abusers, like children, need to experience negative effects for their behaviour. The *Amplified Bible* describes repentance as having four elements:

1 changing your inner self – your old way of thinking;
2 regretting past sins (the 1987 version of this was 'abhorrence of your past sin');[22]
3 living your life in a way that proves repentance;
4 seeking God's purpose for your life.

The Bible makes it clear that human bad choices alienate us from God, yet Christian culture often advocates a change-less form of repentance. When an abuser's apology is accepted without it being accompanied by sustained change in his thinking, abhorrence for his behaviour and living life in a new way, this distorts and devalues the transformative power of repentance. Christians believe that God gives opportunities for new life, but Christian culture's emptying out of repentance to nothing-but-an-apology belittles the amazing gift that God has given for humanity to be changed and restored. Theologian Dietrich Bonhoeffer described this as 'cheap grace'. Unless Christians begin to take seriously the work of repentance, they give an abuser permission for further abuse. Women and children will continue to believe that an apology is enough. They will cling to the false hope that this is the time their husband will stop raping them, hurting them, demeaning them, exhausting them and isolating them. And their church and fellow Christians will be fanning the flames of that false hope.

DIVORCE

Jesus' teaching on divorce seems clear. Matthew's Gospel ('Gospel' is a fancy word to describe the books that are biographies of Jesus' life; there are four, written by Matthew, Mark, Luke and John) states that 'whoever divorces his wife, except for sexual immorality, and marries another woman, commits adultery',[23] while Mark's Gospel explains, 'Whoever divorces his wife and marries another commits adultery against her; and if she divorces her husband and marries another, she commits adultery.'[24]

An extraordinary thing about God becoming human is that Jesus was born into a specific culture. Given that we have 2,000 years' distance from that culture, some of Jesus' teachings are difficult to grasp. In Jesus' time, women's safety and security lay in them having a husband who could provide for them. Women had no access to contraception; childbearing took most of their resources. There was no welfare system, no pensions or care homes. A woman without a husband was either destitute or a prostitute or both. Dr David Instone-Brewer is a rabbinic scholar. His work on understanding the context of Jesus' divorce teaching is very helpful in providing a biblical basis for divorce when a spouse is abusive. He explains:

> A few decades before Jesus' ministry a new form of divorce called 'Any Cause' was introduced by lawyers of the Hillelite party of Pharisees. They derived it from the phrase in Deuteronomy 24.1 where divorce is allowed for 'a cause of indecency' . . . They said that this word indicated a separate type of divorce which was based on 'a cause' which could be any cause from a burnt meal to wrinkly skin . . . Before the 'Any Cause' divorce became popular, Judaism had four grounds for divorce based on the Old Testament: adultery (based on Deuteronomy 24.1) and neglect of food, clothing or love (based on Exodus 21.10f). These latter three grounds were recognised by all factions within Judaism and allowed divorce by women as well as men.[25]

Jesus' teaching on divorce leaves the other reasons for divorce intact: a lack of providing food, clothing or love. Jesus intended to protect women from destitution or prostitution by forcing their husbands to honour their marriage vows. It is ironic that a teaching intended to protect women now perpetuates men's abuse of women. Christianity recognizes marriage as a covenant agreement, seeing divorce as the breaking of that covenant. Abuse or adultery breaks the marriage covenant; when someone is the victim of adultery or abuse, filing for divorce merely makes public her or his spouse's breaking of the covenant.

SUFFERING

Mike Pearl (husband of the aforementioned Debi) published a blog post advising Sarah, whose husband is abusive, 'An angry husband cannot defeat a Spirit-filled wife, nor can he take satisfaction in her silent suffering, for she stands straight and unapologetic as she looks him in the eye with a knowing that pierces to his innermost being.'[26] All the responsibility is yet again on the wife. Jesus' model for how to pray includes asking God to 'deliver us from evil'. For any Christian to tell Sarah she should endure evil while Jesus has exhorted each Christian to pray to be delivered from it seems counterproductive (and extremely dangerous). Surely Sarah's actions should align with God's in helping her to be delivered from evil. The old story comes to mind about the woman who asks God to save her when her home is flooded, but turns down the rescue helicopter in favour of 'waiting for God to turn up'. The reality is that if Sarah's husband is going to kill her, no amount of 'piercing his innermost being' is going to keep her or her children alive.

The New Testament includes various exhortations about persecution and suffering. Jesus was crucified, John the Baptist and the Apostle Paul were decapitated, while St Peter was crucified (possibly upside down). The early Christians anticipated suffering as a necessary part of following the way of Jesus, which was seen by the imperial powers as a threat to their ideals. Thousands of years later we find that, within the West, the imperial powers are generally based on Christianity, with persecution remaining a serious threat for Christians in north-east Africa, south Asia and some of the surrounding countries.[27] Although religious persecution is not a problem in the West, the biblical passages on suffering are often reapplied to other forms of suffering. When it comes to the suffering abu-sive men inflict on their wives, such a reapplication is extremely dangerous.

The temptation of Jesus is described in three of the four Gospel narratives.[28] Jesus fasts in the desert for 40 days while being tempted by the devil, at the end of which he is (rather understatedly) hungry. He proceeds to be tested by the devil in three ways. It's a bit like an early version of *The Crystal Maze*, in which the eternity of civilization hangs in the balance. The devil takes Jesus up to the highest point of the temple and quotes the Bible at him:

> If you really are the Son of God, throw yourself down. For it is written, 'He will command his angels concerning you, and they will lift you up in their hands, so that you will not strike your foot against a stone.'[29]

Jesus is having none of it. He quotes the Bible right back at the devil and says, 'It is also written, "Do not put the Lord your God to the test."'[30] When someone is being subjected to abuse, telling her to suffer for Jesus mirrors the devil telling Jesus to jump off a building: it is putting God to the test. We should be partners with God in enabling people to be delivered from the evil of abuse, not insisting they have a faith that tests God.

PRAYER CHANGES EVERYTHING

Christian culture isn't very sure how to deal with unanswered prayer. All four Gospels give assurances that God will answer prayers. Jesus tells us to 'ask and it will be given to you',[31] 'ask for anything in my name and I will do it'[32] and says that 'whatever you ask for in prayer, believe that you have received it, and it will be yours'.[33] Then there are the cryptic stories he tells of annoying widows[34] and shamelessly audacious neighbours who repeatedly demand justice or bread in the middle of the night.[35] Jesus' teaching seems to be clear: God will answer our prayers if we believe and are persistent. Except he doesn't. Even in Jesus' lifetime, we see him asking for God to save him from crucifixion, yet he still has to suffer. Paul is still beheaded. And Peter crucified upside down. Children die of incurable diseases, and authoritarian regimes destroy lives. Prayers are often left unanswered in each of our lives. When I was with Craig I used to pray all the time for him to change. I would hold on to the verses about asking and it being given to me. If prayer had been a form of physical exercise, I would have been an Olympic-standard athlete. Praying, hoping, believing. And yet he didn't change.

The Old Testament tells the early history of the Jewish people. One of the key players is David. You may have heard how he killed Goliath the giant. Killing the giant brings David to the attention of Saul, Israel's king. Saul utilizes David in both harp-playing and enemy-killing (he had a diverse set of skills). David's exploits (including delivering 200 Philistine foreskins to Saul) cause him to become famous. Saul feels threatened by David's popularity and seeks to murder him. How does David, 'the man after God's heart', respond to Saul's abuse? Does he stay and pray, believing that God will change Saul? No, he doesn't. He runs and hides in a large cave (400 men join him).[36] Saul is out looking for David. Nature calls and he finds a cave to have a poo, but coincidentally Saul's toilet cave happens to also be where David is hiding. Saul assumes the pooping position. From the back of the cave, David's friends silently gesticulate that he should kill Saul while he has the chance − it's clearly God's providence. But David trusts that Saul is God's anointed leader and refuses to harm him. Instead, he creeps behind Saul (who is fully focused on the straining necessary when you have the diet of an ancient Hebrew king) and cuts off the corner of Saul's robe, which has tassels at each corner to help the wearer remember the commands of God.[37] Saul wipes and leaves. David emerges moments later holding up the tasselled corner, proving to Saul that he could have killed him but chose not to. Eventually David becomes king after Saul literally falls on his sword.[38]

When it comes to dealing with an abuser, David's story provides a strategy. If someone is abusing us, we should find a cave to hide in and seek to hold the person to account. Often, as David found, the abuser will not change. But it gives a possibility of safety. My experience is that God can transform all situations, but he may not do what we want him to do.

What would Jesus do? What did he do? What is he doing? What might he say to us if we were to be fully aware of his 'very presence and indwelling'? Luke 4.16–21 tells us how Jesus announced his role:

> When he [Jesus] came to Nazareth, where he had been brought up, he went to the synagogue on the sabbath day, as was his custom. He stood up to read, and the scroll of the prophet Isaiah was given to him. He unrolled the scroll and found the place where it was written:
>   'The Spirit of the Lord is upon me,
>   because he has anointed me
>   to proclaim good news to the poor.
>   He has sent me to proclaim release to the captives
>   and recovery of sight to the blind,
>   to let the oppressed go free,
>   to proclaim the year of the Lord's favour.'
> Then he rolled up the scroll, gave it back to the attendant, and sat down. The eyes of everyone in the synagogue were fastened on him. He began by saying to them, 'Today this scripture is fulfilled in your hearing.'

Jesus is quoting from chapter 61 of the Old Testament prophet Isaiah. Although verse 2 of Isaiah's original text is 'to proclaim the year of the LORD's favour and the day of vengeance of our God', Jesus seems to be unconcerned with God's vengeance. He is concerned with the good news for the poor, release for the captives, recovery of sight, and liberation for the oppressed.

Jesus' entire mission was to bring freedom and liberation. Surely, for women and children living with an abuser, Jesus' primary concern will be their freedom and liberation? Some people have argued that women's earthly submission to an abuser will reap spiritual rewards; however, God made us as whole beings, and living in a relationship with an abuser is incompatible with human flourishing. God intends us to have his peace, a peace that enables holistic flourishing of mind, body, spirit and soul; with the term *shalom*, translated as 'peace' throughout the Bible, referring to 'completeness, soundness, welfare, peace'.[39]

Beyond Jesus' own characterization of his ministry, his relationships with women were extraordinary for the culture he was born into. He chatted to the woman at the well, telling her all about her life.[40] Many people misremember this story as Jesus telling the well woman to 'go and sin no more', but that was part of another story – one in which a woman is to be stoned to death after being caught in the act of adultery. Even though the law required both the man and the woman to be held accountable, it seems only the woman was to be executed. Jesus' response to this imminent execution was to invite those without sin to throw the first stone.[41] Nobody could. On another occasion, a woman who had been bleeding for 12 years secretly touched the hem of Jesus' cloak and was immediately healed. Jesus felt healing power going out from him: 'Who touched me?!' He demands an answer. It sounds unkind. But in fact he is giving the woman a choice. She can choose to sneak off and not admit her position. He could have pointed to her and said, *'You touched me.'* But he doesn't. He gives her an opportunity. He gives her the power to choose.[42] In a culture in which women could not be disciples or learn, we find that he celebrates Mary's desire to learn, much to her sister Martha's irritation.[43] Similarly, Jesus chose women to be the first messengers of his resurrection (the definition of an apostle is 'an authorized messenger'),[44] even if the men didn't believe them. This was truly radical in a culture in which women could not be witnesses in court. In Matthew 23.9, Jesus explains, 'call no one your father on earth, for you have one Father – the one in heaven' (NRSV). Walter Wink has suggested that, rather than Jesus insisting we all call our male progenitor by his first name, this was Jesus removing the power of the father (also known as patriarchy) from human beings. We are to all be siblings in Christian love, nobody having more power than anyone else.[45]

Some argue that Jesus didn't have any female disciples, but it was his female followers who remained faithful, witnessing to his suffering and crucifixion, even after almost all the men had run away. We don't know whether the 72 Jesus sent out were all men (or if it was 70 or 72 people that were sent),[46] but we do know that he and his disciples were financed by Joanna, Susanna and 'many [other] . . . women'.[47]

There is no scenario within the Gospel accounts where Jesus responds to a woman subjected to abuse by her partner. As such we have to follow a trail of breadcrumbs from Jesus' declaration that his ministry was all about freedom and liberation, through his treatment of women and finally to him entrusting women as the first messengers of the full gospel. Are our actions bringing freedom and liberation to women and children abused by men? Or do our actions allow us to imagine we are doing what Jesus would do, while we are in fact covering up wounds of destruction with a brightly coloured bracelet?

This chapter has been rather theological! Hopefully it has made sense and hasn't made your brain hurt. You may have found yourself disagreeing with my views. If you needed to throw the book across the room because it annoyed you, I will not judge! This stuff is really challenging. I am shaking some of the foundations of Christian culture. In the New Testament there is a passage that says only that which is unshakeable will remain;[48] sometimes Christian culture needs shaking to get rid of the stuff that is cultural rather than spiritual. If you are feeling shaken, give some thought as to why. If you are a non-Christian and made it through this chapter, give yourself a round of applause and a pat on the back! Thank you for sticking with me.

Take a moment to pause and reflect. Notice your breathing and what your body feels like. If you are someone who prays, offer up your thoughts to God or feel free to use this prayer:

God, there is so much that I do not know that I do not know. Please show me your truth and enable me to build my life on your firm foundation, able to distinguish between cultural and spiritual. In my struggles with unanswered prayer, help me to be open to your relief and not wedded to my own expectations. Guide me and transform me. Amen.

I would, if I were a man (with my hand on my heart, I say it) take off my hat and stand bareheaded before the most degraded of these women, before I would dare to speak of them as greater sinners than myself, even if I were myself blameless; for, as a man, I should feel ashamed and penitent on behalf of other men, for whom and by whom these helpless ones have been cast forth and branded.

Josephine Butler (1874)[49]

6 Why doesn't she just leave? (The question everyone asks)

'Why doesn't she just leave?' In dinner parties and professional meetings, social gatherings and when chatting with strangers, I am asked this question over and over. Chatting with a dietician who was about to deliver a session on fussy eating in a children's centre, I told her I worked on domestic abuse issues. She commented disparagingly, 'Oh, those women, gluttons for punishment, aren't they?!' I wanted to grab her and shake her but I didn't (I know, I know, my capacity for self-control is commendable). Explaining that it really isn't that simple and that if women could *just* leave then we would *just* leave, I suggested that, as a dietician, she might benefit from doing some domestic abuse awareness training, particularly as many abusers deliberately use mealtimes to abuse their partner and children.

Telling his wife Margery that the food she had just cooked was disgusting, Tony throws his plate of food at the wall. It smashes and spaghetti bolognese slides slowly down the wallpaper as their two small sons hold back tears, their appetites totally gone. Daisy's dad makes her and her mum eat really big portions of food. Even when she feels really sick, he forces her to keep eating. He tells her and her mum that no other man would ever want them.

The word 'just' dominates public charismatic prayer. 'God, I *just* want to ask that you would *just* help us to *just* know you more', punctuated with excessive repetition of God's name. I have this image of God standing up in the middle of the prayer time and roaring,

'ENOUGH WITH THE JUSTS ALREADY.' OK, this might just be me imagining God in my image.

For public praying, the 'justs' provide thinking space for the pray-er to formulate the next sentence. Although highly irritating, they are a benign habit, unlike the 'just' present in the question of a woman leaving her abusive partner. An abuser will minimize his abuse with 'just': 'It was *just* a slap', 'I *just* broke one of your arms.' The 'just' minimizes the statement. When people ask, 'Why doesn't she *just* leave?' they are minimizing the implications present in their question. Just leave? Just leave the father of my children? Just leave the relationship I've invested my life in? Just leave my home, family, friends, community, culture? Leaving any relationship is hard enough; leaving a relationship with an abuser is a thousand times harder.

The perception that it is easier to leave an abusive (rather than a non-abusive) partner is rooted in the idea that the unpleasantness of the abuser will provide greater impetus to leave. That is not the case. Each Biderman behaviour (remember them from Chapter 2?) will be employed by an abuser to keep his partner (and the children) from leaving him. There are three stages to this: the pre-emptive stage, the maintenance stage and the post-separation stage. Taking place in the early stages of the relationship, the pre-emptive stage will be followed by the maintenance stage throughout the relationship, while the post-separation stage refers to behaviours enacted either immediately after his partner has separated from him or in the days, weeks, months and even years later. Let's look at each aspect of the Biderman behaviours that we first explored in Chapter 2 and consider how an abuser may behave during each stage.

THE ISOLATOR

In the pre-emptive stage, the Isolator will undermine his partner's relationships with her friends and family. If he is successful in alienating her then she will have no one to turn to if she does consider leaving him, no one to support her or give her a new perspective that could help her to decide to leave. The Isolator could instead embed himself so deeply within her friendship group or family that, if she was to seek their help, they would be his allies defending him or betraying her confidences. If his partner already has children, he may make himself indispensable very quickly. Establishing a strong relationship with them and offering lots of practical help will make it more difficult for his partner to consider ending the relationship. The Isolator may prevent his partner from controlling her fertility by lying to her about having had a vasectomy or saying he has been diagnosed as infertile. He may prick holes in condoms, convince her to use the contraceptive pill rather than the implant (the pill is much easier to manipulate) or persuade her to have a baby. In recent years, the term 'stealthing', used by men to describe their covert removal of a condom during sex, has gained prominence. Rape Crisis England and Wales quickly pointed out that stealthing is a form of rape.[1] Intentionally interfering with contraception, explains Dr Sinead Ring of the University of Kent, 'is not definitely an offence under English law. It has never been brought as a case. But there is a section in the Crown Prosecution Service (CPS) guidance on conditional consent, and this would be an example of that.'[2] Younger women are particularly vulnerable to this form of abuse as they rarely have the confidence to assert their right to control their fertility. Few will feel confident in insisting on condom use or in refusing to have contraception controlled.

NSPCC research found that 'nearly all' teenager mothers are subjected to controlling behaviour by a partner.[3] When I ask training participants why they think it is so high, many point to the girl's vulnerability and the boy's immaturity, with financial pressure and historic abuse also mentioned. It is rarely understood that the abuse does not begin once the girl is pregnant, but that instead impregnation is part of the abuse. For years, young women have been demonized for 'getting themselves pregnant' to get a council flat. Teenage girls are not artificially inseminating themselves, so it is odd how rarely the fathers of their babies are mentioned. The trope of women manipulating men into a relationship by deceptively becoming pregnant is outrageous given the much likelier scenario where women are coerced into pregnancy by an abusive man. Research on reproductive coercion with women who had abusive partners found that four in ten reported that their partner had tried to get them pregnant against their will or stopped them from using birth control. Eighty-four per cent of them were impregnated by a partner.[4] After manipulating me into sex, Craig refused to use contraception. He told me it wasn't real if there wasn't a risk. Within six months I was pregnant with my daughter. Craig then accused me of having an affair. He lied, telling me that he had a low sperm count and so someone else must be the father. I believed him and, for a while, almost convinced myself that I must have had sex with another man that I couldn't remember. Once the Isolator has impregnated his partner it is very difficult for her to leave. The Isolator knows this. His partner hears about the difficulties fatherless children have and knows that single mothers are vilified (unlike single fathers, who are heroes). She stays with him, hoping that things will improve.

In the maintenance stage, the Isolator controls his partner's access to family and friends. He might time her phone calls, ban her family from the house or accuse her friends of trying to break up the relationship. With no friends or family to turn to, she has nowhere to go. Encouraging her to give up her job, the Isolator tells his partner that he will provide for her. He has full control of the finances and his partner will have no financial independence; she can't buy anything, make phones calls or go anywhere without him knowing.

Despite all of the Isolator's tactics, his partner might manage to leave him. Her family or friends may have persisted in staying in contact with her, or she might gain support from a local domestic abuse service. In the post-separation stage, the Isolator, seeking to control the break-up narrative, may claim that he is the victim, at church, with her friends or in the wider community. He will lie and cry, his tears melting people's hearts. They are not used to seeing grown men cry. Previous to leaving, his partner might have been quite guarded, concerned people might find out what he was doing and interfere. He uses this to his advantage, calling her uptight and controlling. He goes around all their mutual friends and convinces them that she has been treating him badly. Philosopher Kate Manne describes this as Himpathy: the way abusive men are supported and empathized with, rather than being challenged and expected to change.[5] The hurt of him being believed over her pours salt into her wounds. He may alienate the children from her or drag her through the family courts, manipulating professionals into believing him. She goes from being controlled by him to also being controlled by courts and/or social workers.

THE HUMILIATOR

In the pre-emptive stage, calling his partner sexualized names and making jokes about her, the Humiliator desensitizes her to his humiliation and degradation, making it difficult for her to accurately assess what he is doing. He might convince her to pose for naked or pornographic videos or images. He will coax out of her deeply personal information; perhaps about abuse in her childhood, historic situations she is ashamed of or things she feels guilty about. The Humiliator increases humiliation in the maintenance stage. She already feels degraded, and the shame she experiences means she can't even think about the things he is making her do, never mind tell anyone about them. How would she explain to anyone that he makes her say her family members' names during sex and then afterwards calls her disgusting? Occasionally he reminds her that if she leaves him he will send those photos he took to her parents. He tells her she's a terrible mother and that she'd never cope without him. He humiliates her in front of the children and she knows they don't respect her. They will only behave for him. She knows she can't leave him as she'd never manage the kids on her own. When she weeps because of his taunting, he mocks her and tells her she is pathetic. He convinces her that's what everyone thinks about her, and she believes him. She feels incapacitated by shame, doubt and failure.

If, in spite of all this, she finds a way to leave him, the Humiliator's post-separation tactics may include sending her messages telling her she is disgusting, mocking her and telling her no one else will ever want her. He may quickly find a new partner, telling her how much better the new partner is. He will introduce the children to his new partner very quickly, maybe encouraging them to refer to her as Mum. He may release the photographs he has of her, or disclose her secrets to her colleagues, friends or family.

THE THREATENER

In the pre-emptive stage the Threatener may tell his partner about his capacity for violence, the weapons he owns or the way his 'anger' sometimes overwhelms him. Making seemingly innocent comments about how they will be together for ever, he tells her he would never let her leave him. In this stage he is simply establishing that he is capable of harming people – not her, of course, but other people. He will normalize his threatening behaviour in the maintenance stage. Aggressive outbursts will be followed by kind behaviour, which leaves her confused. He will tell her that if she ever tries to leave him, he will destroy her; he'll implicate her in illegal activity, gain full custody of the kids and prove she's mad. 'If you leave me,' says Mervin, 'I will find you wherever you go and I will kill you. And nobody will know, because nobody cares about you.' He will threaten to harm the children, their pets, her family, himself. She will begin to exist in a permanent state of raised adrenaline, walking on eggshells and wondering what he will do next. If she manages to leave, or even suggests to him she might leave, the Threatener's tactics will escalate.

Threatening to kill himself, he will contact mental health services, who do not recognize that he is abusing her. Whether child contact is supervised or not, he will use it to give the children messages: 'Daddy saw you yesterday. He knows where you are all the time.' He might pin threatening notes to the baby's nappy. He turns up at her house or her parents' house and smashes windows, screaming and harassing her and those she cares about. Even if she moves house, he finds her new address and contacts her.

Steve had assaulted his girlfriend Brenda. He had been arrested and charged. His bail conditions banned him from going near her house, but every day she would find that the cigarette butts in the ashtray outside her house had been arranged into a pattern. She knew he had been there but felt stupid telling the police. Greta had the locks changed. She came home and found that he'd smashed the door in. She ran around the house trying to work out what he had done. Eventually she found he had placed a cushion in the freezer. She was petrified.

THE EXHAUSTER

In the pre-emptive stage the Exhauster will gradually desensitize his partner to his exhaustion tactics. He will keep her up late wanting to know all about her and sharing his deepest thoughts and feelings; he will send her thousands of messages every day. The maintenance stage builds on this and he keeps her permanently tired. The tiredness prevents her from thinking straight or accurately assessing the situation. He encourages the children to keep her up and wake her early in the morning. The sleep deprivation and tiredness leave her feeling disassociated and unable to focus. She gets through each day in a zombie-like state. If she does leave him, in the post-separation stage he will harass her late into the night with calls and texts. He may enlist allies in his or her family or friends who wear her down with their (possibly well-intentioned) encouragement that she should restart the relationship.

THE BRAINWASHER

The Brainwasher will gradually erode his partner's confidence in the pre-emptive stage as he seeks to control her reality. The subtext of his communications might be unkind but difficult to decode. He will convince her to follow his dreams rather than hers. Within the maintenance stage, the Brainwasher will reduce her confidence further. Telling her she is stupid, fat and ugly, he will undermine her opinions and competence until she is deskilled and lacks confidence. He will permanently avoid responsibility for his behaviour, blaming her. She will be left feeling she can't cope without him and that nobody else would want her. She is prescribed antidepressants. He hides and moves things in their home so she feels she is going mad. Her capacity to function diminishes. Eventually she manages to leave him. In the post-separation stage, he will point out all her failures. He will use her antidepressant prescription to prove that she is a terrible parent, seeking full custody of the children. He will turn the children against her, telling them she is bad and has broken the family. He might fake not coping; he stops washing and appears dishevelled, presenting to the world the false reality that he cannot cope without her to try and manipulate her into taking him back. He continually dominates her perceptions and undermines her capacity to cope. Constantly changing the goalposts for child contact arrangements, he texts her contradictory and confusing messages.

When my son was born, three months premature, he was transferred to a hospital an hour from our home town. This distance enabled me to separate successfully from Craig. After the first month in hospital I couldn't bear knowing Craig had caused my son's suffering and I reported him to the police. Craig's defence when questioned was that he couldn't remember raping me, but if I said he had done it, he must have done it. Based on this ambiguous statement, the police charged him. His statement was deliberate. He didn't want to alienate me by saying that I had lied, as he knew that would end any possibility of manipulating me back into the relationship. Equally he didn't want to admit rape. He came up with a compromise that best served him. The police contacted me: did I think Craig would threaten me and should they give him bail? After four years of abuse and reporting him to the police I still believed the false reality Craig had woven. 'Of course he should be given bail! He would *never* hurt me.' I hope that the UK police have become more aware in recent years that women subjected to abuse are not really able to fully assess the risk the suspect poses to them; I'm not holding my breath, though. He was released on bail with instructions not to contact me but rang me shortly after being released from custody.

THE ALL-MIGHTY

The All-Mighty is unlikely to do much in the pre-emptive stage. He will bide his time until he has captured his partner with the other Biderman tactics. Within the maintenance stage, he will use violence and extreme control to show his partner that he will always rule her life. Strangling her or otherwise cutting off her airways will show her that he even controls her breath. He will tell her in graphic detail the different ways he will hurt her if she leaves him. He will rape her and force her to perform sexual acts against her will, threatening to hurt the children or their pets unless she does what he wants. He may drive erratically and too fast, proving that he could kill her if he wanted to. He may force her to have an abortion if she does become pregnant. The absolute fear engendered by the All-Mighty may incapacitate his partner from doing anything. She knows he will kill her if she leaves him so she doesn't bother trying. She focuses on the occasional good moments and resigns herself to life always being awful. If she does manage to leave him, the All-Mighty may attempt to kill her. He may kill pets or report her to social services, accusing her of abusing the children. Utilizing spy software, he might turn up outside her work, the children's school or her parents' house, making a scene or attacking her. He may kill the children or attempt to. He may imprison her and subject her to a sustained violent attack. The All-Mighty might succeed in killing himself. By doing this he leaves his partner forever tortured that she caused his death. Whether on bail or having been given an injunction, he will ignore the restrictions, stalking, harassing and threatening her. He may use connections he has in the police, army, church, criminal networks or mental health services to get her arrested, killed, excommunicated or sectioned.

THE DEMANDER

In the pre-emptive stage the Demander subtly begins to assert his dominance, perhaps through withdrawing affection or sulking if he doesn't get what he wants. He will use toddler-esque pester power to get his own way, going on until his partner gives in. In the maintenance stage the Demander creates a situation where he gets whatever he wants and she knows he'll never let her leave. If somehow she does manage to leave him, in the post-separation stage the Demander may continue to act as if the relationship hasn't ended. He won't accept no for an answer. His ex-partner will be left feeling exasperated and frustrated. If there are children involved, the Demander will be extremely unreasonable about contact arrangements. He may demand that she bring the children to him, changing contact arrangements at the last minute, particularly if she is relying on him for work or social commitments.

The Demander will be particularly dominant if his ex-partner starts a new relationship. Romantic comedies generally serve the purposes of the Demander. Films that show the male protagonist engaging in extreme and often hilarious actions to win back his former partner normalize the idea that no woman really wants a relationship to end. Instead, she wants to be convinced back by the man who has (to some degree) ruined her life. These films rarely portray the male protagonist as an abuser, but the sentiment contained within them bolsters the abuser's beliefs and disempowers women from feeling able to assert that the relationship is over.

THE NICE ONE

The Nice One is always present in the pre-emptive stage. He may say things like, 'We'll be together for ever!' Quickly moving the relationship forward, he may rush his partner into moving in together, marriage or having children. It will be because he loves her so much that he can't bear to be without her. The more commitments he encourages her to make, the harder it is for her to end the relationship. He will seek to gain as much information as possible about her under the guise of getting to know her. In the maintenance stage, the Nice One will provide occasional relief from the other Biderman tactics. These nice moments will convince his partner that it's not all bad and persuade her that he is capable of change. The change is always temporary.

If she manages to leave, the Nice One will oscillate with the Threatener. One moment he will be telling her that he is going to kill her, the next he will be telling her how much he loves her and how he can't survive without her. He will switch tactics until he finds which is most effective in getting him what he wants. The Nice One might remind her of the good times and tell her how much the children need parents that are together. He will utilize all the insecurities he has found out about her in the pre-emptive stage to manipulate her back into the relationship. Mark arranged to meet Layla for coffee, just to resolve a few things before he moved out. 'You told me how damaged you were by your parents splitting up,' Mark said softly. 'Why would you want to put the kids through that?'

Sitcoms that portray couples breaking up and remaining close friends lead to unrealistic ideas about how ex-partners should relate. The Nice One utilizes this narrative to push for continued friendship, which is simply an opportunity for him to manipulate his ex-partner back into the relationship.

The question 'Why doesn't she just leave?' is often asked without considering what a woman's partner is doing to prevent her from leaving or what her ex-partner is doing to coerce, manipulate or force her back into the relationship. An abuser's tactics embed hooks into his partner's heart, mind and soul. Leaving him isn't merely a case of ending a relationship, but of painfully removing the hundreds of sharp hooks he has driven into her.

A group of women stand in a circle and I stand in the middle. One woman holds a ball of string. Holding on to the string, she throws the ball to someone else in the circle, and as she does this she states one thing that makes it hard to leave an abusive partner. As each woman does this, the circle becomes filled with a complex web with me stuck in the middle. As the ball makes its way from one woman to another, these words are spoken: 'my children', 'my home', 'my family', 'his family', 'my job', 'financial security', 'my church', 'my life', 'my marriage vows'. Women continue throwing the ball of string. 'I don't want to be a single parent', 'I love him so much', 'I'm disabled, and he's my carer', 'It's soon going to be Christmas and I want the kids to have a good time.' The web grows, and I become more and more stuck. After they've given all their reasons I explain that each of us may be caught in a web just like the one we have made. The work of freedom is one of learning how to disentangle the web and break free. We lay the strings on the floor and I walk out of the web.

When we end any relationship there is a lot to lose, but with an abuser the losses rise a thousandfold. And those losses are generally certain and immediate. The gains will be ambiguous and sometimes far in the future; we might one day rebuild our life, but until then we are certain we are going to lose our home, our community and our financial stability. We are petrified we might lose our children and are disturbed at the idea of becoming a single parent. Public perception of single mothers has been that we are morally loose wasters who got ourselves pregnant. Although this is an entirely baseless trope, it drives many women to stay with an abuser for fear of the stigma of single parenthood. Deidre's husband Phillip lined their five children up against the wall: 'You choose which one is not going to private school this year,' he barked at her. The children stared at the floor. For women in wealthier families financial stability, private education (and/or health care) and a high-flying lifestyle can make leaving extremely hard. As much as she wants to escape, she is willing to sacrifice her well-being to ensure the children have the best education, health care and life that money can buy.

People are generally familiar with the idea of 'Stockholm syndrome'. Criminologist Nils Bejerot coined the term after criminal Jan-Erik Olsson took four people hostage when attempting to rob a Stockholm bank in 1973. The hostages were upset with the way police and other authorities responded and one hostage became friends with Olsson. In 1974 Patty Hearst, the granddaughter of a US newspaper mogul, was kidnapped by a group of armed radicals who wanted to overthrow the US government. Within months she had joined their cause and was sent to prison despite accusing her captors of brainwashing her. In 1979 she was pardoned by US president Jimmy Carter.[6] Elizabeth Smart, Natasha Kampusch, Jaycee Dugard and Shawn Horbeck were kidnapped as children. After they were rescued it emerged that each of them had had opportunities to escape but did not take them. They have all been described as having Stockholm syndrome.[7] Because of the association with kidnapping, I prefer to use the term 'traumatic attachment' rather than 'Stockholm syndrome'. Some of the work done on traumatic attachment refers to it as 'trauma bonding'. I don't use this term, as it is also used to describe a view that women can be addicted to an abuser (they can't). If someone is subjecting us to abuse, whether that be after kidnapping us or when we have chosen to begin a relationship with him, we will form a traumatic attachment to him. This is not something we have any control over. It is our body reacting normally to an abnormal situation.

When we are not in a traumatized state, we imagine that our response to a threat would be actively defensive – screaming, fighting back, running away. However, when we are threatened our decision-making processes are neurobiological and not rational.[8] In any situation where our autonomy is threatened, either through physical danger, emotional difficulty or psychological damage, one of our primary neurobiological requirements is to maintain attachment. This is not limited to abuse but includes any threatening situation: a car accident, a cancer diagnosis or working in a dangerous job. When our body assesses that we are unsafe, we will seek out attachment with other humans. When we make those attachments in a traumatic situation, we bond with those other humans in a quicker and often more intense way. This is why those who work in the army or police force often have a strong and family-type relationship with their colleagues.

Barry and Serena were strangers who happened to be sitting next to each other on a train. When the train crashed, they went through an experience together that bonded them. After surviving the crash, their need for attachment was then worked out in their relationships with their individual families and friends. Bob and Sophie have been in a relationship for two years. Bob quickly rushed to move Sophie in with him. He's gradually eroded her confidence by telling her how stupid and worthless she is. He makes her do things she's not comfortable with sexually and has alienated her from her family and friends. He won't let her work and she fills her days meeting Bob's demands that the house be spotless. If Bob *lets* her out, she isn't allowed to make eye-contact with anyone. Eighteen months into the relationship, Bob assaulted Sophie. He punched her in the stomach, stamped on her head and tried to strangle her. He then urinated on her. Sophie's physiological need for attachment kicked in. The attachment need isn't cognitive. It isn't able to look at Bob's abuse and refuse attachment. Bob has created a situation in which he is the *only* human that Sophie can attach to in a threatening situation. While Barry and Serena can attach to a variety of people, the vast majority of whom will have positive intentions and sincere love for Barry and Serena, Sophie's physiological need for attachment can only be met in Bob, who is the cause of the threat to her. When Sophie thinks about escaping Bob, she feels such a strong connection to him that she can't. She feels stupid: 'What's wrong with me? Why can't I leave him after everything he's done? There's something bad in me that's drawing me to him. Maybe I deserve this.' But she doesn't. Her feelings are entirely normal: it is Bob and what he is doing to her that is abnormal. Trauma expert Zoe Lodrick explains that 'terrified people do not move away from danger toward safety . . . people fleeing threatening situations move toward "home", the familiar, or their attachment object'.[9] The amygdala in the brain is responsible for much of decision-making. Lodrick explains: 'The amygdala will prioritise the preservation of attachment over individual threat response.'[10]

After I had separated from Craig, he would ring me and spew bile about me down the phone. I couldn't stop answering the phone when he called. I couldn't hang up on him. I couldn't even make myself stop ringing him. Whenever my daughter did something new or my son's health deteriorated I would call Craig and tell him. He had spent four years hurting me, culminating in a violent rape that led to my son's premature birth. I had reported him to the police. I had moved an hour away. And still I was under his control.

The police involved in my case thought that Craig would threaten me to keep himself out of prison. But he didn't need to threaten me to keep himself out of prison. He used something much more effective than threats. I was traumatically attached to him and couldn't stop myself from doing what he wanted. Once, he came to visit our daughter but spent the majority of the time alone with me, crying about how hard things had been for him. The voice in my head screamed, *Hard for you?! I'm living in a hospital with a premature child and a two-year-old as a result of your violence and you think it's hard for you?!* but I heard myself respond, 'It must be awful for you.' On another occasion he coerced me into having sex with him. Craig didn't have to threaten me to keep himself out of prison. All he had to do was reactivate the traumatic attachment within me. When we went to court, he was found not guilty of rape after he informed the court that I had slept with him. For years I was petrified of seeing him – not because I thought he would hurt me, but because I wasn't sure I could stop myself from doing whatever he wanted.

Zoe Lodrick's work has found that there needs to be a year with no contact with the abuser to break a traumatic attachment.[11] This includes third-party contact. For a woman whose abuser is her ex-partner, the required third-party contact is extensive: the children, the family court, the police, the criminal court, the divorce solicitor, the church members who are still supporting him, her family, his family – the list goes on.

We live in a culture that idolizes romantic love. If we are dealing with a traumatic attachment, it will often feel much like the description of love in romantic songs. It's intense, all-consuming and dramatic. It seems so totally counter to what our rational brain is telling us (run away very fast) that we assume there must be some sort of deeper reality at work. And the power of the feeling (of the traumatic attachment) leads us to feel it's powerful enough to change the abuser. But it isn't.

Particularly for Christians, there can be an amalgamation of the traumatic attachment and 'what God is telling me to do'. Given that God rarely speaks in an audible voice, we are left to ascertain his will for us in a somewhat complex interplay of Scripture, tradition, reason, experience and church-in-community.[12] The traumatic attachment to the abuser can feel like a spiritual connection; the intensity of it can lead us to conclude that God is clearly giving us a supernatural feeling that overrides all the rationality to run away very fast. We conclude that it is God's will for us to stay with the abuser.

God's calling on our life seems very clear when we layer the intense feeling of love (which is actually traumatic attachment) on to the Bible passages about women submitting to their husbands and the way our church leader and wider church community are advising us to stay with our husband. Christian culture, dubious theology and a traumatic attachment is a toxic and extremely dangerous combination!

Breaking free from a traumatic attachment is extremely challenging, but gaining knowledge of traumatic attachment can be incredibly liberating! By recognizing that our intense feelings of love are actually a physiological process, we can choose to defy them and make new and different choices. We don't have to allow the traumatic attachment to control us; by understanding it we act in defiance of it rather than obedience to it.

It is also useful to gain understanding about the stress hormones adrenaline and cortisol. In a high-stress situation, increased adrenaline is designed to give us the strength to fight back or run away, while higher cortisol levels provide us with increased stamina. Adrenaline junkies seek out leisure activities that will raise their adrenaline levels because this can feel physically amazing. When we leave an abuser, we imagine that we will immediately feel better. However, combined with the traumatic attachment there is likely to be a prolonged period when our adrenaline and cortisol levels will be out of balance. It can take time for our hormones to even out. Our uneven hormone levels can leave us feeling distraught, miserable and depressed. Unaware of the hormonal cause we presume that our misery is emotional, proving that our ex-partner is right, we can't cope without him. If we go back, maybe we'll start to feel better because we didn't feel *this* bad until we left him. Gaining literacy about this can enable us to achieve clarity about our feelings and make more informed choices. For those working with women who have been subjected to abuse, this information can engender greater empathy and understanding.

Another element of understanding why women don't leave is the cycle of abuse (see Figure 3).[13]

The cycle starts with the abuser's beliefs of ownership and entitlement. He has a set of rules for his partner that are kept in place by using the Biderman behaviours. These rules come out of his beliefs that he owns his partner and is entitled to get what he wants from her. The rules might include those listed below.

- You're not allowed any friends.
- You must give me sex on demand.
- You must never leave me.
- You must always have dinner on the table at 5 p.m.
- The tins in the cupboard must always have the labels facing out.
- Nothing is ever my fault.
- The kids are your responsibility.

These rules may be explicitly stated or implicitly understood by his partner, but at some point she will break the rules. There are

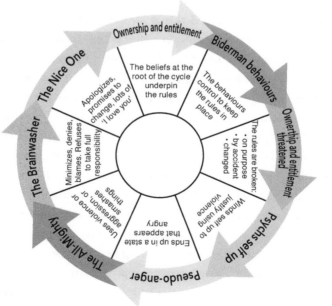

Figure 3: The cycle of abuse

three ways she can do this: by accident, on purpose or because he changes the rules and doesn't tell her. Accidentally breaking the rules includes her children needing hospital treatment (so she can't make the dinner), her friend calling, or being in labour and thereby being prevented from having sex. She can break the rules on purpose by cooking him dogfood pie (I know someone who did this), weeing in his bath (I know someone who did this too), leaving him or simply refusing to do as he says. His changing the rules might mean that he expects her to do as he tells her while also resisting him; for instance, when Craig made me kiss a male friend and then berated me for cheating on him.

Regardless of how the rules are broken, the abuser's beliefs will be threatened. His ownership of and entitlement over his partner is threatened and he needs her to know that she shouldn't break the rules. At this point he will begin an internal (and sometimes external) monologue. Using dehumanizing language about his partner, he will work himself up to a place of pseudo-anger. 'How dare she treat me like this?! I love her and this is how she treats me, the f*cking whore. She needs teaching a lesson.' Most people who have lived with an abuser remember times when he seemed to check out mentally. Usually that's when he's going through the internal monologue.

Once he is in a state of pseudo-anger he becomes the All-Mighty and uses violence, aggression or increasing levels of psychological control. Having done this and established his dominance over us, he will become the Brainwasher, minimizing and denying his behaviour and avoiding responsibility. Becoming the Nice One, he then tells us he is going to change, treating us better than he usually does. This process reinforces his beliefs of ownership and entitlement, and the cycle starts again. It cannot be broken until he changes his beliefs. The cycle is significant in understanding the question of why someone doesn't leave an abusive partner. In particular, there are three aspects within the cycle that we need to consider: her resistance, his escalation and the presence of the Nice One.

HER RESISTANCE

When someone is subjected to abuse she is often assumed to be passive. Comments are made about how she *allowed* the abuse, how she *let* him treat her badly. Yet in reality women always resist the abuser, but usually their resistance either goes unnoticed or is considered dysfunctional.[14] For some women, the only safe place for resistance is inside their head. Part of the way I resisted was to write poems expressing my feelings. Here's one that I wrote while I was with Craig. I'm sorry if the language offends you, but these were all names Craig used to call me, and if the inclusion of this language in a Christian book offends you more than the fact that a significant proportion of women are called names like this by their partners, then I would suggest you may need to reassess your priorities.

I Am Stupid

I am stupid
I am clumsy
A whore bag
And a c*nt face

I'm an idiot
I'm useless
A f*ck face
And a twat

You hate me
I piss you off
You don't care
How I feel

I'm not a princess
I talk too much
I don't know anything
I'll never be good enough

> If this is what you think,
> Why do you stay with me?
> Don't say it's because you love me
> Because it's not from what I can see.

The abuser's partner may break the rules on purpose. This is hugely courageous and is likely to cost the woman greatly. When a woman resists by refusing to obey her partner's rules, do people applaud her? No, they don't. Fiona's partner Harry told her she wasn't allowed to wear a particular dress to the party. 'Did you wear the dress?' I asked. 'Yes I f*cking did!' she exclaimed jubilantly, her eyes sparkling. 'And what happened?' my tentative question came, knowing the likely answer. The sparkle left her eyes. 'We got home and he beat me so bad.' When women resist and their partner chooses to hurt them, they are perceived as responsible for his abuse. Most people react to Fiona's story by telling her she was stupid for wearing the dress. They miss the point. Fiona's dress represents the dignity and honour she is clinging to. While women continue to resist the abuse, they still hold on to some of their self-esteem. Whether their resistance involves a dress, a poem, dogfood pie or a decision to shut their partner out emotionally or takes another form entirely, it should be celebrated as evidence of their dignity. Just as we can build women's understanding of traumatic attachment and stress hormones, enabling them to identify ways they have resisted the abuser can help them to move forward. It definitely helped me to see that I held myself in greater esteem than I had previously realized!

HIS ESCALATION

An abuser's behaviour always escalates. He doesn't punch his partner on the first date; he secures hooks into her first. He gains confidence that he will get away with it, and as previous violence and abuse become less effective and his partner becomes desensitized to it, so his abuse increases. An abuser will see his partner leaving him as the biggest rule break. Women generally know that leaving their partner is the surest way to see his violence or abuse escalate, something which is backed up by research: 'Attempts to end a relationship are strongly linked to intimate partner homicide.'[15] Why doesn't she just leave? Because he might kill her if she does. It sounds extreme, but it is not hyperbole. Two women a week are killed by a current or former partner.[16] In one decade, 29 children were killed by their fathers after their parents' relationship ended.[17] Women and children are killed by men if they try to leave. Even if women are not killed, the absolute certainty that their partner will kill them or their children will keep them trapped.

THE NICE ONE AGAIN

The abuser will use the Nice One's tactics soon after the All-Mighty's violence. We begin a relationship with the Nice One, and as the relationship progresses we see less and less of him. Suddenly the lovely person we fell in love with has come back; hope rises. Eminem and Rihanna's song 'Love the Way You Lie' expresses this much better than I could. Rihanna loves the way the abuser lies because if those lies were true then everything would be perfect and all the effort would be worth it. (Rihanna and Eminem released this song two years after she had been violently assaulted by her then partner, Chris Brown. Eminem has admitted abusing his ex-wife, Kim; one of his most popular songs is about him murdering her.) If we don't believe the abuser when he becomes the Nice One, then we have to accept that we fell in love with a fraud, that the person we fell in love with is a lie, that the hopes and dreams we had for our life have shattered. In their place is brokenness, failure and loss. And yet there is the Nice One. How tempting it is to believe him when he says he's changed. Maybe this time he's telling the truth . . .

Once you bring together the abuser's tactics to prevent his partner leaving, the physiological factors of traumatic attachment and stress hormones and the cycle of abuse, it is amazing that any woman leaves her abusive partner. And yet some of us manage it! Does the world respond to us as extraordinary people who overcame incredible odds to leave the abuser? Do we get offered all the practical and emotional support we need to rebuild our lives? Do our children get counselling? Does the government recognize the enormity of what we have done and ensure that we have a safe place to go and systems that protect us from the abuser? Does everyone recognize that the abuser is dangerous to our children and protect them from him? Does the media treat us as heroes who overcame the worst of human depravity and made it out alive? No to all of the above.

UK domestic abuse refuges rely on fundraising efforts, charitable grants and clients' welfare payments to fund their work. Government funding to services does not include money for children, who account for 50 per cent of those in refuges. Many local authorities have no beds available for women and children fleeing an abuser. Refuges often have to turn away women's older teenage sons because of the risks of them beginning relationships with younger women in the refuge. Women will sometimes arrive in refuges with only bin bags of clothing and possessions, perhaps without shoes or money. It can take weeks for them to be able to claim any welfare payments, and until then they will be reliant on food banks and refuge donations for everything from bedding to sanitary protection. Every day about 94 women and 90 children are turned away from refuges in England and Wales.[18]

The practical reality for women and children fleeing an abusive partner is devastating. There are additional challenges for women whose housing is attached to their partner's job. If a woman's abusive husband is a church leader, she will be dealing with all of the above, knowing that by her taking action he may lose his job while she and her children will lose their home and main income. This is the case for those in the armed forces too. As much as church and military hierarchies may attempt to be helpful (sadly, they often aren't very helpful at all), how many will commit to permanently housing the wives and children of their ex-employees?

Women also have to deal with the social stigma and the emotional and psychological impact of their relationship ending, particularly if they have children or are married. People will consistently say unhelpful things that are difficult to deal with. When I was living in the hospital with my son and daughter, the hospital cleaner asked me where my husband was. After I had explained that I had separated from him, she asked, 'What?! He was such a catch! Why would you let him go?!'

I won't stop working on these issues until the question 'Why doesn't he just stop the abuse?' replaces the 'Why doesn't she just leave?' question in people's minds, hearts and mouths. It will require an entire shift in how we understand these issues, but let's aim high, eh?!

We've made it to the end of this chapter! Hopefully you are now well enough informed to explain why she doesn't just leave. It's a lot of information to take in, and if you need a break, please take one! A lot of what we've covered is stuff that seems really obvious when we know it. If you're reviewing times in your life when you responded unhelpfully to people, as hard as that is, hopefully it will enable you to grow and change. If seeds of discomfort have been planted in you from this chapter, I hope they grow into a new way of understanding the issues. Take a few moments to pray. If a set prayer is helpful, please use this one:

God, there is so much I didn't know. Women subjected to abuse have been put through so much. Please comfort those suffering, and if I can help you to bring them comfort, show me what you want me to do. God, in your mercy, bring transformation to our broken world. Amen.

> It is time to effect a revolution in female manners – time
> to restore to them their lost dignity. It is time to separate
> unchangeable morals from local manners.
>
> Mary Wollstonecraft (1792)

7 Life can be beautiful (Dealing with sexual harm and betrayal)

This chapter is about sex. Dear reader, please do not skip past it. God invented sexuality, and yet Christian culture is not comfortable with it. I would love to write a whole book on how awesome sex can be and how much God loves sex (publishers take note!); however, in the UK one in five women has been subjected to sexual violence, so before I write a tome about awesome sex we must reflect on sex at its most depraved.

This chapter comes with a warning. It will be unpleasant. If your personal history includes having been subjected to sexual abuse, please take care. You are in control of how you read this book, and if you do need to skip some pages don't feel bad. Please refer back to page 12 for some self-care strategies if you need them. There will be some graphic descriptions of sex and some swear words in this chapter. These are necessary to adequately understand the topic. Christian culture loves to euphemize difficult issues; however, remaining ignorant to the realities of sexual violence prevents us being a safe person to disclose to. If your eyes bulge at my use of the f-word or you look disgusted when I tell you what I have been subjected to, I may never share my story again. Disclosure is always gradual and people are testing our reactions to their least worst pain.

Ephesians 5.4 instructs Christians to choose thanksgiving over 'obscenity, foolish talk or coarse joking'. This chapter is not foolish talk and God sees the worst of human behaviour. Jesus is intimately acquainted with evil; he endured the cross to overcome it. If we are to walk with people in their pain we have to be willing to witness the brutality, not shutting our ears when the stories are horrifying or the language offends us.

Christians believe God created sex but are taught that we should avoid thinking about it until we get married. This is an odd situation given that there are no guarantees we will ever get married (particularly for Christian women, as there just aren't enough Christian men to go around). Our sexual organs do not appear at puberty or on the wedding night, suggesting that God intended sexuality to be an integral part of human life. Our sexual scripts start at birth, as writer and sex educator Dr Emily Nagoski explains:

> On the day you're born, you're given a little plot of rich and fertile soil, slightly different from everyone else's. And right away, your family and your culture start to plant things and tend the garden for you, until you're old enough to take over its care yourself. They plant language and attitudes and knowledge about love and safety and bodies and sex. And they teach you how to tend your garden, because as you transition through adolescence into adulthood, you'll take on full responsibility for its care.[1]

Christian culture generally seeks to ignore the garden entirely until adulthood. The resulting landscape is mainly populated with the shrubs of wider culture. And cacti, spiky cacti. This is particularly true for girls and young women, as Nagoski explains:

> Medieval anatomists called women's external genitals the 'pudendum', a word derived from the Latin *pudere*, meaning 'to make ashamed' . . . The reasoning went like this: women's genitals are tucked away between their legs, as if they wanted to be hidden, whereas male genitals face forward, for all to see.[2]

Women's vulvas were literally called shameful. Sadly, this mentality is not relegated to history: while the negative words to describe sexually active women are seemingly endless, the labels for men are all positive. When Christian youth events do the Sex Talk, girls are taught to 'protect their hearts' with a focus on purity and modest dress to avoid being a 'stumbling block' to men and boys. Modest dress ranges from high necklines and long shorts to avoiding shoes that show 'toe cleavage' (this is an actual thing a youth leader said to a girl because of his foot fetish).[3] With the boys, there will be an assumption that they are generally sex-obsessed, with a focus on avoiding masturbation. This is not the model for sexuality evident in God's creation or in the Bible. Jesus doesn't tell a man that if his eye causes him to sin because of a woman's toe cleavage she should be forced to change shoes. Instead, if a man's eye causes him to stumble he should 'gouge it out and throw it away'.[4] If we followed Jesus' teaching, there'd probably be a lot of blind men stumbling around. Jesus is clear, girls and women are not responsible for men's lust or men's sexual violence, and while sexual attraction was designed by God and has its place in human relationships, the distortion of healthy sexuality lies in the heart of each individual and not in the object of that person's desire.

The clitoris has been discovered a number of times by men (this comment is not a joke stereotyping men being unable to find the clitoris; in 1559, Realdo Colombo officially identified the clitoris, with other men rediscovering it at various points).[5] The only organ in the human body designed solely for pleasure, and God gave it as a gift to women. Scientists have struggled to explain the purpose of female orgasm. It was thought that the female orgasm helped transport the sperm to the egg, but it does not: 'it turns out sperm is transported most efficiently through a completely unstimulated uterus!'[6] How extraordinary. God designed women to enjoy sex in a way that is counterproductive for conception. Evolutionary biologists are going to have a hard time explaining that. God designed women with the capacity for great sexual pleasure. Most male orgasms are followed by a 'refractory period' when the penis cannot become erect again. This can take minutes or even hours.[7] Women can have multiple orgasms without any refractory period. That is how awesome God's intention for female sexuality was!

At its best, sex is not about power; it's about love, mutuality, intimacy and grace, two people who love each other connecting and committing themselves in a beautiful and sacrificial way. This is not the dominant model of sexuality in society; it's also not the dominant model of sexuality in the Bible. Both represent sexuality as male dominance. They say that 'sex sells', but what they mean is that 'products which are advertised by women-as-sexual-objects and men-as-sexual-agents sell' (which isn't such a catchy phrase!). Car tyres, deodorant, protein milkshakes, bank cards, shoes, perfume and more have all been advertised using sexually objectified women.[8] Women's necks are stretched and bare, the same stance taken by animals submitting to a predator, while their eyes look at the camera and say, 'Take me to bed.' Barely clothed and pouting, they are digitally altered to remove flaws; the girl in the magazine doesn't even look like the girl in the magazine. They look perpetually adolescent. Men are generally clothed and presented in powerful postures. Even when they are unclothed, their eyes say, 'I'm going to take you to bed.' This model of sexuality is at its most extreme in pornography.

Before taking us into the hideousness of pornography, I must warn you that it is rather vomit-inducing. You may not want to know what happens in pornography, but people you know (both men and women) are watching it. Children and young people you know are stumbling upon it. And women subjected to abuse are often dealing with the impact of pornography on their abusive partner's (or their own) sexual expectations. You may not want to know, but how can you adequately support them unless you do?

The web's biggest pornography site, Pornhub, found that in one year its viewers consumed 4.5 billion hours of pornographic videos. That's 5,246 centuries of time spent on one porn site in one year, five millennia of time invested in pornography.[9] The year 2017 saw over

4 million pornographic videos uploaded to the site, and the top five search terms on the site were lesbian, hentai,[10] MILF,[11] step mom and stepsister.[12] The videos available in these search terms include:

- incest: 'Step mom uses her step son for a fuck toy';
- aggression: 'Perfect fit teen gets fucked hard';
- sexual abuse: 'Perv dad takes advantage of young daughter';
- anal sex: 'College teen in yoga pants gets quickie deep anal'.

At the side of videos there are adverts implying child sexual abuse. One reads, 'First real adult game, play for free'. Another advert has a photograph of a girl who looks approximately 13 years old[13] with the caption 'Young teen sluts; blow your load to tiny teens videos for free'.[14] The prominence of teenage girls in pornography cannot be overstated, while the prevalence of violence and aggression is almost ubiquitous. Many scenes include a selection of the following:

- deep throat: a woman is seen choking as a man forces his penis down her throat;
- bukkake: a number of men (usually about eight) ejaculate on a naked woman;
- creampie: seminal fluid leaking out of the woman's vagina or anus;
- facial: men ejaculate on a woman's face;
- double penetration (DP): either a woman being penetrated simultaneously both vaginally and anally or with two men's penises in one orifice, usually her vagina or anus; she will often also be penetrated orally at the same time.

The videos show women enjoying these degrading and violent acts. By the age of 16, 65 per cent of British young people will have seen online pornography as described above.[15]

Online pornography could be dismissed as something far outside the norm of human sexual experience. However, the sheer number of people viewing material across the world says otherwise. Usually while watching they are masturbating until ejaculation.

What does it do to an individual to regularly reach orgasm while watching women being degraded and violated (even if they seem to be enjoying it)? More importantly, what does it do to the pornography performers?

Online pornography does not exist in a vacuum. It sits within what I describe as 'the spectrum of pornographies'. At one end is the graphic sexual violence we've just considered. At the other end of the spectrum is sexualized culture: the Moschino perfume advert with a naked woman, face covered, clasping a bottle while squeezing her breasts together;[16] the advert where 'sexy angels' fall from the sky and smash their haloes because the man is wearing Lynx deodorant; the proliferation of children's accessories plastered with the Playboy bunny logo. When my daughter was three years old, our local shopping centre's face-painting stand had an option for children to have the Playboy bunny painted on their faces. When I complained, the centre manager assured me that the Playboy bunny was now unrelated to pornography; he was wrong.

Other media are included on the spectrum: music videos with objectified, scantily dressed women, Instagram accounts filled with selfies of self-objectified pouting girls, desperate to get enough likes. In feature films, the Bechdel Test considers whether a film has more than two named female characters who speak together about something other than a man,[17] given that in many films women's roles are limited to being sexual objects or the wallpaper of men's lives. Each year only around half of the top 25 films pass the Bechdel Test.[18] The media as a whole perpetuates harmful ideas about sexuality. Pornography is not an aberration; it is the logical conclusion of patriarchal sexuality.

The Song of Solomon is the only book in the Bible that consistently presents sexuality in a more positive light than porn–ography, describing the erotic love between a young bride and bridegroom (it is depressing that the only biblical text that has a consistently positive view of sexuality was written by a man who probably had 700 wives and 300 concubines).[19] The garden in chapter 4 of the Song of Solomon should have the prefix of 'lady' (i.e. lady-garden, otherwise known as a vulva). The book's eight chapters contain barely veiled references to cunnilingus (for those who – like me – received religious sex education, cunnilingus means oral sex performed on a woman), breasts like twin gazelles and the groom's head being wet with dew.[20] It's a veritable feast of erotica. Mutual pleasure is clearly important, and the presence of this book within Scripture can show us that erotic love is holy and that God created women and men with the capacity for sexual pleasure.

The rest of the biblical canon seems to do sexuality huge harm. *'He came into her* and then she had a baby' is generally how sex is described, with occasional stories about people like Onan, who refused to provide Tamar (his widowed sister-in-law) with a baby by ejaculating on the ground, and Lot's daughters (as usual, we are not told their names because they are women), who get him drunk and rape him to impregnate themselves (though we might suggest that it seems odd Lot was so drunk as to not remember this but was able to perform the impregnation act).[21] Leviticus is filled with laws about how *not* to have sex, but doesn't mention how *to* have sex or that it should be enjoyable. Where infertility is mentioned in Scripture, it is always the woman's fault; not once is a man's fertility the cause of childlessness. But the New Testament seems slightly better. In the first letter to the Corinthians they are told it is better to marry than to burn (with lust), with instructions for a husband not to 'deprive' his wife of sex.[22]

The most disturbing theme in Scripture about sexuality, seemingly condoned by Hebrew law, is men's sexual violence.[23] In Deuteronomy, we are told that a man who rapes an unbetrothed virgin must marry her.[24] No amount of cultural analysis or fancy hermeneutics seems to make this passage any easier to take. However, I know that God did not condone my husband raping me, and my experience of God's love and transformation sits in sharp contrast to the Hebrew law. I can't explain the passage, so I live in the tension of choosing a faith which has Scripture that remains offensive and unexplainable to me.

'In those days Israel had no king; everyone did as they saw fit.'[25] This is the ending of the Old Testament book of Judges. Ignoring God and his laws, the people sink into ever greater depravity, culminating in two very different offences. Judges 17 tells of Micah, who employs one of God's priests to be his own personal priest to minister to a statue-god he has had made. Two chapters later, and a different priest throws his concubine on to a street full of men who want to rape him. These men rape his concubine (possibly to death). Taking her body, the priest cuts her into 12 pieces (possibly while she is still alive) and posts them throughout the country.[26] Nothing can sugar-coat this horrifying story, but it highlights that communal disobedience to God will result in more men being sexually violent and in more idolatry. Within the UK, 85,000 women and 12,000 men a year are raped by men,[27] while globally the rates are much higher. My experience has been that sexual violence grieves the heart of God and that, just as Judges evidences, human depravity is at its greatest when combined with sex.

Anti-war activist Stan Goff explains: 'Sex is routinely practiced, portrayed and understood as a form of aggression and power. This is recognized in everyday speech.'[28] Going on to quote a friend, he states,

> Men – in the 'man talk' they speak . . . often use metaphors of rape (male–male rape, for example) to indicate aggression, anger, submission, domination. Just bend over . . . we really took it in the shorts that time . . . check out the Web site today, Juan Cole just ripped Goldstein a new ass . . . I've got a hard-on for that SOB . . . he just rolled over for it . . . he thinks I'm his bitch . . . and of course, the routine uses of 'to fuck' as in 'fuck you', 'we are so fucked', 'that's fucked', plus the pejorative applied to the submissive/receptive role, as in . . . 'he's such a scumbag' (recipient for sperm) . . . 'that sucks' . . . 'what a cocksucker' . . .

and so on. The very texture of the vernacular expresses every-thing a sociologist could want to know about the association of sex, and aggression, sex and ranking, etc.[29]

Given this rhetoric, it seems unsurprising that some men become sexually violent. Yet often their violence is explained away as either lust or love. There is a widespread myth that sexual violence is about lust. Just as anger and passion are used to minimize the control an abuser has over his actions, so uncontrollable lust is the presumed driving force for rapists. That someone would subject another person to sexual assault if he was in full possession of his faculties seems so unbearable that lust provides a way of reducing the culpability of the offender. Lust is not responsible for rape. Rapists are. Diana Scully and Joseph Marolla's interviews with convicted rapists found that

> these men raped because their value system provided no com-pelling reason not to do so. When sex is viewed as a male entitlement, rape is no longer seen as criminal . . . Justifications particularly, but also excuses, are buttressed by the cultural view of women as sexual commodities, dehumanized and devoid of autonomy and dignity. In this sense, the sexual objectification of women must be understood as an important factor contribut-ing to an environment that trivializes, neutralizes, and, perhaps, facilitates rape.[30]

Sexual violence perpetrated within a relationship is often mis-understood. The abuser's partner thinks, 'I wouldn't have sex with someone that I didn't love (or at least like), therefore if my partner is willing to have sex with me, then he must love me, or at the very least like me.' This was my view of Craig; there was no way he would have sex with me or engage in intimate physical activities with me unless he actually liked me. I didn't realize that his view of sex was different from mine. I didn't realize that it wasn't about intimacy or mutual pleasure. It was evidence to him that he owned me and had total power over me. Sex wasn't primarily about desiring me; it was about conquering me. Realizing that the person we believe loves us actually sees us in a totally different way is extremely painful. But we must let go of the false notion that our sexual relationship is evidence that our partner loves us. Until we see the abuser as he really is, devoid of the assumptions we have made about him, we will find it very difficult to move forward.

There are two aspects to sexual abuse perpetrated by a partner: there's the context he creates to get his partner to do what he wants and there's the sexual abuse itself. Let's look at how each Biderman tactic operates.

THE NICE ONE

After he has encouraged his partner into sexual activity through spending intensive time with her, showering her with affection and possibly gifts, she will often be more than willing to engage in sexual activity. The Nice One's love bombing will leave his partner feeling emotionally overwhelmed, with her committing to increasing levels of physical intimacy without the time or space to make an intentional choice. As other Biderman behaviours increase, during sexual activity might be the only time that he's nice to his partner. Starved of love and affection, she may be so desperate for affirmation that she acquiesces to his sexual demands. In fact, their sexual relationship may be entirely non-abusive. In this way, the Nice One causes her to think that he's not 'that bad' and she feels unable to leave him. Theological objections to sex before marriage can leave the Nice One's partner vulnerable to his suggestion that they rush into marriage after sex. This makes it even harder for her to leave him.

There is a story that is often used when working with perpetrators of domestic abuse. A man brings home flowers for his partner. After dinner, he makes sexual advances towards her. She refuses. He begins touching her sexually and she pushes him away. He grabs her, slaps her and rapes her. The question perpetrators are then asked is: when did he become abusive? The answer is: if he bought her flowers with the intention of making her have sex with him, it started with the flowers (buying flowers in and of itself is not abusive, obviously!).

On first meeting Craig, I made it very clear that I did not believe in having sex before marriage. All my friends and my entire education had been Christian until I began a childcare qualification with an entirely non-Christian cohort. As a passionate evangelist, I would tell them all about Jesus. My proud virginal status was one of the many cultural delineators evidencing that I was different from them. Grateful for Craig's verbal support of my choice to abstain, I was oblivious to the fact that his actions did not match his words. He was the most beautiful man I had ever seen and was extremely experienced sexually.[31] In my naivety and with a lack of robust sex education, I was unable to see that when he pushed me to be naked in front of him, that was a disrespect of the clear boundaries I had stated. I didn't know that his incessant requests for greater levels of intimacy were undermining my ability to consent. He did it all gently and eloquently. I didn't feel forced but I did feel permanently uncomfortable, which I put down to having begun a new relationship. With the 20/20 vision of hindsight I can see that I was feeling highly anxious. Nobody had mentioned consent to me. After clearly articulating my commitment to abstinence, I was unaware of how manipulation and coercion could nullify my assertions. If Craig had violently forced me into sex, I could have identified that it was not my choice. As it was, he made me believe that I had made a choice, even though I couldn't remember choosing sex. After sex, I assumed that I had to marry him. The only way to redeem my 'choice' to betray Jesus was to stay with Craig for the rest of my life. I was 17 years old and had been in the relationship for 12 days.

THE BRAINWASHER

By permanently sexualizing his partner, the Brainwasher will cause her to blame herself for her lack of interest in sex. Expecting sex multiple times a day, he will tell his partner she has a low sex drive for not meeting his sexual 'needs'. Cara began marking the calendar with a cross every day that she and Hans had sex because he insisted they hardly ever did. After a month, every day had a cross in it. The Brainwasher might put his partner down sexually, telling her that she's dirty, a slut, a whore, frigid. Directing insults at particular parts of her body, he may say her genitals smell foul or capitalize on her own fears about her appearance, telling her she's worthless and ugly. If his partner suggests attending marriage counselling, the Brainwasher will put her off, telling her the counsellor will side with him, telling her that she's weird and wrong. Pornography has increased men's expectation of anal sex, without giving the details of how to safely prepare with enemas, anal dilation and lubrication. For many women, anal sex is both painful and totally unpleasurable. The Brainwasher may convince his partner she has to 'let him' have anal sex with her, or may anally penetrate her 'accidentally'.

If she initiates sexual activity, the Brainwasher will mock her and tell her she's disgusting. Arousing and then rejecting her, he may also move her close to orgasm and then stop. He might reduce her to a sexual object whose only value is in performing sexually for him. Telling her she is disgusting and that she's lucky he bothers having sex with her at all, he may tell her that his ex-partners performed better in bed, or will have affairs and force her to listen while he tells her what he did with the other woman. Craig regularly slept with other women. On one occasion he told me he had cheated on me, having sex with his friend Yvonne. I was distraught. Later that day he told me he had made it up, he hadn't cheated on me. When I asked him why, he told me, 'I wanted to see you in pain. I wanted to hurt you.'

THE EXHAUSTER

In her book *The Power of a Praying Wife*, Stormie Omartian suggests a 'better' option for Christian women dealing with their husband's more frequent desire for sex:

When your husband communicates to you what he has in mind, as only a husband can do, don't roll your eyes and sigh deeply. Instead say, 'Okay give me fifteen minutes.' . . . During that time do something to make yourself feel attractive . . . Comb your hair. Wash your face and prepare it with products that make your skin look dewy and fresh. Put on lip gloss and blush. Slip into lingerie you know he finds irresistible . . . Whilst you're doing this, pray for God to give you renewed energy, strength, vitality, and a good attitude. Hopefully when you're ready, your husband will find you were worth the wait. You'll be surprised at how much better a sex partner you are when you feel good about yourself. He'll be happier and you'll both sleep better.[32]

Men who aren't interested in sex and are sexually neglectful of their wives are advised by Omartian to seek professional help. Apparently men don't have to make their faces dewy! Stormie Omartian would argue that her advice is not for women with an abusive husband, but so many women don't *know* their husband is abusive. This counsel from a woman who has literally trademarked the phrase 'the power of a praying wife' is unhelpful and simplistic, presuming that all women are not actually exhausted, that their husbands are not ill-intentioned and that this solution will actually work.

The Exhauster will use pester power to get what he wants sexually, going on and wheedling until he succeeds. If she later objects, he will become aggressive, stating that she agreed, so now she has to. Utilizing her existing exhaustion, he will ask her to agree to sex acts when she is tired, convincing her it is easier to 'let him' have sex with her, perform oral sex on him or watch pornography rather than endure his incessant moaning. He will wear her down with complaints and constant requests. She may avoid being in a state of undress around him because she knows he will immediately begin touching her sexually. His constant demands are exhausting, as is the amount of sex he wants. He seems incapable of non-sexual affection and she is intimacy-starved while he pushes for more sex. It doesn't matter to him whether she is tired, ill or busy; he will expect her to meet his sexual needs, something that is rarely (if ever) reciprocated. Many abusers will initiate sex when their partner is asleep (this is known as sleep rape); waking to find their partner penetrating them, many women fake continued sleep to avoid a confrontation. Although women rarely identify that this is a form of rape, if someone is penetrating us without our consent (which we can't give when we are asleep), it is sexual assault.

THE DEMANDER

Sex will simply be demanded. The Demander's partner will become aware that his expectations have to be met. Stating that he wants sex *now*, he expects her to stop whatever she is doing and give him whatever he wants. He may become aggressive if she refuses or does not perform to his standard. Only his needs and pleasure will matter; she is expected to sexually serve him. The aforementioned Debi Pearl writes:

> Don't talk to me about how uncomfortable or painful [sex] is for you. Do you think *your* body is special and has special needs? Do you know who created you, and do you know he is the same God who expects you to freely give sex to your husband? Stop the excuses![33]

These messages in Christian culture reinforce the Demander's attitudes and behaviours and are often predicated on the false assumption that all men have a high sex drive and all women are uninterested in sex.

THE HUMILIATOR

'Humiliation almost always happens unexpectedly, even if the victim has been living in fear of it. It involves a breach of law, norms or values that both the humiliator and the victim believed were binding,'[34] says Phil Leask, in his research on humiliation. Fundamentally, sexual abuse is humiliating. Opening ourselves up to sexual intimacy involves a level of vulnerability that intensifies the potential for power misuse and particularly for an abuser's humiliating tactics to be effective. When we believe that someone loves us, the impact of his humiliation of us is even harder to deal with. Through the abuser's manipulation and traumatic attachment we might repeatedly enter contexts where he humiliates us: 'See, you love it when I treat you like this – you keep coming back for more.' But as Phil Leask points out, 'Can humiliation be refused or rejected by the intended victim? Because of the power relations involved, this appears unlikely.'[35]

There are seemingly endless ways that an abuser will use sexual abuse to humiliate his partner. Jane's new boyfriend Byron invited her round to his house. Assuring her that his flatmates were out, he convinced her to perform oral sex on him. His male flatmate walked in. Jane tried to move away, but Byron forced her to continue while he and his flatmate had a conversation about coursework.

Either forcing his partner to enact scenes from pornography or hiding his pornography consumption, the Humiliator's sexual expectations of his partner become pornography-inspired. If her partner admits his pornography use within a pastoral or church context, he will often be treated as a victim of addiction. The potential that he is sexually abusing his wife or that she is affected by his betrayal will rarely be considered, even though research has found that a partner's pornography consumption can lead her to develop post-traumatic stress disorder.[36] Most of those who watch pornography are not addicted to it. Responses to pornography consumers which do not build empathy for pornography performers or the consumer's partner are deficient. Using an addiction model can collude with abusers and enable their tactics of minimization, denial and blame. Anti-pornography academic Robert Jensen points out, 'Let's talk about why men can be aroused and achieve orgasm to images of women being treated as less than fully human.'[37]

The Humiliator may ridicule his partner during sexual activity. Mocking her sexual performance or her body and humiliating her when she initiates sex, he tells her she is disgusting. His comments may include references to Christian literature which state that women are uninterested in sex or that God is disgusted with her sexual urges. Forcing her to remain naked, he will deny her access to clothes. Penetrating her with objects (bottles, vegetables, children's toys), he may leave her feeling degraded or disgusting. He may cause her pain during sex, either through being too rough or through forcing (or manipulating) her into painful acts, such as anal sex or 'deep throat' oral sex. If these acts result in the presence of faeces or vomit, he may tell her she is disgusting. He may laugh at her or humiliate her by telling others about the incidents. By forcing her to clean herself or clean up after sex he tells her that she is dirty and disgusting. He may make her have sex on the toilet or call her vile names during sex. Many women describe the acts of humiliation as being much worse than the sexual violence. People understand violence, they can comprehend it, but his degrading tactics will often be so far outside people's frame of reference that their shocked responses compound her existing humiliation. How does a woman tell anyone that her partner made her have sex with animals? Or that he urinated on her during sex? Or that he made her agree to be strangled? Or that he coerced her into group sex?

Leanne waited at the STD clinic. The previous day, she had discovered that the deficit in their bank account was a result of her husband Gary paying women for sex. He'd cried and begged for her forgiveness. She felt God wanted her to stay with him. He cried, so she ended up comforting him. She'd suggested they come to the clinic together, but he had become defensive and shouted at her. She waited alone in the clinic, unsure how she would make it through the humiliation of the examination.

THE ISOLATOR

Through his isolating her, the Isolator's partner doesn't have anyone to advise her about what he is doing. When he tells her that his sexual requests are normal, nobody can verify this, and if they watch pornography together this seems to prove that he is right; anal sex is clean and painless; brutality is arousing; everyone wants group sex. The Isolator's sexual abuse might *cause* his partner to withdraw from others. Telling people about the sexual relationship in great detail, he embarrasses her so badly that she doesn't want to see them any more. The shame of what he has been doing, or making her do, leaves her feeling depressed and unable to maintain other relationships. Particularly if she is part of a faith community, his premarital sexual coercion will leave her feeling she has betrayed Jesus. She may feel unable to continue going to church or may be asked to stop participating in ministries in the church because she is 'sexually active'. She becomes more isolated.

THE ALL-MIGHTY

Using violence and extreme control, the All-Mighty will force his partner to do what he wants sexually. There may be brutality or the use of weapons. He might penetrate his partner with objects that injure her, or force her to have sex after surgery or childbirth. Forcing his partner into sexual exploitation, he will make her have sex with other men for money. Child sexual exploitation is often seen as totally separate from domestic abuse, but perpetrators of both use all the Biderman tactics. Often the only behaviours that his partner can identify as sexually abusive are those of the All-Mighty. There were only two occasions with Craig that I immediately labelled as 'rape', and they both involved being held down, physical violence and me explicitly saying no to him. He abused me sexually most days for four years, but it took a lot of therapy to reframe everything else as 'abuse'.

Nancy White, a black female domestic worker, spoke about losing money after rejecting the sexual advances of white male employers: 'When you lose control of your body, you have just about lost all you have in the world.'[38] I know this to be true.

THE THREATENER

It took years to say the r-word out loud. It would reverberate around my head but I couldn't say it. Yet the implications of the first rape resulted in Craig getting whatever he wanted sexually from that moment on. Knowing that he could physically force me again led me to acquiesce to all his sexual requests. The mind is an amazing thing: I convinced myself I wanted to do whatever Craig demanded, as at least doing it with some form of consent made it 'not rape'.

The Threatener need never threaten us. One act of physical or sexual violence, and a line has been crossed that could be crossed again. We will change our behaviour to try and prevent him doing it again. In reality we are not able to prevent him: it's all a façade he creates to enable us to feel we have some power. Using explicit threats to get what he wants, he may hint at violence or having affairs. He might threaten to hurt or abuse the children if she doesn't do what he wants. Or he could threaten to tell people sexual details about her unless she does what he wants. This will be especially effective if she is unmarried and Christian. Often the threats alone are enough to make her do what he wants.

Whether in sexual sadism or constant sexual put-downs, sexual abuse produces intense feelings of shame and guilt. Recently, the British Psychological Society developed a new approach to mental ill health entitled *The Power Threat Meaning Framework*. It identifies shame as

> both the most social of emotions and the most hidden and 'un-speakable' . . . We feel shame when we judge ourselves through the imagined disapproving eyes of others, and thus it

functions as a powerful social regulator in promoting or discouraging certain beliefs, experiences and behaviours.[39]

Expert on shame Brené Brown explains:

> I believe that there is a profound difference between shame and guilt. I believe that guilt is adaptive and helpful – it's holding something we've done or failed to do up against our values and feeling psychological discomfort. I define shame as the intensely painful feeling or experience of believing that we are flawed and therefore unworthy of love and belonging – something we've experienced, done, or failed to do makes us unworthy of connection. I don't believe shame is helpful or productive.[40]

This is a particularly useful distinction for Christians. Our teaching on sin and the need for redemption can make it very difficult for us to grasp the concept of shame. We are so invested in a narrative of having 'sinned and fallen short' that we have no space for those who have been sinned against. In recent years, mega-church pastor Andy Savage admitted that as a youth pastor he had sexually abused a girl in his youth group.[41] This girl is now an adult and, empowered by the #metoo movement, she shared on social media how Andy Savage had coerced her into performing oral sex on him.[42] After he had made his statement, Andy Savage's church gave him a standing ovation and his lead pastor told the congregation: 'We are so grateful for your support. I know when you support Andy in that way [by giving him a standing ovation], you are also supporting [his victim]. You are supporting her healing.'[43] What does our redemptive narrative mean for people who have been abused? If a hypothetical abuser tells a church he has changed, do we consider how his victims will be affected by our treatment of him?

The redemption narrative makes it difficult for those subjected to abuse to distinguish between shame and guilt. We blame ourselves for what the abuser has chosen to do. This aids the abuser in avoiding responsibility for his behaviour and is utterly debilitating. It makes relating to ourselves and to the world extremely difficult and painful. Brené Brown's research has found that the key to overcoming shame is 'the willingness and capacity to be vulnerable'.[44] This is impossible while remaining in an intimate relationship with an abuser. Regardless of our willingness to be vulnerable, our capacity will be less than 0 per cent. The abuser will use any vulnerability to further abuse us, thereby compounding the shame. Dr Rana Awdish explains:

> Shame doesn't strike like a fist. It rots its way in. Shame unravels us at our most fragile seams. It burns holes in our façade and allows light to shine on our self-doubt. It whispers to us, reminding us that we are imposters and, by the way, are not actually fooling anyone. It's unique in its devastating ability to make us feel exposed and worthless.[45]

The tireless work of campaigners, including Christian activist Jill Saward,[46] to change the law and ensure its enforcement has transformed the legal landscape for women subjected to sexual abuse and rape. Until 1991, men could rape their wives with impunity. Until 1992, those who reported rape or sexual assault to the police were not entitled to anonymity. Until 1994 juries had to be warned that women who accused men of rape could be lying. Although we have moved a long way, women's sexual histories, their actions, their clothing, their conversations with their counsellor and their communication history are all interrogated. Within the UK criminal justice system, anyone accused of a crime is entitled to legal representation. Your solicitor communicates with you throughout the case and you are given copies of all the statements and evidence against you. Those who report a crime, including women who have been raped or sexually abused, are not given legal representation. Under the UK system, it is the Crown versus the defendant. Although this system is not in and of itself problematic, it does mean that, during a criminal case, the woman is simply a key witness in the case. She is not allowed to speak with the prosecution barrister until the case is in court. She is not allowed a copy of her own statement and is certainly not allowed to see the defendant's statement. It can take days, if not weeks, for her to be informed whether the defendant has entered a guilty plea, and while the police often do their best, the system is not designed to support women who have been subjected to sexual abuse.

Every so often there are calls for anonymity for suspects in rape cases, claiming that the effect of such allegations is so awful there should be anonymity. Until an alleged rapist is charged, his anonymity is protected under libel laws[47] and he will only be charged if the Crown Prosecution Service accepts that the weight of evidence is likely to lead to a prosecution. Given that many sexual offenders commit offences against multiple people, the release of their name after they are charged is important for public protection. No other crime (including murder) warrants anonymity for the defendant; it is important that the justice system is consistent with all crime. False reporting of sexual assault is lower than for other crimes, with conviction rates for sexual offences also much lower.[48] It is interesting that those most passionately arguing for anonymity for defendants are rarely outraged that although approximately 97,000 people are raped every year in the UK, just under 10,000 people each year (10 per cent) are convicted of rape.[49] Under UK law, only men can be convicted of rape, but for all other sexual offences 97.3 per cent of defendants are men.[50]

This is perhaps the most brutal chapter so far. It is likely that much of what you have read is out of your frame of reference. If it is not, please know that my soul bears scars similar to your own. It is hard to continue existing in a world where abusive men practise sadism that so brutally breaks God's beautiful gift of sexuality to each of us. The impact on women can feel endless and all-consuming. And for a time it might be. But as someone who has walked that path, I can assure you that it doesn't have to be. I once attended a training event that included a craft activity. We cut out pictures and made personal slogans that were then laminated. Mine is still tacked to our kitchen cupboard: a photograph of the open road sits underneath the words 'Life Can Be Beautiful'. Life *can* be beautiful. I know that to be true even though life can be brutal, I can be broken and the darkness sometimes seems never-ending.

This chapter has primarily focused on sexual harm, but the truth that life can be beautiful includes that sex can be beautiful. It is *because* sex can be such a profoundly beautiful, intimate and liberating part of life that the misuse of it can so totally break us. *Eros* is one of the four ancient Greek words for love and is the form of love that God designed for people to share in sexuality. It is God's good gift to us. God gave women the gift of the clitoris, which means that, unlike with men, our sexual pleasure doesn't have to be linked to the part of our genitals designed for procreation (the vagina). After the horror of this chapter it can be easy to lose sight of the beauty of sex and the gift that it can be, but we must hold on to the truth that life (and sex) can be beautiful.

Take some time to pray or pause, or both.

God, there is so much brutality and evil. I don't know how to handle it. Please help me to know you in the midst of this. You are entirely good even though you have witnessed such evil; teach me to hold on to your goodness even as I feel overwhelmed by the pain. Amen.

> We are all meant to shine, as children do. We were born to make man-
> ifest the glory of God that is within us. It is not just in some of us; it
> is in everyone. And as we let our own light shine, we unconsciously
> give other people permission to do the same. As we are liberated
> from our own fear, our presence automatically liberates others.
>
> Marianne Williamson (1992)[51]

8 We did the best we could (Bringing up children with a co-parent who is harmful)

It wasn't what Craig had done to me that led to me reporting him to the police. Rather, it was watching my tiny son's chest rise and fall mechanically, a ventilator pumping air into him while other tubes provided him with intravenous nourishment. People usually don't know that premature babies have paper-thin skin. Subconsciously, most people will want to stroke them, but this can be painful. My son was three weeks old when I first held him and three months old when I first breastfed him, before which I expressed milk multiple times daily. My daughter was only two and a half when he was born. It was a great blessing to be able to live in hospital with him, as our home town was an hour from the hospital. I would take my daughter to children's centres, parks and libraries. We made a scrapbook recording what we did each day. My son would not remember how much time I spent with him, but my daughter would. Her whole world had changed; she had lost her daddy, her home and her stability. She needed to know I was the same, even if I wasn't the same. I tried to make life normal for her. I was 21 years old.

My experiences are unique only in that they belong to me and my children. Countless babies are premature as a result of men's violence; many will not survive; some will be left with serious health problems or learning difficulties. Pregnancy increases the risk an abuser poses to his partner. More than 30 per cent of violence starts in pregnancy, and existing abuse may escalate,[1] while, as we've already considered in Chapter 6, pregnancy itself can be a result of the abuser's tactics.

Why does an abuser's behaviour escalate when his partner is pregnant? People often presume it is about her hormones, financial insecurity, a lack of sex, stress. These are *not* the reasons. A woman is in no way responsible for her partner's choice to abuse her, regardless of her hormones or lack of interest in sex. Abuse increases in pregnancy because of the abuser's beliefs of ownership and entitlement. His partner's pregnancy changes the following two things.

1   Because of her desire to provide her baby with a two-parent family, his partner is less likely to leave him.
2   The pregnancy gives her someone to fight for other than herself, and she may resist his abuse more overtly and challenge him more. This means his beliefs are more likely to be threatened, so he reasserts his dominance and ownership.

Pregnancy should be a special time and, just as with any special time, the abuser wants to destroy it and further hurt his partner. She may give him less attention and, like a small child, he will demand she focus on him. He's not a small child; he's a grown man and a father-to-be.

'I don't understand!' the training participant stated sadly. 'Surely when a man's partner is pregnant he would want to look after her? Why wouldn't he support and love her?' I wanted to send her away then; such a lovely woman should be surrounded by kittens, not exposed to the brutality of abusers. But, in reality, her sister, friend or daughter may need her support, so she needs to know the truth. Women do need extra care in pregnancy, and when they are in a relationship with an abuser that need is undermined and remains unmet.

An abuser's use of isolation leaves his partner without friends or family members to ask for advice. Controlling her access to medical care, he might prevent her from checking whether the baby is growing safely and well. Telling her she is fat and disgusting every time she eats, he may thwart her efforts to eat healthily. His financial control leaves her unable to buy healthy food or maternity clothes and she may panic about whether the baby will have enough equipment and clothing. She will be unable to get the sleep and rest she needs as he exhausts her. A supportive partner would make space for her needs, massaging her feet, taking on extra hours at work and going out at 2 a.m. to buy craving-satisfying gherkins. An abuser does not meet his partner's pregnancy needs. He tells her she is being selfish and demanding. She remains alone and unsupported in what should be a beautiful and precious time. Where a single pregnant woman might be supported by family and friends, her partner's presence means those who know her are oblivious to her unmet needs. Her partner will threaten to hurt the unborn baby if she doesn't do what he wants. Many women recount how their partner punched or kicked their abdomen while they were pregnant. An abuser doesn't care about his partner or their baby; he is only interested in getting his own way.

While his partner is in labour, an abuser may berate and demean her, controlling her options. He may force her into a caesarean to 'preserve' her vagina. An abuser may force a specific name on their child, perhaps insisting she be named after a woman he had an affair with. He may force his partner to breastfeed, or may tell her she is not allowed to. Once the baby is born, this small human being may become a weapon the abuser uses to get what he wants while remaining totally uninterested in his child. His partner will have to do everything for the baby while still being required to meet all of the abuser's needs, including sexually. Her exhaustion increases, her ability to breastfeed diminishes and the baby is significantly affected by the abuser's behaviour.

If you, dear reader, were brought up with an abusive parent, please take care as you read on. This is brutal and painful, but hopefully it is helpful to know that you are not alone. Dear reader, if you have children and my description of an abusive partner is something you recognize in the behaviour of a current or former partner, then this chapter is going to be extremely hard. In pregnancy we desire the best life for the human growing inside us. When we bring that small person into the world, we will want to give him or her everything we can. Even if the conception was painful, brutal or not our choice, by the time we see the baby's face our ambiguous feelings are usually dominated by hope for this new child's life. And, almost always, we will do everything within our power to meet our baby's needs. Yet an abusive father means we won't have very much power.

It is hard to write this chapter in a way that helps everyone. For those who want to understand more about abuse there is a need for lots of information. For women who have small children, becoming aware of the harm your partner is causing the children may give you the knowledge you need to make new choices. However, for women with adult children, that knowledge is years too late, yet it may be helpful in enabling you (and your children) to make sense of the past. Each of us has different needs. Yet regardless of how you experience the rest of this chapter, please hold on to this truth:

We

All

Did

The

Best

We

Could.

We really did.

Research shows that even before a baby is born an abusive father can have an impact. Marion recounts, 'My partner used to shout and scream at me. I left him when I was seven months pregnant. When my daughter was a few months old, my ex came to visit me. The moment she heard my ex's voice, she started screaming. She wouldn't stop until my ex left.'

An abuser could prevent his partner from caring for the baby. Dave seethes as he pushes Marjory away from their three-day-old son, Simon. 'Don't touch him; he needs to self-soothe. I don't want a sissy-boy!' If Simon's mother cannot give him the care and love he needs, the bond between them is undermined. The health visitor visits, raising concerns about Marjory's lack of attachment. Dave scowls at her behind the health visitor's back and Marjory stays silent. She feels she is being judged as a bad parent. She does the best she can.

Researchers on childhood trauma have found that

> The experience of overwhelming and often unanticipated danger triggers a traumatic dysregulation of neurobiological, cognitive, social and affective processes that has different behavioral manifestations depending on the child's developmental stage, but is usually expressed through problems of relating and learning in the forms of aggression, hyperarousal, emotional withdrawal, attention problems, and psychiatric disturbances . . . [these] may alter a child's biological makeup through long-lasting changes in brain anatomy and physiology.[2]

Lundy Bancroft suggests five aspects to an abuser's parenting:

- undermining the mother's authority;
- retaliating against the mother for her efforts to protect the children;
- sowing divisions within the family;
- using the children as weapons against the mother;
- creating role models that perpetuate the violence.[3]

Let us now consider the impact of the Biderman behaviours on the abuser's children or stepchildren. We will do this with hypothetical children, Ay (girl) and Zed (boy).[4]

THE ISOLATOR

It is not only his partner that an abuser will isolate; it is also his children. When they are small, he may prevent their mother from joining parent and toddler groups. Cutting ties with her family and his own leaves Ay and Zed with no wider family, which is deeply distressing for their grandparents and other relatives, and Ay, Zed and their mother are left isolated and alone. When they grow old enough for school, the Isolator will not allow Ay's schoolfriends into the home. Even though Zed might be allowed friends home, he doesn't want to invite them because his dad might fly into a rage. He tells his friends he's not allowed friends round.

His dad always wants Zed to tell him what his mum has been up to. Sometimes his dad jokes and asks, 'Has your mum been out with her boyfriend today?' Even though his dad is laughing, it doesn't seem very funny. Ay continues to wet the bed even though she is seven because she is too frightened to get out of bed at night. Her mum hides this as they know her dad will punish her, so she is sent to school without being washed. She doesn't have any friends because she smells bad. Zed sometimes gets invited to friends' houses, but he doesn't like going as it upsets him to see how different their families are and how kind their dads are. Ay isn't allowed to go to friends' houses. Her dad mocks her and tells her no one would want to be her friend – she's too ugly. Ay's mum tries to tell her that's not true, but once Ay's dad saw it and she heard her mum screaming later.

THE HUMILIATOR

Ay and Zed hate dinner times. Their dad always makes their mum feel really bad about her cooking. He calls their mum bad names all the time. Zed is so angry with his mum for not fighting back that sometimes he calls her those names too. He is nine years old. His dad likes it when he does that and Zed likes it when his dad is nice to him. Their dad shames Ay and Zed if they do badly on school tests, but never congratulates them if they do well. Zed never cries, no matter what his dad does, because then his dad tells him he must be gay and mocks him. Sometimes their dad tells Ay she's his princess and sits her on his knee. She likes that, but then when she smiles he laughs unkindly at her and tells her he was lying.

Their dad tells their mum she is fat all the time. When they go out as a family, their dad whispers things in their mum's ear that make her look really sad. She rushes to the toilet and when she comes back her eyes are red as though she's been crying. Ay asks if she's OK and she says she's fine, even though they know she's not. Their dad took all the doors off their hinges. He said he wanted to see what they were all doing. Ay didn't like seeing her dad in the bedroom with her mum and would close her eyes when she had to walk past their room.

THE THREATENER

Ay and Zed are really frightened of their dad. He regularly threatens to smack them if they don't do what he wants. It's not safe to be angry with their dad because he might hurt them, so they feel angry with their mum for staying with him. Zed shouts at her and Ay kicked her the other day because her mum asked her to do homework. Sometimes Ay pretends she's too poorly to go to school so she can stay at home to check her mum is safe. Zed struggles to do his work at school because he's worried his dad might be at home hurting his mum.

THE EXHAUSTER

Their dad gets angry in the evening, shouting at their mum and smashing stuff. Neither Ay nor Zed gets much sleep when he does. In the morning, their mum pretends she's fine and they know she's been up half the night tidying up so that they can't see the mess. They find it hard to concentrate at school because they're so tired. Sometimes their mum tries to make them keep to a bedtime, but their dad lets them stay up watching scary films and eating sugary sweets. Sometimes he only lets Zed do it and sends Ay to bed. Zed loves his dad; Ay hates him. Their mum knows if she leaves she will break Zed's heart, but if she stays her husband will continue to hurt Ay. Most of the time, their mum is too tired to play with them. She tries to help them with homework and stuff, but then their dad comes in and rips it up.

THE BRAINWASHER

Although their dad works a lot, he doesn't give their mum enough money to buy what they need, yet sometimes he buys them special presents. They like it when he does that. Their mum never buys them presents. Even though their dad is usually horrible to their mum, he makes them think it's their mum's fault. He says that she winds him up and doesn't do what he wants quickly enough. Their mum tells them that their dad really loves them and doesn't mean to be unkind. That makes them think it's definitely her fault. Ay begins to really hate herself; she believes her dad when he tells her she's useless and worthless. Zed feels angry all the time. He can't cry because then his dad will think he's gay.

THE ALL-MIGHTY

When Zed was little, his dad said he could see him in every lightbulb so he had better behave. Zed is petrified of doing anything wrong because there are lightbulbs everywhere. Their mum knows she can't cuddle them as their dad will fly into a rage, so she keeps her distance from them, even though it breaks her heart. At Christmas, their dad smashed up the Christmas tree. One year he smashed all their presents before they even had dinner. His dad never stops play-fighting even when Zed wants him to; he's always too rough. If Zed shows he is scared his dad mocks him and tells him he is girly. Their mum knows that if she tries to leave their dad, he will find her and kill her. Even though she hates the way he treats the kids, she doesn't know how else to stay safe. Once her husband pulled out a knife and said he was going to cut off her fat. Then he laughed and put the knife on the kitchen unit. Another time, when they were supposed to be asleep, their dad locked their mum out of the house and made her stay outside until the morning.

Once they heard their mum choking and they rushed in to find their dad strangling her. Zed tried to pull their dad off while Ay rang the police. Their mum sat them down and told them they needed to forgive their dad – that's what God wanted. They feel really confused about it.

THE DEMANDER

Their dad makes their mum do all the housework tasks more than once. She sometimes asks them to help, but if their dad sees them helping he starts shouting. They know that they have to behave or he will get really angry. Neither Ay nor Zed feels safe to be naughty. Ay hates the way some of the children are mean to her, so she sometimes steals their stuff. Her teacher found out and called her parents in. Her dad made a massive scene and started screaming at the teacher.

THE NICE ONE

Sometimes their dad is really nice to them. He is a vicar and sometimes lets them help him with the service. After he has hurt their mum, he immediately cheers up. Their mum will often be upset for days afterwards. She is always moany and sad, whereas sometimes their dad is really good fun. He lets them do stuff their mum won't and buys them sweets and chocolate even though their mum says the dentist is worried about their teeth. Sometimes he swings Ay round and round and it's magical and she knows he loves her. And when he's in a good mood and ruffles Zed's hair, Zed is sure his dad is OK and things are going to be all right. Even though they're not.

Ay and Zed's family does not offer an exhaustive example of how an abuser uses the Biderman tactics, but hopefully it does provide a representation of how an abuser damages his children and partner. There is an enduring myth that 'just because he is an abusive partner, that doesn't make him a bad father'. This is not true. A good father treats the children's mother with respect and value, encouraging the children to value their mother too. If the relationship breaks down, a non-abusive man will seek to have a positive relationship with his children and their mother, and recognizes that meeting their mother's needs will help his children's needs to be met.

Ryan and Luke Hart's father killed their mother Claire and sister Charlotte after years of control. They described him as a 'bored prison guard'.[5] Luke reflects on his childhood:

> 'Well, he's not drunk and beating us every weekend, we're not failing at school, we don't have behavioural problems.' Those were the signs I was looking for . . . And because it hadn't happened, we didn't recognise our suffering, or that he was dangerous. From the outside, we were three healthy, intelligent children. No one seemed concerned that much was wrong, because we were doing so well.[6]

We presume that if a child has an abusive parent, it will be obvious: he or she will be dishevelled or unhappy. There are various roles children may enact to deal with the abuser.

- The Informer tells the abuser what her mum has been doing. This may be accurate information or could be lies told to win favour with her dad.
- The Peacekeeper tries to calm situations. She or he may get between the parents when the abuser is being violent or may feel responsible for their mum, seeking to make her feel better after their dad's abuse.
- The Copy Cat may become abusive like his dad, treating his mum, siblings, friends or girlfriend abusively.

- The Scapegoat feels responsible for the abuse. In this role children blame themselves and will try to direct their dad's abuse towards themselves and away from their mum.
- The Invisible hides away. Children will try to make themselves smaller and quieter to avoid being caught up in their father's abusive behaviour.
- The Star Pupil is well behaved. Driven to achieve, Star Pupils seek to block out the abuse and perhaps hope to gain their father's approval.
- The Problem Child will be badly behaved at school and home. Potentially misdiagnosed as having ADHD, he or she will act up to gain attention.

Most of these roles are not easily observable from the outside. It is only the Problem Child, the Copy Cat and perhaps the Invisible who conform to the picture that comes to mind when we think about children subjected to abuse. However, rather than looking for a particular type of behaviour, we need to build safe spaces where children feel able to talk about their lives. Their family is their norm. Without exposure to other families or to information about how people should behave towards one another (with respect, kindness, gentleness), they have no family model other than their own norm. They will have no reason to disclose what goes on in their home because nobody has told them that it is unusual or wrong.

ALEX'S STORY

My friend Alex has kindly shared some of her story of growing up with an abusive father:

> My own experience as a child, I suppose it is one of overwhelming responsibility (I grew up Irish Catholic and in my early years this faith was very pronounced). I was an only child and the eldest of four close cousins, and my nanna always held me

up as the one who would be OK and would make things OK. I barely remember my dad and the aspects I remember overwhelmingly are feelings and atmospheres. I developed PTSD very young and even now, almost 30 years on, specific memories are patchy. I remember feeling constantly 'aware' and hearing noises. Screams and thumps were written off as 'a bad dream' or a horror film. I witnessed his violence towards my mam only a handful of times (possibly more but my memory fails me here). I have learned that my father was controlling (explained away as OCD) so if I made any mess as a child, he would beat my mam (if my mam found me making a mess she would – understandably – scream hysterically at me, knowing what was about to come).

Our home was full of terror at all times. He worked away a lot but even his absence created a culture of fear – my mam was tracked, reported on, called at specific times of the day. If I fell over, she would be punched. If I became ill, kicked. The levels of his violence I can only imagine. My father was infamous in our town – his violence well known within the community and accepted. Remarks such as 'Here comes (my mam) showing off her panda eyes' were forever echoing.

My nanna despised him. Every time she mentioned him it was with anger and fear. And I absorbed this – he was *my* father, *my* responsibility – I came from him. So I tried to be a good kid – keep order, obey, clean up. But I also needed to protect my mam – who else could? We fled so many times and each time he would find us. We would change our names, move to isolated areas, but it made no difference – we were never safe. The only time he stopped trying to access her or me was when she met a man who raped me and brutalized her throughout their relationship.

My father dying was the greatest thing he ever did for me. It was a harrowing and horrifying death for him and for me, but I finally became free – at least from him – and my relationship with my mam became much less heightened, less fight or flight.

I am so incredibly fortunate to know and believe that she did the best she could, despite being terrorized for decades – she's a remarkable woman. Every choice she made she believed was best for *me* – every single one. I am lucky to have her.

But the legacy male violence has left is acute – her ability to meet her own needs is flawed. In many ways, she remains child-like – naive and reactionary and often lost. So, as a 30-something adult, I continue to try and look out for her in all aspects of her life. We have a reversal of roles that I imagine will last until one of us passes on. Before my nanna passed away, she asked me to 'take care' of my mam – make sure she was OK financially, emotionally, physically. But she need never have asked – I have done so since I was seven years old.

The caretaker part of me extends beyond my mam – I have this core 'belief' that it is my responsibility to look after those that are in need, and there is hope attached that I can leave them once their needs have been met – support to empower. Sadly this has meant unhealthy relationships lasting much longer than they should and me not valuing my own needs enough, but mostly (certainly within my career) this has worked well – support until no longer required. I can't see this ever ending with my mam and we are both painfully aware of it.

I was speaking at a large social work conference a few years ago with another speaker who was an expert in child neglect. Using attachment theory, her presentation focused on mothers' neglect of their children, presenting a picture of women as the only influence on children. She never once mentioned fathers.

David Mandel is an expert in the fatherhood of abusive men. He talks about how social care (also known as social services), parental support, education and other services will often erase the perpetrator in their work with women who have been subjected to abuse by a partner. Their expectations of the woman are that she exists in a vacuum, unaffected by the abuser, when the abuser is often controlling her for years after the intimate relationship ends.

Mandel shares stories of social workers questioning him about how to deal with mothers who 'fail to engage' with them. When he asks where the father is in the situation, the social workers often state that the father is irrelevant: only the mother's behaviour matters. Inevitably it would turn out that the father was still involved, controlling the mother or the children. In schools, it is the mothers of children with challenging home lives who are expected to change. The fact that it is the children's father who is responsible for their issues is either ignored or leaves professionals fearful of engaging with him.

We must not erase fathers. David Mandel's work is evidence that the best way to keep children safe is to enable them to stay 'safe and together' with the non-offending parent, working as a partner with her and doing robust assessments (with practical outcomes) of abusers.[7]

Diana had separated from her partner Jamie. Social care and the police were involved. She was placed in a refuge but had returned home with her small kids to pick up some clothing. Suddenly there was a loud banging on the door. Her ex-partner was outside screaming, swearing and smashing his fists against the door. The kids were really frightened. She didn't know what to do. She opened the door to him, thinking that she could calm him down. He began punching her in the head. The police arrived and arrested him. Diana arrived at the hospital. Social workers were waiting and placed her children in foster care. They said she had failed to protect them by opening the door. Diana was devastated.

An abuser will often manipulate professionals. Social care's standard for fathers is often much lower than for mothers, and the abuser may cause his partner to think that she can 'manage' him. This façade is designed to get him what he wants and to implicate her in his behaviour. Diana was doing the best she could.

An abusive partner diminishes our ability to co-parent. Regardless of our parenting skills, our partner's constant undermining and his turning the children against us makes it very hard for us to parent effectively. My two-year-old daughter was sitting on Craig's knee. 'What is Mummy?' he asked her. In her sweet little voice she answered, 'Skanky.' Craig had not trained her to say that but it was what she had consistently heard him call me. Children do not have to witness physical violence to be damaged. Merely having a parent who is an abuser and having to spend time with him can harm them. Our children are damaged, our relationship with our children is damaged and we are damaged by the abuser's behaviour.

An amendment in Section 31(9) of the Children Act 1989 states that harm to a child can include 'impairment suffered from seeing or hearing the ill-treatment of another'.[8] In British law it is recognized that domestic abuse is harmful to children. If we become aware that a child has a domestically abusive parent we have a statutory responsibility to report it. We can assume that a man's abuse of his partner has a minimal effect on her children, but that really is not the case.

What constitutes 'bad enough' abuse? A man may control his partner in various ways but there is no physical violence and the children seem to be doing well. Is there a threshold before we see the man's behaviour as damaging the children? No one could draw such a line in the sand as we do not know the impact of the abuser's behaviour on the children. We may think that we know enough, but we only have the information we have been given. Disclosure is always gradual, and abusive behaviour generally escalates. It is both foolish and dangerous to label any man as 'not that abusive'.

Many will be unhappy with me stating this. If someone is in a relationship with an abuser and he is the father (or stepfather) of her children, she may feel that I am dealing in absolutes in too complex a situation. She will feel that I don't know what her partner is like, that he loves the children, that it isn't that bad and that the children don't even know what's gone on. She feels angry and hurt that I would suggest she consider depriving her children of a father, finding it particularly outrageous that a Christian book is advocating separation of families. She was perhaps hoping that this book would give her strategies to help her partner change and here I am, telling her that her children's father is a problem that cannot be solved. I am sorry not to be able to tell you what you want to hear. I have walked a similar path and held similar views. I believed Craig could be redeemed and that my child was better off with him. Children need their father, don't they?

When my son was released from hospital we lived in a flat in the north-east of England where people affectionately call you 'pet' and their accent is The Best. I was preparing food. My three-year-old daughter was chattering away – 'Mummy sleeps in Daddy's bed and Gabby sleeps in Daddy's bed and everyone sleeps in Daddy's bed' – doing a big circle with her arms as she said 'everyone'. Gabby was one of the teenage girls Craig had been abusing. I asked her why she hadn't told me about Gabby sleeping in Daddy's bed when we lived with Daddy. 'Daddy told me it was naughty to tell you.' I don't know what else Craig told her was naughty to tell me, but I do know he created a context that made her vulnerable to abusers. If someone sexually abused her, she had already been primed to accept the idea that it is naughty to tell her mummy.

I can't tell any mother how to deal with an abusive partner. The facts remain very clear: children are negatively affected in countless ways when their mother is abused and when they have an abusive parent. That is not their mother's fault. We choose a partner with good intentions and want our children to have a loving, caring father. Yet we cannot live in denial. We cannot simply imagine that situation into existence. An abuser who is a father needs significant intervention to improve his parenting. Without his attending an accredited perpetrator programme, change is extremely unlikely. As hard as it is, our children need us to choose *them*, not through a misplaced belief that we are choosing them by maintaining a relationship with their father but to really choose them, even if that means ending our marriage. God wants life in all its fullness for us and our children. An abuser stands in the way of God bringing that to us and them.

I reported Craig to the police because my son was born prematurely. I didn't care what he did to me, but I cared about my son and what had been done to him. Very often, it is not until our partner hurts someone else that we take action. Valerie's husband hit her mother, and she reported him to the police and left him the same day. It is an amazing testimony to the strength of women that, no matter how many hurdles they have to overcome, when someone they care about is being hurt they will take action, no matter the cost.

There was a time when I couldn't imagine leaving Craig. I thought I would never survive alone. Yet living in a hospital with a premature baby and a toddler was easier than living with him. Parenting without being constantly undermined, I was able to help my children to develop values of honesty, kindness and gentleness. I could cuddle them and spend time with them. We could do arts and crafts, we had enough food in the house and I learned to cook after previously being scared of messing the recipe up.[9] I could take control of my finances and save a small amount of money. Accessing support services and counselling, I began to see that Craig's treatment of me was abuse, not my fault. My son's health improved and, although my daughter was extremely sad about losing her daddy, I was able to be honest about his choices and give her a framework to make sense of the hurt. I was able to rebuild a relationship with God.

Craig attempted to eradicate my faith, forcing me to do things that went against my values. I became isolated from my church after he sexually abused a teenage girl connected to the church community. Utterly broken, I had nothing to give God. After my son was born, we were living in a hospital. I had lost my home and my husband. It was then I began to hear God speak.

This is a wackiness warning for non-Christian readers! This is where my story gets quite crazy. It probably sits outside your frame of reference, but I hope you can find a way to honour my experiences. You may need to stop occasionally and yell out 'What the . . .?' *If this is the case, you may need to wait to read this until you're alone!*

On one occasion God said to me, 'Stop praying for your son to live, and instead pray for my will to be done. I need to know you will love me the same whether your son lives or dies.' I considered this for a long while. Could I choose God if my son died? I had endured four years of utter depravity, unable to have a relationship with God. It was hell. That experience of godlessness led me to choose God, not because he had promised my son life but because I knew the alternative involved a different kind of death, a death that would kill my soul as well as my body. From then on, I chose obedience to God regardless of the cost.

Months after this epiphany I was visiting my friends Andy and Alice for a New Year's Eve party. Our mutual friend was there. We all knew him as Baggy (I'm going to leave you all to guess why he's called Baggy). While I was chatting to him God told me, 'You're going to marry Baggy.' My immediate response was, 'I am not going to marry Baggy. I am not marrying anyone. Ever.' Just to clarify, I said this *inside* my head, not out loud. I was shocked at this extremely unwanted revelation. Over the next 14 months, Baggy and I chatted on the phone occasionally (he lived in south-east England). Baggy had been single for 13 years and (unlike many Christians) he was extremely happy with his single status. He was convinced God had called him to a life of childfree celibacy. God had basically told me I was going to marry a monk. The more I thought I wasn't going to marry Baggy, the more I knew, deep down, that I was going to marry him. It was very surreal. Eventually I informed God that he would need to tell Baggy that he was supposed to marry me, because I *certainly* wouldn't be telling him.

Soon after this, God called me to move to the south-east to join Baggy's church. I saw this as unrelated to the never-going-to-happen divinely arranged marriage. Baggy helped me move house. I would later learn that while Baggy was driving my removal van

God informed him that he was to marry me. Apparently it was a total shock to him, but seemingly he was slightly less opposed to the plan than I was. After a couple of weeks, we found ourselves having an extremely awkward conversation.

'Would you like a cup of tea?' (Yes. This is the way all important British conversations start.)

'No, thank you.'

'Oh. Right. Erm. Would you like a cup of tea?'

'Are you OK?'

'Erm. I don't know. I'll talk about it in a minute. Erm, would you like some tea? Oh no, you wouldn't. Erm, well. Erm, do you know what I'm trying to tell you . . .?'

'Well, I might. Is it good?'

'Erm, I don't know. Maybe. I'm not sure. Erm . . . Erm . . .'

Awkward silence, followed by Baggy blurting out, 'I like you. Do you like me?'

'Well, erm. Yes. Well, actually I think I'm supposed to marry you.'

'Yeah, me too.'

'So shall we get married?'

'Yeah, we should.'

There are a lot of caveats regarding this experience. Most Christians get together in the normal way. They date, they dump, they date some more, they find a special someone and there's a proposal. If you're single and waiting for a new partner, our experience is unlikely to be yours.

Baggy and I have been married over a decade now. We believe that the way our marriage began was truly a gift from God. If I'd had the normal experience of being attracted to Baggy, I would have been scared that I was wrong. I'd spent four years being destroyed by someone I'd fancied. It was God's grace to make his way clear for our lives. My son was only 18 months at the time and he oddly began to call Baggy 'Daddy' without any prompting. We gave my daughter the choice of how to refer to Baggy and she too chose to call him Daddy. When we got married, we also had a ceremony to dedicate the children to God. Once married, we felt they became our babies. God directed us not to have children together naturally.

We are very blessed that Craig has no contact with the children. A combination of his lack of interest, asserting strong boundaries and living at the other end of England has helped with this. It is possible for some abusive fathers to safely have contact with their children, but mothers need to have power and control for it to work. Many fathers will use contact to further abuse their partner and children (as we read in Chapter 6).

Our daughter is an excellent 16-year-old and our son is a brilliant 13-year-old. Both are age-appropriately aware that Craig is dangerous, that he hurt me and caused my son to be born prematurely. They are on their own journeys and it is not my place to tell you their stories; maybe one day they'll write their own books!

God was in the end of my marriage to Craig. He can provide for us in ways that fit outside our theology. God is always bigger than our vision of Him but is gracious enough to meet us in whatever space we give Him. It's a bit like having a duvet in a box.[10] Dragging a bit of it out of the box we could warm our feet, while pulling more out might cover the lower half of our body. Removing it from the box entirely means we can snuggle our whole selves within it. We usually put God in a box. He loves us enough to meet us in the small space we give Him. Yet there is so much more of God. He's just waiting for us to take Him out of the box.

Entire books have been written on understanding the effects of abusers on children. This chapter is merely a metaphorical toe in the deep dark swamp of the harm abusers cause children. If you would like to learn more I recommend these books:

- Nicky Stanley and Cathy Humphreys (eds), *Domestic Violence and Protecting Children: New thinking and approaches* (Philadelphia, Pennsylvania: Jessica Kingsley, 2015)

- Marianne Hester, Chris Pearson and Nicola Harwin, *Making an Impact: Children and domestic violence* (Philadelphia, Pennsylvania: Jessica Kingsley, 2006).

We have come to the end of this chapter! Take a moment to pause and reflect. What was most helpful about this chapter? What has challenged you? What has been positive for you? What do you need to do to move forward in your understanding? If you're up for it, let's pray . . .

God, the children and partners of abusers suffer so much. Please would you guide me to know your will more. Show me your ways and enable me to be a light for those struggling. Bring justice and freedom to women and children, and show me how to bring your truth and love to them. Amen.

> Dear refuge of my weary soul,
> On thee when sorrows rise;
> On thee, when waves of trouble roll,
> My fainting hope relies.

> While hope revives, though pressed with fears,
> And I can say, 'My God,'
> Beneath thy feet I spread my cares,
> And pour my woes abroad.

> To thee I tell each rising grief,
> For thou alone canst heal;
> Thy word can bring a sweet relief,
> For every pain I feel.

> Anne Steele (1791)[11]

9 It's all in your head (Trauma, emotional harm and all the sciencey stuff)

Christians are often taught that in death our soul will shed our body (a bit like a caterpillar shedding its chrysalis) and float to heaven. This is sometimes coupled with rather dubious research by Dr Duncan McDougall (published in 1907) who claimed to have proven that the soul was a physical entity that left the body on death.[1] Christian culture's relationship with the body is ambivalent at best and self-loathing at worst.[2] Theologian Paula Gooder has written an entire book on the body. She explains, 'Treating our bodies as though they are a precious gift from God, rather than an encumbrance to be endured or ignored, lies at the heart of a Christian theology of the body.'[3]

God made our bodies. Jesus came to earth in a human body; in Communion we remember His *body* that was given for us. C. S. Lewis explains that 'this new life [of Christianity] is spread not only by purely mental acts like belief, but by bodily acts like baptism and Holy Communion'.[4] Our Christian faith is not merely orthodoxy (which means 'right opinion') but also orthopraxy (from the Greek for 'right conduct'): 'faith by itself, if it is not accompanied by action, is dead'.[5] God did not design us to be floating souls, imprisoned within a body, finally liberated from that body upon death. He made us as integrated beings with soul and body interconnected, intertwined, interdependent.

Human understanding of itself has generally followed human understanding of the wider world. Robert Epstein, former editor-in-chief of *Psychology Today*, explains:

> The invention of hydraulic engineering in the third century BCE led to the popularity of a hydraulic model of human intelligence, the idea that the flow of different fluids in the body – the 'humours' – accounted for both our physical and mental functioning. The hydraulic metaphor persisted for more than 1,600 years, handicapping medical practice all the while. By the 1500s, automata powered by springs and gears had been devised, eventually inspiring leading thinkers such as René Descartes to assert that humans are complex machines. In the 1600s, the British philosopher Thomas Hobbes suggested that thinking arose from small mechanical motions in the brain. By the 1700s, discoveries about electricity and chemistry led to new theories of human intelligence – again, largely metaphorical in nature. In the mid-1800s, inspired by recent advances in communications, the German physicist Hermann von Helmholtz compared the brain to a telegraph.[6]

As the body came to be understood mechanically, philosophers began to separate body and soul. In 1641, the philosopher and mathematician René Descartes was trying to work out what he could be certain of. Philosophers were postulating that everything we perceived could actually be a dream. Descartes concluded that if he was able to think, able to reason, then he could confidently assert that he did in fact exist (otherwise translated as 'I think, therefore I am'). Separation of soul and body grew as rational thinking became the key to truth, many rejecting the idea of a soul altogether. Regardless of whether you are reading this with a view of the soul as integrated with the body, as separate from the body or as non-existent, I hope we can all agree that our physical body is not irrelevant and that our physicality, thinking, experiences and humanity affect each other.

Our bodies have an inbuilt system to manage threats.[7]

Historically, when faced with a lioness, Wilma the cavewoman's brain shifts into 'threat response mode', or the Survival State. This takes place in the brain stem, the lower part of the brain. In a split second, Wilma's brain assesses the best response for survival. Could she fight it? Should she run away from it? Or failing that, should she stay very still and hope the lioness assumes she is a tree? Imagine a control panel in Wilma's brain with three siren lights, labelled Fight, Flight, Freeze. Her Survival State is triggered and her brain whirs, calculating the best option; the corresponding light flashes and her body responds. As this happens her body automatically pumps her full of adrenaline and cortisol to prepare her for running or fighting.

Fast forward thousands of years and, within the West, lions are no longer an issue – it's other human beings that are the problem. Yet our Survival State continues to operate in the same way. Confronted by a rude stranger while we load our shopping on to the conveyor belt, our Survival State will kick in. Our brain makes a split-second decision to flight, fight or freeze, our body releasing high levels of adrenaline and cortisol. This results in heart rate increase, tunnel vision, shaking, dilated pupils, flushed face, dry mouth, slowed digestion, hearing loss and bladder relaxation. Most people will recognize this process. Trauma expert Zoe Lodrick suggests that our brain has two additional Survival State settings: Flop and Friend.[8] Flop involves playing dead, while Friend tries to befriend the threat, turning the lion into a large pet cat or frantically apologizing to the rude stranger. Flight, Fight, Freeze, Friend and Flop are known as the Five Fs.

Among its many parts, the brain has three areas.

1   The upper brain (also known as the prefrontal lobe) is the most advanced bit. It deals with language, imagination, reasoning and rational thinking. When our brain is operating from here, we call it the Executive State.
2   The mid-brain (usually called the limbic system) deals with emotions, memories, habits and basic decisions. When we utilize this part of our brain, it's called the Emotional State.

3   The lower brain (which is also known as the brain stem) is the least developed part and it deals with trauma response and the times we go on autopilot. If our brain operates from this part, it's called the Survival State.

The lower brain does not have the same processing capacity as the more developed mid- and upper brain, but it is the part of our brain that deals with threats. If the aforementioned Wilma's upper brain had to deal with threats as the lioness approached her, it would still be trying to work out whether the lioness was a soft toy while the animal was merrily chomping through her arm. However, the lower brain's primitiveness may cause us to enter the Survival State in response to non-threats. Seeing a spider in the kitchen we panic, then realize that it is just a tomato stalk; the split second between perceiving a spider and recognizing the tomato stalk is the time between the Survival State response of the lower brain and the Executive State response of the upper brain.

Many of us will have watched nature documentaries where a lioness is out hunting. The quiet authority of a David Attenborough-esque voice narrates the scene. The grazing antelope moves slightly away from the herd, then, smelling the lioness as she leaps from the bushes, his brain kicks into Survival State. His adrenaline and cortisol levels shoot up as his brain stem selects Flight, Fight or Freeze. The lioness catches him and we watch as she drags him along. We assume he is dead. Distracted, the lioness places the antelope on the ground. Suddenly the antelope jumps and runs. As he runs his limbs shake and judder. We cheer at the screen, 'You can do it, Arnold! Run like the wind!' The lioness realizes she has been fooled and, after trying to chase him, she leaves Arnold and begins her second attempt to catch dinner.

Freeze and Flop are the brain forcing the body to play dead. However, the body will have still released adrenaline and cortisol in case Fight or Flight is selected. When the antelope shakes and judders, he is discharging the unused adrenaline and cortisol. But, unlike wild animals, both humans and domestic animals do not naturally do this.

It is often assumed that if someone is attacked she will immediately fight to escape a potential rapist. The police deem many rape cases 'No Further Action' because the woman (or her attacker) had no wounds to prove she had fought back. A lack of attempt to run away or fight an attacker is not evidence that an attack did not take place, but rather shows that the victim's Survival State designated Freeze, Flop or Friend as the best chance for survival. Many people blame themselves for not fighting or running away from an attacker when they could not have done anything differently.[9]

Trauma expert Dr Robert Scaer has found that women's brains are much more likely to have a passive response to a threat (Freeze and Flop), while men are more likely to actively respond (Flight and Fight).[10] Scaer suggests this is as a result of women's higher likelihood of having been subjected to childhood abuse or medical trauma, and alongside this women and girls are often socialized to be passive. The Survival State takes into account the woman's physical strength and size compared to her attacker's in designating her response. If she is most likely to survive by freezing, that is what her body will insist she does. If someone has been subjected to historic trauma (either in being abused or through invasive medical procedures) her body is much more likely to repeat whichever of the Five Fs kept her alive previously. The body of a small child who has been raped or held down to be intubated (put on a ventilator) will deem Fight and Flight impossible. Even if as an adult she is strong enough to fight back, her brain may continue to use previously successful strategies. Friend is an active response to a threat, but it goes against what is considered rational.

Katy's husband George had assaulted her. Their children were in bed and she could hear them whimpering quietly. He had stormed downstairs. Rushing after him, all she could think about was moving him away from the kitchen, particularly the knives. She spoke quietly and kindly, 'Darling, why don't you come here and we can go to bed.' Feeling eerily calm she successfully pacified him and they went to bed. He wanted to have sex and, although her ribs ached and her face was swelling up where he'd hit it with a heavy book, she did what he wanted.

Katy's brain was in Survival State; she couldn't risk George accessing knives, so she used Friend to de-escalate the situation. She didn't have a choice about sex, but later may not identify that George raped her because she didn't say no. When her brain enters the Executive State she may feel guilty for not fighting back, confused as to whether she encouraged George's behaviour. She won't talk to anyone for fear that people won't believe her or will shame her for not running away or fighting.

Rosie's boyfriend Vinny had gone to church. He had told her that if she left he would kill her. Rosie quickly packed her bag. She was jittery with adrenaline and it took her three attempts to zip it up. She left the house, but as she rounded the corner she saw Vinny coming towards her. Dragging her back to the house, he hurt her badly all night. It was the worst he had ever done to her. Afterwards she felt so stupid. Why had she tried to run? She couldn't tell anyone what had happened; they'd only tell her she should have done as he said.

Roberta woke up to find her husband Mike touching her sexually. She didn't want him to touch her. Hours earlier he had told her about his most recent affair with her sister. She wanted to push him away, but her arms felt too heavy to move and her body was a dead weight. She kept her eyes closed and pretended to be asleep. Her thoughts turned to the book she had been reading, her work as a GP – anything to avoid being present. When he'd finished, he rolled off her and fell asleep. Her body felt like lead, her head fuzzy. Mike snored. Roberta felt utterly disgusted with herself; why hadn't she pushed him away? Why had she been such a coward? It wasn't sexual assault because she hadn't told him no. She couldn't talk about what he'd done, no one would understand. Rushing to the bathroom, she vomited and spent hours trying to wash him off her. But he was still there.

Hayley's boyfriend Jamie flew into a rage, smashing up the house. As she tried to push him out of the door he grabbed her face. She bit down and she felt his blood in her mouth as he screamed. She let go. Grabbing his phone, he ran upstairs and locked himself in the bathroom. She could hear him talking quietly. Twenty minutes later there was a knock at the door. Jamie pushed his way past her and told the two police officers at the door that she had attacked him, showing them the bite mark. Arresting her, they took her to the police station. Hayley was mortified. She didn't know why she had thought she could fight him. Now she would get a criminal record and lose her job working at the nursery school. She felt so ashamed.

Wendy's boyfriend Charles set the webcam to record. She had told him she didn't want to do it, but he had told her he would kill Tigger, her ginger cat, if she didn't. He barked at her to take her clothes off. She couldn't get her fingers to undo the buttons, her whole body was rigid. He pushed her on to the bed and stripped her. She felt him doing it to her, but her body had stopped working, it didn't feel as if it belonged to her. She was frozen. Finishing, he switched the camera off and told her she was a dirty whore. After he left, she gradually felt her body unfreeze. Her limbs felt heavy and her brain couldn't compute what had happened. She felt totally alone. How could she tell anybody she hadn't wanted to do it? He'd said he was going to show the video to his mates. She felt so ashamed: why hadn't she fought back? Why had her body betrayed her so badly?

Our responses to threat are normal. We are responding normally to an abnormal situation, but no matter how we respond we are likely to blame ourselves. If we are supporting someone who has been subjected to abuse she may express feelings of self-blame. Our first response may be to invalidate the self-blame: 'It was not your fault. You couldn't have changed it.' It is not wrong to encourage someone to know that she is not to blame. However, understanding *why* someone may blame herself is really important.

There are two primary reasons why someone may blame herself. First, in order to avoid responsibility the abuser will blame his behaviour on his partner and she will believe his version and take on responsibility for his behaviour. Second, self-blame can be a subconscious coping strategy; an abuser's behaviour is utterly disempowering, and his partner's feeling utterly powerless can be psychologically very dangerous. As autonomous beings, we need to feel that we have power and agency, that we can make choices and feel able to protect ourselves. Self-blame allows us to feel we have power: if it was my fault, then I have the power to change it and I can prevent it happening again. Accepting that I don't have the power to change it and cannot prevent it happening again is a very frightening reality, and self-blame can help to avoid that reality.

This is the rationale behind much victim blaming. If women's clothes cause men to rape them, then I can protect myself by ensuring I wear the right clothing. If men only abuse women with low self-esteem, then I can protect women by building their self-esteem. If all abusers look like weirdos, then I can spot them and keep me and mine safe. Nobody wants to live in a world where they cannot control their life or where they can't protect themselves and those they care about from abusers.

Understanding self-blame as providing psychological distance from powerlessness can help us to make sense of it. It can help us be better supporters. Rather than telling someone it is nonsense for her to blame herself, we can empathize with her, gently helping her to know it's OK to identify powerlessness; she is safe now and she can increase her power.

Soldiers in the First World War described their post-war trauma as 'shell shock'.[11] In 1941, psychiatrist Abram Kardiner described it as 'traumatic neuroses'.[12] At that time it was perceived that 'The soldier who developed traumatic neurosis was at best a constitutionally inferior human being, at worst a malinger and a coward.'[13] Forty years later, Vietnam veterans successfully lobbied for a new diagnosis, 'post-traumatic stress disorder' (PTSD),[14] to be added to the third edition of the American Psychiatric Association's *Diagnostic and Statistical Manual of Mental Disorders* (DSM-III).[15] Medically, PTSD is recognized as being caused by many traumatic incidents, including war. Yet general perception continues to see PTSD as solely about war, demonstrated when provocateur Piers Morgan condemned musician Lady Gaga's PTSD diagnosis: 'Enough of this vain-glorious nonsense . . . I come from a big military family. It angers me when celebrities start claiming "PTSD" about everything to promote themselves.'[16]

The typecasting of PTSD as a 'military thing' leaves many people ignorant of how common it is. PTSD can be caused by war, car accidents, abuse, rape, medical procedures, childbirth, assault, terrorist attacks, natural disasters, diagnosis of a life-threatening condition or the unexpected death or severe injury of a close friend or family member.[17]

Disorder can be defined as a 'lack of order or regular arrangement',[18] which is definitely how trauma affects people. Disorder can also be described as a disturbance in physical or mental health or functions. Post-traumatic stress disorder is not a disturbance of mental health function, but is rather our body and mind functioning exactly as they were designed to. A PTSD diagnosis should not suggest that we are 'disordered' but rather that our body responded normally to an abnormal situation.

To receive a PTSD diagnosis, someone must have either experienced a traumatic event or have witnessed it (either directly or indirectly). This can include the sudden death, serious injury or wider trauma of a family member, friend, client or patient. Three types of symptoms must be present for over a month.

1   **Re-experiencing** You have unexpected memories of the trauma, including flashbacks (this is where you feel physically transported back to a traumatic incident and fully re-experience it) and/or memories triggered by particular stimuli, including sounds and smells.

2   **Avoidance and numbing** You avoid situations, locations or stimuli that lead to feeling retraumatized. Feeling numb or disassociated, some people forget chunks of time or lose the ability to function normally once the trauma is triggered.

3   **Arousal** You are irritable, have difficulty sleeping, experience hyperarousal and hypersensitivity and are constantly assessing danger. Jumping at unexpected movement or sound, you may become angry quickly or have difficulty concentrating.[19]

A diagnosis of 'complex PTSD' may be given for those subjected to sustained trauma over a prolonged period by someone close to them, often in childhood. The nature of complex PTSD is wider distortion of core identity, with more intense and long-lasting symptoms. It is much less well understood than PTSD.[20]

PTSD is linked to the Five Fs. Confronted with a threat, our brain goes into Survival State and designates a Fight, Flight, Friend, Freeze or Flop response. Particularly with the passive responses of Flop and Freeze, the brain stem may not be able to free itself of the trauma. Without an active response of Fight, Flight or Freeze, the hormones and stress response are not discharged and remain 'stuck' in the body. If the trauma gets stuck, it cannot be processed. The primitive brain stem cannot recognize the incident as historical, seeing it as continuing even after it ends. This is what causes the symptoms of post-traumatic stress disorder: the trauma is stuck in the wrong part of the brain. Hypervigilance and hypersensitivity are a result of the undischarged energy as the brain continually tries to respond to the trauma. As the brain tries to deal with the stuck trauma, disassociation, numbness and 'spaced out-ness' result. Our brain may block out the memory of the trauma. Any stimuli that remind us of the trauma may trigger our brain into overdrive, transporting us into the stuck trauma; these are experienced as flashbacks and/or nightmares.

Using the Adverse Childhood Experiences (ACE) scale,[21] it has been found that adults with high levels of childhood trauma are at significant risk of chronic depression (66 per cent of women, 35 per cent of men), suicide (a 5,000 per cent greater likelihood), alcoholism (seven times more likely), IV drug use (4,600 per cent more likely) and cancer (twice as likely), with a 15 per cent greater chance of developing chronic obstructive pulmonary disease (COPD), ischaemic heart disease and liver disease[22] and greater occurrences of autoimmune disorders including fibromyalgia and chronic fatigue.[23] There is no doubt that abuse and trauma seriously affect both mental and physical health.

Trauma expert Bessel van der Kolk explains, 'Trauma is much more than a story that happened long ago. The emotions and physical sensations that are imprinted during the trauma are experienced not as memories but as disruptive physical reactions in the present.'[24] Brain scans of traumatized people have shown that:

- the time and perspective areas of the brain go blank, as do the areas of the brain that integrate sounds, images and sensations (dissociation);[25]
- for those with multiple traumas, 'almost every area of the brain has decreased activation, interfering with thinking, focus and orientation (depersonalization)';[26]
- stress hormones (adrenaline and cortisol) take longer to return to baseline, spiking quickly and disproportionately;[27]
- viewing images of past trauma activates the right hemisphere of the brain (intuition) and deactivates the left hemisphere of the brain (rationality and logic);[28]
- when scans were done during a flashback, the brain could be seen to shut down speech in the same way as after a stroke; 'the effects

of trauma are not necessarily different from – and can overlap with – the effects of physical lesions like strokes'.[29]

This robust neuroscientific research giving evidence of the physical effects of trauma can be hugely liberating for people who are traumatized. Instead of being told that their issues are emotional and psychological in a way that insists they should simply 'pull themselves together', the research shows us that trauma fundamentally changes the way someone's body works. But that is not all! The research indicates that there are a number of ways to recover from trauma which are currently not being utilized by healthcare professionals.

First, though, let's start with what *doesn't* work.

1 **Cognitive behavioural therapy (CBT)** Despite the success of CBT in various types of counselling, it is not appropriate for treating trauma. Developed for dealing with phobias,[30] CBT enables those with irrational fears (as of spiders or flying) to process their irrationality and compare them with the reality. PTSD is not irrational fear, it is rational fear. CBT may help with the wider by-products of trauma, but will not help with the core PTSD symptoms.

2 **Talking therapies** Where someone's brain is shutting down speech or causing disassociation or depersonalization, talking therapies are basically useless. Trying to talk about the trauma is likely to trigger trauma, thereby increasing someone's incapacity and retraumatizing him or her.[31]

3 **Prescription drugs** Designed to alleviate the symptoms of mental health disorders, the symptoms of PTSD are actually the body responding normally to an abnormal situation. Bessel van der Kolk explains, 'All too often, however, drugs . . . are prescribed instead of teaching people the skills to deal with such distressing physical reactions. Of course, medications only blunt sensations and do nothing to resolve them or transform them from toxic agents into allies.'[32]

So, what *does* work? Excitingly there are lots of different ways that trauma and PTSD can be resolved. One of the basic theories is that in order for the brain stem to release the trauma, the body needs to be physically relaxed while recalling the trauma. Once the brain notices that our body isn't having a physical reaction to the trauma, it can release it. This allows it to be 'unstuck' and processed in the Executive State of the prefrontal lobe.

Various therapies have been developed to aid this process, including the Rewind Technique. Carried out by a trained therapist, this process does not require the traumatized person to talk about the trauma. Moved into a relaxed state by the therapist, she is encouraged to imagine a TV screen and video-cassette recorder (VCR) in her mind. (For those born in the 2000s, a VCR is a bit like a DVD player but with a plastic tape. Magically, this stays at the same place when you take it out of the player!) After imagining this, she visualizes herself floating out of her own body and watching herself watch the TV screen. This leaves her two places removed from what she is watching. Instructed to imagine the trauma playing on the TV screen in forward, rewind, fast forward and fast rewind, she is able to remain physically relaxed. Having achieved this, she can take the tape out of the VCR and throw it away before being moved out of the relaxed state. This process alone can cause dramatic recovery from PTSD.

Eye Movement Desensitization and Reprocessing (EMDR) is a technique used by a trained therapist, who encourages the traumatized person to follow a moving finger with her eyes while remembering the trauma. If the person experiences new memories, feelings or sensations, the therapist asks her to notice what they are. EMDR does not require someone to talk about her trauma. It 'loosens up something in the mind/brain that gives people rapid access to loosely associated memories and images from their past. This seems to help them put the traumatic experience into a larger context of perspective.'[33] Developed by Francine Shapiro in 1987, this is an extremely successful therapy that requires few sessions to make a huge difference in people's lives.

Somatic Experiencing has also proven successful in treating PTSD. It provides opportunities for a traumatized person to discharge the energy that can get stuck during Freeze and Flop.[34] Developed by trauma expert Peter Levine, it provides opportunities for someone to physically experience what it would have been like to fight back or run away.

Internal Family Systems Therapy was developed by Richard Schwartz and sees each human as a 'family' of different selves. Particularly in traumatized people, these selves are often working in unhealthy ways, as they came into existence to help the person cope with traumatic experiences.

Beyond the specifics of these therapies, there are more general therapeutic methods that can help traumatized people. Both mindfulness and yoga are somewhat contentious among Christians, with some concerned that they originate in Hinduism and Buddhism. Evidence has found that both are hugely beneficial for traumatized people, and it is possible to utilize the methods without subscribing to Hindu or Buddhist theology. Trauma-aware yoga teachers and mindfulness coaches can help traumatized people to remain in the present, while yoga helps people reconnect with their physical bodies. Sexual and physical assault and invasive medical procedures can leave people highly disconnected from their own bodies, and yoga enables them to rebuild trust and confidence in their physical selves. Two other extremely important resources in recovering from trauma include building self-awareness and having positive relationships.

I am not aware of any research into how prayer can contribute to healing trauma; however, a key part of recovering from trauma is to be relaxed while recalling the trauma. If someone remembers a traumatic incident while God's peace is on her, this may have a similar impact to the Rewind Technique. Some have had prayer that involves remembering the traumatic incidents, imagining Jesus as present there with them, while others have felt the Holy Spirit descend on them as they have prayed. Although it is unlikely that any scientifically robust research will be able to prove the power of prayer in healing trauma (it seems that God requires there to be an element of faith in his work . . .), many people are able to testify to the healing power of prayer, whether that be with the Bethel Sozo healing ministry[35] or healing prayer after a local church service.

You may have thought that marrying Baggy was a happily ever after for me and the children. It wasn't. As soon as I had someone safe to rely on, I fell apart. I would lose the ability to move and speak. Once Baggy called the emergency services as I was totally unresponsive; the ambulance crew arrived and declared me totally well. Baggy had gone from 13 years of singleness to having a crazy wife and two vaguely traumatized children. It wasn't that fun for him. Sometimes I would cry hysterically; sometimes I would wish I could cry but felt utterly numb. On occasions, I was suicidal and would be up late into the night telling him the worst bits of what Craig did to me. It was horrific, brutal and unquestioningly necessary.

Baggy didn't really have any support. No one knew how to support him. For the new partners of women who have been subjected to abuse there is no handbook or advice line they can call. Baggy and I have thought about writing a book on this (publishers take note . . .). New relationships often have unspoken rules about leaving the past in the past, avoiding too much talk about previous relationships. When someone has PTSD or is traumatized, the past is not in the past, it is in the present, affecting the majority of life.

If you're supporting someone in a new relationship where the history of one or both partners includes abuse, it is so important to support each of them. Ask them what they need. The normal rules for Christian relationships will often be unhelpful. People advised Baggy and me that we shouldn't spend too much pre-marital time alone, but

I couldn't leave my sleeping children to go to social gatherings, and sometimes I would lose the ability to function for most of the night, causing Baggy to have to stay with me.

People at our church were both amazing and difficult. They offered such intense and loving support, but sometimes the 'words of knowledge' people offered during prayer times would be unhelpful or wrong. One female leader advised me to change my clothing style because my husband wouldn't want me showing my midriff – Baggy was appalled by this advice. During marriage preparation we were told that sexually men are like gas cookers (turn them on and they are on full) and women are like electric cookers (they take a while to warm up). I wanted to know who got to be the microwave.

Sex was complicated as we chose to wait until we got married. Our honeymoon was interesting. Baggy had been single and had avoided thinking about sex for 13 years, while I'd been married to someone who wanted sex multiple times a day. To say we were sexually incompatible is an understatement. We weren't only on different pages, we were on different bookshelves in different continents. I spent night four of the honeymoon crying hysterically and extremely loudly after realizing that my son could have died numerous times. It was the longest I'd been away from the kids, and as I wailed, 'HE COULD HAVE DIED, BAGGY! HE COULD HAVE DIED!!!' with snot and tears plastering my face, Baggy gently asked me if I could maybe be a little quieter because other hotel guests might think he was hurting me. 'NO, BAGGY, I CAN'T,' I wailed. 'IT NEEDS TO COME OUT NOW!'

A decade of marriage, including a season of sex therapy, deep and abiding confidence in God's plan to call us to marriage and a friendship that allows us to laugh with each other (a lot) has brought us to a place where sex is more of what God intended it to be and less of a complete and utter nightmare.

When I left Craig, people were hugely supportive, but once Baggy and I were together and things seemed to be OK they thought

I was better. But it was only when I was in a safe place that my brain could shut down. Until then I had full responsibility for two small children. Baggy's love and support opened the floodgates for the trauma to come spilling out. I had lots of counselling and prayer sessions; becoming hysterical, I would vomit up air and at times my body contorted in twisted painful ways.

As the months and years moved on, the number of episodes I had decreased. Yet every time I was triggered into an episode it would feel as though I would be stuck there for ever, disassociated, unable to think clearly, sometimes totally disconnected from my body. Once I lay in bed under the covers, staring at my hand. I knew rationally that it belonged to me but it felt like an alien entity. My friend once likened life with PTSD to walking across a stage not knowing when a stage door will open underneath you. I would go for months feeling like a normal human being and then BAM! I would be floored. A new reminder that I was still broken; that my life would always be tainted by Craig.

About five years ago I was watching a TV programme. The scene shifted to violent rape. My brain immediately shut down. I could barely speak, my limbs felt heavy, my head was fuzzy. This went on for weeks. I would drag myself through the days, unsure that I was ever going to feel normal again. I had paid to attend a five-day facilitator training event held by the Right Use of Power Institute, whose work seeks to transform personal and professional ethics around power use.[36] I couldn't afford to lose the money and so attended while feeling disassociated and disoriented. The first night I got chatting with a therapist who specialized in trauma. Over that evening and the subsequent days she explained trauma theory to me, the way I have explained it to you in this chapter. It made total sense. She told me about the Rewind Technique, and a few days after the training I found a local therapist and had a session with her. Within hours I felt totally normal again. It was amazing.

I have since had a couple more sessions when I have been

triggered into a traumatic space. I'm down to about one episode a year now. I deal with them by trusting that God is in the timing. Rather than fighting for control of my body, I relinquish myself to whatever has been raised, making space for it and trusting that God will enable me to overcome it; so far, He always has.

Some of the counselling I have had has positively changed my life,[37] but not all of it. When married to Craig I was referred to a psychologist. When she asked me what I wanted to get from the session, I told her I wanted to leave my husband. After patronizingly nodding at me, she asked, in her soft counselling voice, 'Well, shall we start by looking at your childhood?'

There is much within psychotherapy that is damaging, particularly for women. Founder of psychoanalysis Sigmund Freud wrote a paper in 1896 entitled *The Aetiology of Hysteria* in which he argued that it was men's sexual abuse which 'triggered the onset of hysterical symptoms [in women]'.[38] However, as Freud considered the implications of a society in which men's sexual abuse of girls and women was endemic, he repudiated his theory and 'Psychoanalysis became a study of the internal vicissitudes of fantasy and desire, dissociated from the reality of experience'.[39] Carl Jung founded analytical psychology. Dutch theologian Riet Bons-Storm has said, 'It is very obvious that Jung looks upon women as illogical creatures. None of the four aspects of the [female] anima contain any rational insight.[40] Although psychotherapy and counselling have moved on from Freud and Jung's original work, trauma-informed practice remains a niche specialism rather than a core part of all counselling practice. We have a long way to go!

Understanding neural plasticity (explained in Chapter 4) can be very helpful in moving towards recovery. I liken our neural pathways to a river running down the side of a mountain. At the top of the mountain is a lake, and a stream forms as the drips from the lake trickle down the mountain. This gradually becomes a river as more water trails down the slope. As the water flows more strongly, a riverbed forms a path down the mountain. This is like a neural pathway. The more we do an action, the more a neural pathway develops. We get to a point of almost automatically repeating the same pattern. Driving to work the same way year on year, we get to a point of not remembering the journey we've just taken. Yet neural pathways can change if we opt to make different choices. Set yourself a task: move something in your kitchen – tea, coffee, bin or something else. Count how many times you go to the old place before you start going to the new place. When you finally get it right first time, that's the point where you've made a new neural pathway!

Understanding that our brains are not fixed can bring great hope. Christians believe in free will, and it turns out God made our brains with the capacity to change deeply embedded ways of living. When we are traumatized or feeling beholden to a traumatic attachment (Chapter 6), things can change. It may take more than simply moving our kitchen cupboards around, but it is a reminder that our brains and lives are truly not fixed.

We've made it to the end of this chapter! There's a lot of information to take in. Much of it involves sciencey terms that may be unfamiliar. Please don't let that put you off! It is a lot to absorb and you may need to take some time to process it. If you are already familiar with this stuff, hopefully it was a helpful refresher. Let us take a moment to pause and to pray (if you're that way inclined . . .).

Dear God, the human body is so amazing! We really are fearfully and wonderfully made. Thank you for those people who have worked tirelessly to bring to light knowledge that enables us to understand ourselves better. Please help me to make sense of this stuff for my life and be with those whose lives are overwhelmed with trauma. Bring your healing and transformation to them. Amen.

Emotions are tunnels. You have to go all the way through the darkness to get to the light at the end. And if you just keep putting one foot in front of the other, you'll get to where you want to go. Some of us know how to go through the tunnel because we grew up in families that taught us how. Some of us know how to go through the tunnel because we learned that skill later in life. And some of us haven't had a chance to learn that skill yet. But we can always learn . . .

Emily Nagoski (2015)[41]

10 Help! I don't know how to help (You can make a difference)

Niamh approached Marion during the women's event ministry time (for the uninitiated, ministry time is a part of Christian events when Christians can ask someone to pray with them). She spoke tentatively about her husband's abusive behaviour and Marion responded, 'What you need to do is put a little love note in your husband's pocket every morning before he goes to work. That will sort things out.' Then she began to pray.

A LITTLE LOVE NOTE?! *What?!* Niamh's husband was abusing her. A little love note was *not* going to stop him abusing her. Niamh eventually left her husband, and Marion's well-meaning advice Niamh her mistrustful of churches for years. But Marion's advice seems tame compared to Julia's friend's church leaders mentioned in *Raped by a Partner: A research report*:

> Julia said, 'My best friend wouldn't help because her church told her not to. They said, when I confronted them and told them [he] was hurting me, they said to pray about it. It wasn't just the rape, it was hitting and verbal abuse and theft and drugs. It was a textbook abusive marriage. I said to them, "What if he kills me first?" They said, "At least you'll go to heaven" . . . They don't believe in rape within marriage. The people I spoke to were ministers and high people and they just didn't want to get involved and kept telling me to pray about it and if I died I'd go to heaven.'[1]

In the same report, Louise explains,

> I told him [the priest], and he actually was awful. He actually
> told me that my responsibility as a wife was to do whatever my
> husband told me to do, and so that put me in a worse place than
> I was before because I felt that it was my [fault] – because my
> husband told me all the time that it was my fault anyway – so
> that just reaffirmed the fact.[2]

Research has found that 'abused Christian women are more likely to
remain with or return to unsafe [partners], citing religious beliefs
to support avoidance of "family break-ups" despite abuse'.[3]

Women and children who are subjected to abuse by men need
supportive churches. This begins with the wider church cultures.
While most of the examples I have given have been of churches compounding abusive behaviour, many women have positive stories to tell
about how their church helped them and held the abuser to account.
Women have shared with me how their churches helped them move
house, paid for legal fees and counselling sessions, babysat children,
accessed expert advice and generally were a rock throughout horren-
dous trauma. However, this is sadly not yet the norm. We need all
churches to create a safe *context*. If a church culture implies (either
implicitly or explicitly) that men are entitled to certain things because
of their headship, if it bemoans divorce rates and the 'fatherless
generation' and advocates forgiveness without appropriate boundaries, it will collude with an abuser's narrative. While a woman is being
subjected to abuse and sits within a congregation where she is being
told that divorce is the most harmful thing in society, she will think
that she must try to make her marriage work. Teaching that forgiveness requires she be a doormat will leave her feeling compelled to
accept his behaviour. If her church never mentions abuse, or only
mentions it as a problem for *those people out there,* her church is not a
safe place for her to disclose abuse.

Churches should only bemoan divorce rates if they also mention that divorce is sometimes the only option to deal with an abusive spouse. Teaching on forgiveness must always include a caveat that forgiveness doesn't mean enabling sin. Where sex is discussed in sermons or small groups, it must always be acknowledged that some sex is damaging and that some husbands are sexually abusive. The implications for the partners of pornography consumers must be addressed whenever pornography is mentioned by churches. Churches need a culture where abuse is recognized as a significant issue. Every church leader, preacher, pastoral support worker and congregation member should assume that there will be women and children in their congregation who are being subjected to abuse. And that there are men in the congregation who are abusive. Would you change your sermon message if you were aware it could be misconstrued as telling a woman to stay with an abuser? How would you run a small group if you knew that a man in the group was using the community to further abuse his wife? Would you run a marriage preparation course differently if you knew that the man was raping his fiancée every week? Presuming that abuse is present within our congregation is a big shift in thinking, but is the only way to ensure that our communities become safe contexts for those subjected to abuse. Only then can we ensure that we do not collude with abusers.

Alongside making shifts in church culture, it is of utmost importance that we are able to effectively support someone who is being subjected to abuse. Most people would like a list of dos and don'ts for pastoral support. But lists are never exhaustive. It's taken until Chapter 10 for us to think about how we support people, because if you really accept the fundamentals within the earlier chapters your ability to support people will improve exponentially. The *overwhelming* reason people get it wrong is their misconceptions about abuse. Building understanding about abuse enables us to more ably offer support. It is a lot to get our heads around. Jesus said, 'The mouth speaks what the heart is full of.'[4] If we want our mouths to speak helpfully to those subjected to abuse, we need to get our hearts right.

We need to understand how abusers operate and how their partners are affected. Understanding the wider societal messages that collude with abusers helps us to understand our own propensity to do just that.

I'm going to trust that you've read the previous ten chapters and haven't *cheated* by flicking through to here. We've all heard that song about not building our house on the sand but instead building on rock (and the rain came down and the floods came up. WHOOSH!). This chapter will not help you to support women without reading the rest of the book. Don't build your support on sand, dear reader. Women are worth a lot more than just one chapter of your time!

Let's consider some of the reasons why people feel apprehensive about supporting those who are being subjected to abuse. I've identified nine different reasons.

1   **Lack of knowledge** By not understanding the issues well enough, we might feel out of our depth and fearful of getting it wrong. We feel inadequate, avoiding the topic so we don't alienate women subjected to abuse. Gaining knowledge can help with this. Acknowledging that we aren't knowledgeable but want to learn, we can give them permission to correct us if we're wrong.

2   **Social convention** Abuse remains taboo in 'polite company'. Abuse remains associated with the private sphere (mentioned in Chapter 3), despite costing England £16 billion every year.[5] Overcoming social conventions isn't easy. Risking being ostracized requires courage. However, be encouraged. I've been doing it for years and it's extremely liberating!

3   **Culture and community** Christians are often taught to emulate Jesus in being meek and mild, even though that's not in the Bible.[6] Christianity is mostly hierarchical, with church leaders seen as the final authority on faith and practice. How do we respect earthly authority while following Jesus' model of challenging religious leaders?[7] The writer of the biblical book of James lived

when there were no support systems for widows and orphans. He explains, 'Religion that God our Father accepts as pure and faultless is this: to look after orphans and widows in their distress and to keep oneself from being polluted by the world.'[8] In the West, widows and orphans are generally supported, yet women and children subjected to abuse are often abandoned by society. They are among the widows and orphans in distress that we must care for to have a pure and undefiled religion.

4   **Personal experience** Our experience of abuse may leave us unwilling to speak about it, with trauma limiting our capacity to help. That is OK. Setting boundaries is important and our own recovery must be prioritized; however, it may be wise to avoid taking on pastoral responsibilities until then.

5   **Awfulness factor** Abuse is awful and listening to people's stories can even lead to vicarious trauma (also known as 'compassion fatigue' or 'secondary traumatic stress').[9] People's pain can be overwhelming and we shouldn't feel guilty if we are struggling to cope; denying the cost of supporting others will not help them or us. We cannot reduce the awfulness, but we can look after ourselves in the midst of it.

6   **Myths and 'othering'** Viewing those who are subjected to abuse as 'those people over there' means we 'other' them, making them different from us. This gives us a huge blind spot, making us unsafe for someone to disclose to. It is inadvisable to respond with open-mouthed shock: 'Are you sure?' 'I don't think he would be abusive!' 'Really?! I think you're exaggerating.' The only way to overcome this is by owning our tendency to distance ourselves and choosing to begin identifying with them.

7   **Lack of resilience in managing the issue** We may have offered support in the past and found it really difficult, and this may have put us off helping. Someone who has been subjected to abuse doesn't have to be a nice person. She may grate on us, she is very likely to have complex needs and make demands on our

time. Refusing to help isn't sustainable if we want to build a safe community. Building resilience in responding is important and we can do this by increasing our people–work skills, ensuring our own needs are met and setting positive boundaries.

8   **Fear of the unknown** The unknown can fill us with dread. Gaining understanding about abuse can increase the number of unknowns. Outside our comfort zone, we are left fearful, and courage is needed. Remaining in the present with the known quantities can help, as the unknowns might not even happen.

9   **Fear of the consequences** The majority of men who kill or seriously injure their partner do so post-separation. We don't want to make things worse, and also may be fearful of the abuser hurting us or our family. However, it rarely serves the abuser's purposes to harm us, as he wants us to be his ally. Most abusers do not directly harm anyone other than their partner and children. Action should be taken cautiously and after seeking advice from specialist services, but the consequences of not getting involved are likely to be even more severe than us remaining uninvolved for fear of the consequences.

Most people will not self-identify their experiences as 'abuse'. Acknowledging their current or former partner's abuse can seem too painful or life-shattering. Many women's lives remain 'unstoried'.[10] As Riet Bons-Storm explains:

> [Women's lives] cannot be given a meaning that somehow fits in the fabric of a developing self-narrative. This happens to those experiences that are painful and shameful: they are put in a closet, the door shuts. To put those experienced events into words and to tell another person the story would mean not only letting the experiences but also the pain and shame attached to them, out of the closet. One can only do this if one is absolutely certain that the listener will both understand and acknowledge

the pain and shame and nevertheless accept the person who tells the story.[11]

Can you be that listener? Enabling someone's experiences to become storied as part of her wider self-narrative, will you 'understand and acknowledge the pain and shame and nevertheless accept the person who tells the story'? Or will you compound her unstory through disbelief, shock or rejection?

In supporting someone who has been subjected to abuse, I have a six-step system.

1 Believe.
2 Ensure safety.
3 Empower (don't rescue).
4 Support.
5 Understand your limitations.
6 Signpost well.

BELIEVE, BELIEVE, BELIEVE

Research by US criminologists Carole Anne Burris and Peter Jaffe in 1979 found that the women they studied had been assaulted an average of 35 times before first reporting their partner.[12] The charity Safelives found that on average 85 per cent of those subjected to abuse had sought help five times before getting effective help.[13] You may be the fifth person a woman seeks help from after she has been assaulted 35 times. Believing her is the first step to ensuring you don't become the sixth unhelpful person.

Disclosure is always gradual; the woman will start with the tip of the iceberg to test how we handle the 'least worst' details. Do we believe her? Do we look shocked? Are we safe? Disclosure is often accidental. Claire bumped into her church friend June after her partner Sam had locked her out. She was crying. She didn't intend June to know. How would June respond? Would she be open and believing or minimize the abuser's behaviour? By siding with the woman, we undermine the abuser's belief that no one will believe his partner. Our belief and validation weakens the Brainwasher's narrative. If the abuser is a church leader or holds a position of authority, it is even more important to believe his partner. In disclosing his abuse, she has probably overcome more barriers. You may feel uncomfortable about this, concerned about assigning blame with only one person's perspective. In Chapter 7 we established that the rate of false disclosure for abuse is lower than for other crimes. The shame and pain are often so great that women do not disclose at all. Within court, someone should be considered innocent until proven guilty, but an abuser is not going to admit his behaviour if he is confronted. In fact, by confronting him we put his partner and children at greater risk. We can support his partner and enable her to work out how she wants to proceed without condemning him to prison. The Church of England's policy on domestic abuse is to believe the person disclosing abuse,[14] and all other church safeguarding policies will presume that the person disclosing abuse is to be believed. Regardless of your personal opinions, your church's policy will require you to operate from an assumption of belief.

SAFETY

My dear friend Susan King describes women receiving support as 'smelling different'. A woman who is listened to, believed and supported is likely to feel less powerless. Her partner will smell that difference and potentially escalate the abuse to re-establish power. Just because his partner feels more powerful this does not make him less dangerous. Best practice includes helping someone make a plan to increase her safety, particularly if she is considering leaving; a model safety plan can be found in Appendix 3. The basis of a safety plan is the question, 'If I was living with a mass murderer, how would

I behave?' I would avoid him going near knives, and I would park my car facing out. Seeking to keep my communications about his behaviour secret, I might also give my children the skills needed to stay as safe as possible. No matter what I do, he might still kill me, but by putting preventative measures in place I might be able to escape alive.

If you are part of a church denomination, you may find that your church has a policy for dealing with domestic abuse. You could contact your regional safeguarding team to find out more about this. In doing so, I'd recommend researching online the name of your church organization (e.g. Methodist, Baptist, Church of England), the area you live in and the word 'safeguarding', and information should be available. If you are a part of an independent church, you may need to contact your local domestic abuse service for further help and support.

A woman might discount the risk her abusive partner poses to her as a result of his minimization tactics or her coping strategy of self-blame. It is almost impossible to function psychologically while accepting the full risk posed by an abusive partner. If a woman is telling us that she is worried her partner is going to kill or seriously harm her, we should take this extremely seriously. Extensive research has found that there are 16 risk factors that suggest an abuser is at risk of killing or seriously injuring his partner.[15] These are:

- the victim's perception of the risk the abuser poses to her;
- separation (particularly where there is continuing child contact);
- the period from pregnancy until the baby is 18 months old;
- escalation of the abuser's behaviour;
- the abuser isolating his partner;
- being part of a community with additional needs, e.g. LGBT people, those with disabilities, those from ethnic minorities, asylum seekers;
- stalking (including persistent and consistent calling, texting, sending letters and following);

- sexual assault;
- strangulation (including choking/suffocation/drowning);
- credible threats to kill;
- use of weapons (including threats of weapon use);
- controlling and/or excessively jealous behaviour;
- child abuse;
- abuse of animals/pets;
- the abuser's misuse of alcohol or drugs, and/or him having mental ill health;
- the abuser threatening or attempting suicide.

These 16 risk factors form the Domestic Abuse, Stalking and Honour Based Violence Risk Checklist (DASH), a checklist developed to measure an abuser's risk to his partner. The DASH is a series of questions that all police officers and domestic abuse services across the UK use with women to assess the abuser's risk to them. Within my work I have identified an additional three risk indicators.

- **Power differential** This occurs when the abuser's status gives him more power than his partner, including the abuser being significantly older than his partner,[16] the abuser having a powerful job or being from a wealthy or upper-class family, and/or the abuser being a community leader.
- **Speed of relationship** This is relevant when the relationship has moved extremely quickly to cohabiting, getting engaged/married, having children, etc.
- **Disregard for consequences** When an abuser seems unperturbed by the consequences of his behaviour (injunctions, criminal charges, prison), he poses an extreme risk to his partner and children.

Regardless of how many of these risk indicators are present in an abuser's behaviour and choices, he is always a risk to his partner, ex-partner and children. There is no such thing as a 'low-risk' abuser.

Understanding these indicators may enable you to more effectively support women, but please don't disregard your own gut feelings if few indicators are present.

EMPOWER (*DON'T* RESCUE)

When someone discloses abuse to us, we may go into full Jack Bauer mode (yes, this is a blatant reference to the US TV series *24*). Dedicating ourselves to fixing the woman's life, we may neglect our family and other commitments. Using all our best rhetorical skills we try and convince her to leave him. When I was pregnant with my daughter, I mentioned to my family that Craig was seeing another woman. They told me to ring him and force an ultimatum: choose me or I would kick him out. He refused to choose me. As my family helped me to pack his possessions into bags, they encouraged me, 'This is it, right?' I nodded, too tired and miserable to muster any certainty. Days later he was back in the house. I stopped telling my family about his behaviour after that. I knew I'd only let them down by taking him back. When we are supporting someone, we need to *do* the opposite, not just *say* the opposite, to the abuser.[17] If the abuser demands that she stay with him and we demand that she leave him, we are doing the same as the abuser even as we are saying the opposite. We cannot *make* someone leave an abuser. We can only seek to open her eyes to the abuse while undermining the abuser's intentions.

If we take the Biderman behaviours, we can identify how to act in the opposite way to the abuser. While the Brainwasher distorts his partner's reality, we can present her with the truth: she is valuable and important, his behaviour is not her fault, she matters. Reminding her of the hopes and dreams she had for the future before he squashed them, we can build her confidence and show her that she is competent and capable. Where the Exhauster tires her out, we can provide opportunities for sleep and rest, offering to babysit her children and supporting her as a parent. We can cook her a nutritious meal and invite her round to have a night of fun. The Threatener leaves her feeling unsafe and scared, but we can welcome her into our home and let her know she has a safe place to come to whenever she is able. The Humiliator fills her with shame and disgust; we can tell her she is precious to us. Remaining unshockable if she tells us what he has done, we can honour her and show her she is worth loving. When the Isolator seeks to alienate her from us, we can continue to visit her no matter how rude he is to us. If the only thing we do is maintain a relationship with her regardless of what he does, that might be just the lifeline she needs. Craig tried to alienate me from all my friends. A couple of them stuck around, particularly my wonderful friend Lora Dora. She would always visit. Though I learned later that she hated him, she never said anything to me. She didn't allow him to undermine our friendship and would spend time with me and my daughter no matter what was going on. She remained stable and kind throughout, never treating me as fragile – she was simply present. And I love her for that.

When the Nice One tries to convince his partner that he has changed, we can gently remind her that he's tried before and nothing is different. We can be a safe place for her when the All-Mighty smashes the house up or hurts her, without getting enraged if she returns to him days later. The Demander is constantly taking from her, but we can reduce our expectations of her, simply remaining available. An abuser shrinks her world so that she feels she has no choices; we can't make her leave, but we can show her that the world is bigger than he has made it and that she does have choices. We empower someone by enabling her to have access to all the information before making a decision. We may want to rage about how much of a (insert swear word here) he is, but that is about *us* getting what *we* need. Curiosity is a helpful tool within this. It's hugely unhelpful to be negative about her partner, but we can utilize curiosity in gently questioning his intentions.

Barbara's boyfriend Jack had accidentally wrecked her phone by leaving the lid off a bottle of water in her bag. She told her friend India about it, saying that he had also jokingly hidden her handbag in a kitchen cupboard, making her late for work. India paused for a moment, then gently asked, 'Do you know it was definitely accidental? I mean, I'm not saying that it was deliberate, but do you think it could have been? I don't want to question his intentions, but it may be worth thinking about . . .' India hasn't called Jack names. She hasn't alienated Barbara, but she has planted a seed. Our role is not to rescue but to plant seeds. We have to trust that those seeds can grow into trees of confidence, literacy about abuse and a desire for a different life. We cannot guarantee that they will, but hopefully we will be able to maintain a relationship with them.

Although our role isn't to rescue women, we do have a responsibility to any children. As mentioned in Chapter 8, witnessing abuse is a safeguarding issue and we must pass on safeguarding concerns. There is now more understanding within safeguarding about 'vulnerable adults', and it may be that the woman who is being subjected to abuse fits into this category. You could contact your local safeguarding team to find out more about this. If the woman and her children are part of our church, we can do that through our church's safeguarding systems.[18] If we know her and the children socially, we may have to report the situation to our local children's social care department or via the NSPCC helpline.[19] We can do this anonymously if necessary. If someone is in immediate danger, whether child or adult, we must dial 999. Keeping a record of everything that is disclosed may be really helpful if the woman decides to report her partner at a later date.

The work of Professor Liz Kelly, who is Director of the Child and Woman Abuse Studies Unit at London Metropolitan University, provides evidence that when a woman leaves an abusive partner she builds 'space for action'.[20] By taking steps to expand the space for action, a woman's supporters increase her capacity to recover and move on. The steps to moving on are long and arduous, with the space for action being reduced through the abuser's post-separation abuse, social care intervention, insecure (or non-existent) housing, financial instability and lack of emotional support. By helping to meet women's practical and emotional needs, we can exponentially increase their space for action.

UNCONDITIONAL SUPPORT

Very often women feel that the support offered to them is conditional even though this may not be an explicit message from those supporting them. It wasn't my family's intention, but after they helped me to pack up Craig's things I felt that their support was conditional on me doing what they wanted. Our support must be sustainable. If it takes a woman two weeks, two years or two decades to leave her abusive partner, how do we sustain a relationship with her? When there is a crisis, do we drop other commitments to support her? What about when the crisis is over? Will we still be able to sustain that level of support?

'Nobody cares about me unless there's a crisis,' Faye announced bitterly. 'When he's kicked off and things are really bad, everyone rushes to help me, but when things go back to normal, they're not interested.' Faye cannot see that people are willing to offer a greater commitment when there is a crisis because of their concern for her. She thinks they only care about being involved in a drama. Trying to maintain regular contact when things are going well is really important, even though it can feel utterly infuriating, knowing the abuser is continuing to get away with harming her.

This model of empowerment rather than rescue can be extremely difficult. We need a support network to let rip to when things get really difficult. Someone who is being subjected to abuse is often unable to meet her own needs; she's certainly not going to be able to meet our needs. We need to look after ourselves and avoid getting caught up in the cycle of abuse. One of the ways to do this is by changing our measure of success. Most people identify 'success' for a woman with an abusive partner as her leaving him. Rather than seeing success as leaving, we can begin to see the incremental differences in a woman's life. If she starts recognizing her partner's abusive behaviour, that's a success. When she saves the number for a local service in her phone, that's a success. Getting a secret pay-as-you-go phone that her partner doesn't know about, building her confidence, spending time with friends, starting counselling, getting a job, telling us more about her partner's behaviour, setting herself goals – all of these are successes! She may or may not leave him, but each tiny step towards freedom can be celebrated.

I was on a train. A couple got on and sat nearby. His body language was intimidating and she looked frightened. Speaking to her quietly, his face was contorted with hate, while she remained still, staring at the floor. A fellow passenger stood up and confronted the man. I stood up too. I asked her if she was OK. She started crying: 'I just want to get away from him; he won't let me go.' The man grabbed hold of her. I asked her if she'd like to come and stand with me. She began nodding as he whispered something in her ear. I pulled my phone out of my pocket and called the police. The man started shouting abuse at me, calling me a Ginger C★nt. (I don't have ginger hair. Not that there's anything wrong with ginger hair . . .) I pulled the lever to stop the train at the next station. The police were waiting for us. The train continued as the couple, the other passenger and I spoke to the police. At this point the woman said she was fine and didn't need help. The police said there was nothing they could do. They waited with me until another train arrived, just in case the man became abusive again. I don't know what happened next. But I do know that the woman on the train was shown that her partner's behaviour wasn't OK. Two people had stood up and told her she was worth fighting for. It might be days, months or years before she leaves, but we planted a seed. And that is enough.

UNDERSTANDING LIMITATIONS

As good as this book is (even if I do say so myself!) it is not going to make you an expert in domestic abuse issues. It is important for you to understand your limitations. People presume that because they know abuse is wrong, they will automatically make good choices in supporting those being subjected to abuse. That is incorrect. If you have not had prolonged specialist training or experience in understanding abuse, you will need to seek the advice and support of those who have.

After reading this book, if you recognize the abusive behaviours described in men you know, or if you see the impact of an abuser on the lives of women you know, it is important to seek professional advice. This book will take you some of the way, but if you feel out of your depth that is a good thing! It will cause you to be cautious. What the world does not need is more people making hasty uninformed decisions. Many of the services listed in Appendix 1 will offer training and advice.

If you are a church leader or counsellor, or in another pastoral care role, those you support will often presume you are the expert on their lives. As a faith leader, you will be seen as someone who knows God. People may take your words authoritatively. If you are asked to pray with someone who has an abusive partner, be careful! If you pray for her partner to change, this may give her a false sense of hope: 'A holy person has prayed for my husband. He'll definitely change now!' Focus instead on asking God to give her strength, freedom and hope (and there's no reason why you can't pray for her husband privately).

It is extremely important that we own the power we hold as leaders. One of the best things we can do is to explain that we are not qualified to fully support her, but we know a place that may be able to. Which brings us to our final step . . .

SIGNPOST WELL

It is important to become familiar with the wider landscape around domestic abuse issues. There is no national domestic abuse service. In the 1970s, groups of women around the country began establishing safe houses and other services for women and children who had been subjected to abuse, with many becoming registered charities. By 1974, the Women's Aid Federation of England had been set up to coordinate these local charities. This remains the structure for Women's Aid. The national federation supports local domestic abuse services, lobbies the government and raises awareness about abuse. Separate federations were set up in Scotland, Northern Ireland and Wales.[21] The separate charities within each federation are autonomous, supporting women and children in their local area (many also offer support for men).

These charities receive little statutory funding. When women and children flee to a refuge they either need to pay rent or, if unemployed, are entitled to housing benefit to cover some of the costs of living in a refuge. If a woman's partner has controlled the finances she may not have access to a bank account and will have no money until this is resolved. The government provides no money for children living in refuges, even though they are 50 per cent of the refuge population. Refuges rarely have funding to provide for women and children's practical needs. When families arrive with no food, sanitary protection, clothing or toys, they are reliant on donations, fundraising and food banks. Their wider provision of counselling, advocacy, legal advice, support with attending court and psychological support for children is funded through grants, trusts and donations. Some services can be accessed while a woman is still with her abusive partner, whereas other resources are only available once she has left. In recent years, the national domestic abuse strategy has recognized that where a woman's partner or ex is identified as high risk (according to the risk indicators mentioned on pages 197–8), the woman will benefit from additional support. She will usually be assigned an Independent Domestic Violence Advisor (IDVA), a trained professional who can keep her updated about her case, advocates for her in meetings and offers her more intensive support. Independent Sexual Violence Advisors (ISVAs) support women and men who have been subjected to sexual violence. Usually based at either domestic abuse services or police stations, ISVAs and IDVAs are often managing large caseloads, limiting how effective they can be. One of the many flaws of a 'risk-based model' is that some women who are ready to leave find that their abusive partner is not deemed sufficiently high risk, while a woman who is not yet ready to leave and is entirely resistant to any intervention may have a partner who is designated high risk. The woman who is ready to leave will not be entitled to IDVA support. If an abuser is deemed high risk, his partner (or ex-partner) will have her case referred to a Multi-agency Risk Assessment Conference (MARAC). This monthly meeting involves all professionals in domestic abuse cases: police, probation, social care, education, health, etc. The woman herself is not allowed to attend MARAC, but her IDVA will represent her at the meeting (this is obviously problematic in itself, as she should be able to be in meetings that are *about* her). Her case will be discussed and any actions that can be taken to increase her and her children's safety will be planned and put into action.

If a woman reports her partner to the police, or if he is reported through a third-party witness (a neighbour, church leader or family member), the police will investigate the report. An investigation is unlikely to take place unless someone actually reports the crime to the police. (A few years ago, when a photograph of Charles Saatchi strangling Nigella Lawson in a London restaurant was plastered across British newspapers, I contacted the police local to the restaurant to report the assault. Although the newspapers had presented evidence of the assault, unless someone reported it to the police it would be unlikely to be investigated.) If the police investigation reveals that a crime has taken place, they may arrest the abuser. On questioning him, they may decide to offer a caution, warning or penalty notice – although these shouldn't be used with domestic abusers, they often are – otherwise the police may send the case to the Crown Prosecution Service (CPS). The CPS will evaluate the evidence and decide whether there is enough evidence to secure a conviction. If there isn't enough evidence, there will be no further action (NFA). If there is, the abuser may be charged and given bail (or remanded in custody, which means placing him in prison) until the case goes to court. There may be various conditions to the bail, usually including not contacting his partner. If he doesn't adhere to these conditions, he can then be remanded in custody. The case ought to proceed to trial in a criminal court and, depending on the severity of the crime, it will either be tried in a magistrates' court (under a district judge or a panel of three lay judges) or in a Crown Court, with a jury and a judge. The prosecution legal team must prove beyond reasonable doubt that the abuser committed the crime.

Civil and family courts are the other courts relevant to domestic abusers. Both civil and family courts make judgements based on probability rather than the absence of reasonable doubt. Within the civil court a woman can apply for a civil remedy to prevent her partner from contacting her, harassing her, living with her or removing the children from her (or from the country). These orders only become a criminal matter if the abuser breaks the order. He can then be arrested, fined or taken back to court.[22] Family courts deal with matters pertaining to children, including custody proceedings, when separated parents seek a ruling if they are unable to agree on their children's residence or visitation arrangements. Family courts also deal with cases where social care staff have removed a child into a fostering placement. In the UK, means-tested legal support is provided to defendants (the abuser) in criminal cases. In the majority of civil and family court cases, no free legal support is available unless a child has been taken into foster care, in which case the parents are entitled to free legal representation. This forces many women to represent themselves in court, and requires a woman to confront her abusive ex-partner.

If your brain is feeling fried right now, imagine how difficult it is for someone to navigate these different services and systems while also dealing with an abuser! It is extraordinarily difficult. Gaining literacy about the different services will help you to signpost more effectively. It is imperative that you find out the details of your local domestic abuse service. After reading this chapter, Google 'domestic abuse service' and include the town or county you live in. Navigate to the domestic abuse service website and familiarize yourself with their work. Make time to call them and ask them the following three questions.

- What will happen if someone discloses abuse to me and I refer her to your service?
- Can you send me posters and leaflets advertising your service that I can put up in my church or workplace?
- What can I and/or my church do to support your work?

If Ursula tells you that her husband is abusing her and you give her the number for the local domestic abuse service, she may phone them. However, if you are able to tell Ursula the names of some of the workers at the service and what sort of resources they have available, that will give her much more confidence in contacting them. They may have waiting lists or only answer the phones at certain times of the day. It might take all of Ursula's strength to phone them, and if nobody answers or if their waiting list is two months long she may never bother calling them again. If you can temper her expectations by telling her about their limitations, she is much more likely to phone them when they're available and not be put off by the long waiting list. You can make the promotional literature available in your church. Placing posters in women's toilet cubicles may be helpful, as is putting materials on your noticeboard. Making people aware that these services exist may lead someone to take action, regardless of whether you ever know about it.

Domestic abuse services are desperate for financial support. The British public donates more money to a Devon-based donkey sanctuary than to all the main domestic abuse services in the UK put together.[23] When I told my Colombian friend Carolina this, she exclaimed, 'Money for sick donkeys?! In my country, we barbecue them!' I'm all for supporting sick donkeys, but there is something wrong with our nation's priorities when supporting donkeys is more important than supporting the women and children that men are abusing. Seeking to support local services will make a huge difference to women and children, and builds links with those services for you in supporting women and children who need them.

That brings us almost to the end of this chapter. I know what you're thinking, dear reader: you want to know how we should respond to abusers. This entire chapter has focused on how we help women and children who have been subjected to abuse, while offering very little idea as to what to do with the abusers. This has been deliberate. Work with abusers requires extensive training and skill, and sits outside the scope of this book. Hopefully reading this far has given you significant insight into the nature of abusers and how they will seek to turn us into their allies.

A woman approached me at a conference. She was a counsellor and told me that an ex-client had admitted to her that he was abusing his wife. Apparently he was very angry with his mother, and she had told him in a counselling session that he needed to let his anger out. He left the session. Days later he had killed his wife. Abusers are dangerous, and responding to them requires skill and training. Within the UK, the Respect phoneline[24] provides advice for both perpetrators and those engaging with them. You can call Respect or access their website[25] for further information. Other books you can read are:

• Lundy Bancroft, *Why Does He Do That? Inside the minds of angry and controlling men* (New York: Berkley Publishing Group, 2002)

- Evan Stark, *Coercive Control* (Oxford: Oxford University Press, 2007)
- Kate Iwi and Chris Newman, *Engaging with Perpetrators of Domestic Violence: Practical techniques for early intervention* (London: Jessica Kingsley, 2015).

This chapter is full of information, but hopefully it feels manageable. Please make sure you do contact your local domestic abuse service – you could even give yourself a slice of cake or at least a pat on the back once you've done it. As with every chapter, let us pause for a moment. Have a think about what has been most useful to you. What has been difficult to process? Has anything felt unacceptable to you? Why is that? How can you move to a new understanding? Take some time to pray if that's something that is helpful to you.

Dear God, there is so much at stake in being a good friend to someone who is being subjected to abuse. It can feel totally overwhelming. I don't want to get it wrong. I don't want to collude with abusers. Please give me wisdom, and help me to overcome the myths and prejudices that get in the way of me responding appropriately. Thank you that you do call us to care for the widows and orphans. Please open my heart to those who need my care and love. Amen.

You started a fire in her soul
But tomorrow came
And you left her shivering in the cold
So she gathered what little embers left of her
As she carefully whispered love to her dying self
Now she's a burning forest, as bright as the sun
And all you could do is look at her with awe
For you'd never imagined that a girl
Looking so fragile and naive
Would one day become a fire
That you could never ever put out.

Cynthia Go (2017)[26]

11 There is no chrysalis season (Making a difference for the next generation)

Dear reader, there will be some references to graphic sexual content in this chapter, so please do take care when reading.

Very few of us have a life devoid of young people. Whether as parents, aunties, uncles, congregation members, teachers, youth workers, neighbours, friends of parents or church leaders, we are all likely to have relationships with young people. This chapter is important for us all. If you only come into contact with smaller children you may think this chapter can wait until they're teenagers. I hate to break it to you, but those children are going to grow up!

Babies and small children are often seen as entirely separate entities from adults, tiny cute humans with entirely separate lives from the full-grown people. They aren't. Adults' primary role in children's lives is to help them grow into functioning adults. All children are on a trajectory to adulthood (via their teenage years). We cannot avoid difficult topics and hope these tiny humans will simply wrap themselves in a chrysalis, one day emerging as a grown-up with whom we can then have adult conversations. Everything we do with children contributes to the adults they will become; this is a daunting and possibly even horrifying truth. There is no chrysalis season. Thank the Lord that humans are vaguely autonomous and equipped with neural plasticity, so that there is always hope for those whose childhoods were filled with grown-ups who did not help them become functioning adults.

Dear reader, do not be tempted to skip this chapter. Yes, it is difficult to accept that those adorable tiny humans we cuddle and sing nursery rhymes with will potentially be subjected to abuse by a partner or may go on to subject a partner to abuse, but we cannot bury our heads in the sand. In the UK 72 per cent of girls will have been abused by a boyfriend by the time they are 16.[1] We recognize the need to teach children road safety; it does not defile their innocence to tell them that cars can be dangerous. We don't avoid telling children that fire will burn them. Part of an adult's job is equipping children to make good choices and protect them from harm. Helping them to recognize abusive behaviours and make good choices in relationships is part of that job.

I wrote the DAY Programme almost a decade ago. It is a programme providing awareness about domestic abuse and sexual exploitation for young people. Over 300 practitioners across the UK, the Isle of Man and South Africa have trained to deliver the material to young people. I developed the programme after working with adult women who had been subjected to abuse by a partner, concluding that we all really needed the information when we were 12. Researching existing resources, I developed a replicable programme that required practitioners to attend a three-day training course. Four of the eight principles explored in the programme are particularly relevant to us.

- 'Power and control are the motivation for domestic abuse.'
- 'Ownership and entitlement are the roots of domestic abuse.'
- 'Challenging societal messages is integral to understanding domestic abuse.'
- 'Encouraging critical thinking' in young people will enable them to make life choices.

Understanding the nature of abuse to be about power and control and ownership and entitlement enables us to educate children to be non-abusive and to recognize abusive behaviour. Encouraging critical thinking in children and challenging societal messages with them opens up their capacity to be more effective human beings and to make informed choices.

Doing this doesn't make life particularly easy. Teaching children to think for themselves and not blindly accept the status quo leads to them asking difficult questions and challenging our inconsistencies. If we encourage them to understand power and its misuse, we may be shocked when they point out ways that we are misusing our power. Building children into functional adults is the surest way to become brutally aware of our own dysfunction!

What does this look like in practice? It starts with encouraging children to know they own their bodies and letting them choose their own clothing, and goes on to make it clear that we should never force them to hug or kiss adults or other children. Building understanding that their body and life belongs to them helps. (Some Christians may object to this, in that our bodies belong to God.[2] However, that is the case for those who have made a commitment to follow Jesus, and they can only give their bodies to God if they know their bodies belong to them in the first place.) When they are little and need help dressing, you can play the 'Who does this belong to?' game. As you put their socks on, ask, 'Who does this foot belong to?' You can make suggestions: 'Mummy?' 'Daddy?' 'Grandma?' Each time the answer is no. But when you say the child's name, the answer is *yes*! This may result in weird clothing combinations and awkward conversations with family members who demand a kiss goodbye, but other forms of affection can be offered – waving, smiling or high fives. We might have to relinquish our desire for children who look like catalogue models, but they are human beings and not mannequins.

Giving children the skills to recognize power misuse isn't as complicated as it may sound. If we define bullying as 'trying to make someone do something they don't want to', this can include everything from shouting or hurting to saying, 'I'm not going to be your friend unless . . .' and diminishing someone. We often excuse power misuse as kids being kids, but most adults vividly remember hurtful childhood comments; they didn't hurt any less because we were small and they can affect our developing core identity.

Assuming a lack of intention is usually our main motivation in not taking children's power misuse seriously. When little Jonny hits Millie, we assume that he didn't mean to do it. Asking children why they have been naughty, we suggest that if they give us a good reason, they won't get into trouble. But the impact on Millie doesn't change based on Jonny's intention.

Dr Thomas W. Phelan has over 35 years' experience as a clinical psychologist working with children, young people and families. He explains,

> [children] are not born reasonable and unselfish. They are born unreasonable and selfish. They want what they want when they want it, and they can have a major fit if they don't get it. Consequently, it is the parent's job – and the teacher's job – to help kids gradually learn frustration tolerance.[3]

He also explains the 'Little Adult Assumption':

> The Little Adult Assumption is the belief that kids have hearts of gold and are basically reasonable and unselfish. In other words, they're just smaller versions of grownups. And because they are little adults, the idea goes, whenever the youngsters are misbehaving, the problem must be that they don't have enough information in their heads to be able to do the right thing.[4]

When we minimize power misuse and unkind behaviour in children, we do so because we want to believe that children are fundamentally good and kind. They are not. Little Jonny isn't a mass murderer in the making, but as a human child he needs help becoming reasonable and unselfish. Minimizing or tolerating his behaviour will not help him. The dinner lady responds to little Jonny by telling Millie, 'It's just because he likes you.' We could respond to this by writing a letter to the school stating that such sentiments are damaging. When my children's primary school established a 'Battle of the Sexes' to encourage boys to read by competing with the girls for extra playtime, the head teacher received a three-page letter from me. The scheme immediately ended.

My son was in hospital and the play therapist skipped past all the pink bravery certificates, telling him he wouldn't want a girly one. He was five and immediately said he did want a pink one. We can make our children aware of sexism and racism. Watching films with the children we will critique with them how many women and people of colour are in lead roles and discuss whether the characters are stereotyping girls and women. Listening to music lyrics we will consider the messages they give about relationships and gender.

Having positive role models is important; children struggle to be what they can't see. They need to see men and women in non-stereotypical roles and people of colour and those with disabilities achieving success – in other words, role models. Self-confidence alone is not enough. After being taught that they can succeed and see others like them succeeding, they may be shocked to discover all the barriers they face. If they are female, black or disabled they will have to overcome many additional barriers, and they need to be prepared for this and encouraged to build resilience. Otherwise they may give up when things inevitably get unjustly hard.

Intentionally bringing up children to be aware of sexism and racism, able to recognize and reject gender stereotyping and identify power misuse, will cause them to experience the world differently from many of their peers. When my son wanted to attend church with his hair in pigtails, we warned him that other children might be unkind. We regularly explain to the children that not everyone believes that boys and girls can wear whatever they want. Learning that people have different beliefs and ideas helps them to make sense of the world. Recognizing that there are market forces seeking to push them to like certain products helps them to understand the ways their choices are influenced by those who are uninterested in their flourishing. Many adults don't understand the lengths to which companies will go to target advertising. Sites like Facebook are free to use because they sell our data to companies who want us to buy their products.[5] If we're not paying for a product, we usually *are* the product.

Road safety training won't guarantee that our children will never be in a road traffic accident, and there are no guarantees that our children will be protected from abusers (or from becoming abusers). Yet, just as we continue to teach children road safety, we can reduce the likelihood of abuse and give them the potential to become kinder people who seek to create a more just society by bringing them up to understand power, control, ownership, entitlement, critical thinking and societal messages.

Some people will be reading this and thinking, 'What nonsense! Boys should be brought up to be boys and girls brought up to be girls. Children shouldn't be exposed to information about abuse. End of.' If that is you, I applaud you for making it this far through the book! Your tenacity and resolve are admirable given our differing views. Thank you for sticking with me! In response to your thoughts, I have a couple of suggestions. First, if boys and girls are that distinct, giving them options will not matter; they will still maintain their distinct maleness or femaleness. Why should we limit their choices unless we are fearful they won't adhere to gender stereotypes? Second, honesty is the best policy with children. Talking about children and grief, Dr Phyllis Silverman writes, 'Our impulse is to protect children, to shield them from the pain and perhaps from the facts of death. However, perhaps the best way to protect children is to involve them, in ways that respect their age.'[6] And guidance for adoptive parents explains:

> Even children as young as 2 or 3 can be given simple explana-
> tions which are truthful and which will help to prepare the child

should reunification not be possible. There may be a tendency, arising from the best of intentions, to be over-protective and to feel that very young children in particular should not be exposed to the harsh reality of their birth family's situation . . . This marks the beginning of the first phase of life story work, which helps the child to understand the reasons why they are unable to return home and to express their feelings about this.[7]

The vast majority of children will not be brought up in the ways described above. The proportion of girls abused by a boyfriend remains incredibly high. What are the specific issues facing teenagers in relation to abuse? Are teenage abusers different from adult abusers? What do we need to know about abuse within teen relationships?

Young people may be adult-sized but they are not adults. When delivering DAY Programme training I include a session entitled 'Youth: an alien race'. Young people operate not only in a different cultural and social framework (complete with their own language) but are also physically different from adults. Their body is altering, with boobs and beards changing the way the world sees them. Girls begin being sexually harassed by adult men; black boys become perceived as a threat, with security guards often following them in shops. Young people's hormones overtake them, with sexual decisions driven by attraction alone: 'Is he hot? Then I should go out with him.' Their capacity to assess whether a potential partner is non-abusive is overshadowed by their hormones.

Young people begin seeking approval more from peers than parents. In intimate relationships, they seek advice from barely more experienced friends rather than speaking to their parents or other adults. If their boyfriend or girlfriend uses the Biderman tactics, their friends rarely have the skills to support them, and having a girlfriend or boyfriend will often increase their status, leaving them reluctant to end the relationship. Years after leaving Craig I was speaking with one of my school friends. 'The thing is,' she said thoughtfully, 'if I'd known then what I know now about relationships, I would have known he was dangerous.' We need to equip young people to be good friends, able to recognize and respond to abusive behaviour.

Young people struggle to understand subtext. While running groups with young people I have found that they will generally think it is nice for my husband to say, 'You look good, but you'd look better if you went on a diet.' (Don't worry, this is a hypothetical statement! Baggy wouldn't say such a thing!) They miss the subtext: he is telling me I am fat. Recognizing subtext comes with maturity, but many of the Biderman behaviours, particularly the Brainwasher and the Isolator, operate within the subtext. An adult can hear intonation and the underlying message; a young person may miss this, accepting at face value the abuser's statements. This remains the case into adulthood for many on the autistic spectrum. The human brain isn't fully developed until around 25 years old.[8] Author of *The Teenage Brain* Professor Frances E. Jensen explains,

> Parts of the brain connect to each other through synapses, which are insulated, just like electric wires. That insulation is a fatty substance called myelin, which is created over time. The process takes years, and it starts at the back of the brain and slowly moves forward. The last bits of the brain to connect are the frontal and prefrontal cortices, where insight, empathy and risk taking are controlled. This means that very smart adolescents will do very stupid things in a very impulsive way.[9]

Young people's brains have 'not yet matured to the point where risks can be adequately assessed and control over risk taking can be sufficiently exerted to avoid unhealthy outcomes'.[10] When a young person starts a relationship, the capacity to recognize the potential danger the new boyfriend (or girlfriend) poses will be significantly lower than an adult's.

Young people are utterly self-conscious. Psychologist and educator Dr David Elkind coined the phrase 'imaginary audience' in 1967 to describe the experience of young people (and some adults) that they are the main focus of other people's attention. When a young person's boyfriend (or girlfriend) tells her that everybody hates her, her imaginary audience leaves her assuming that absolutely *everybody* does hate her. Adults can generally differentiate between hyperbole and truth; young people rarely can. Young people are also developing their independence and sexual identity. A lack of visible gay or lesbian relationships may leave LGBT young people assuming a boyfriend or girlfriend's abusive behaviour is simply the way queer relationships work.

Layered on to adolescent development is youth culture. Previous generations had subcultures: mods, rockers, goths, chavs, skaters, soulboys, grebos, metalheads and emos. Youth culture is much less delineated now, mainly thanks to digital culture and consumerism.[11] Clothing, music and accessories remain relevant, but free online music sites and low-cost clothing mean young people's tastes morph and change quickly. The use of Instagram, Facebook and Snapchat leaves girls in particular vulnerable to obsessive selfie-ing, driven to increase the 'likes' on their photos. Increasing numbers of boys and young men are being diagnosed with 'bigorexia'; body dysmorphia which leaves them feeling small despite being big and muscular.[12] Anonymity in online interactions lulls young people into sending naked images of themselves to others (in the UK, if a young person is under 18, owning naked images of him- or herself or of others who are under 18 is illegal and could lead to a conviction of sexual offences). Through technology young people can have intimate relationships without speaking offline, declaring their undying love for one another without needing to converse face to face.

It is a parental imperative to be intentional about our children's technology usage, so much so that I think intentional technology usage should be covered in prenatal classes. As babies become toddlers it is so tempting to give them our smart phone or tablet. In the café when we want to chat with a friend or if we're out for dinner, a YouTube video or children's game keeps our toddler quiet, but is done without intention. Both my children were given smart phones at 11 years old, on starting secondary school. We explained that the phone belonged to us and that we were letting them use it with conditions. We avoided giving them a phone as a gift, as this would result in them viewing the phone as belonging to them. The conditions included:

- limiting usage to public areas of the house (this rule applies to their visiting friends' devices too; their friends found this weird at first, but our kids have a better time with their friends);
- providing us with their password;
- never deleting messages;
- asking permission before downloading apps;
- never communicating with strangers;
- communicating online with the same boundaries as face-to-face interactions;
- never accessing porn.

Parents are usually clear about stranger danger with their children. Many children are not allowed to play outside because of fears of kidnapping, yet are given an unlimited portal to the most despicable aspects of humanity. Our children will never be allowed Facebook, while Instagram and other apps are removed from their phones if we find them using them inappropriately. We keep a cheap non-smart phone available in case they break the rules and are banned from using their smart phone. Many parents only talk with their children about technology when they, as parents, need help with operating it. It is so important that parents gain literacy about digital culture so they can effectively support their children.

Most young people have watched pornography. The NSPCC has found that 65 per cent of 15- to 16-year-olds have seen online pornography, with 44 per cent of boys stating that they wanted to emulate scenes.[13] These young people are learning how to have sex by watching multiple men penetrate women, ejaculating on women's faces. Their expectations (those of both girls and boys) are shaped by pornography. Boys think they should ejaculate on their girlfriend's face, girls think they should enjoy it. Leading adolescent gynaecologist Dr Naomi Crouch has expressed concerns at the rising number of girls, some as young as nine, who want cosmetic labia surgery to modify the shape of their genitals.[14]

Research has found that 13 per cent of girls have post-traumatic stress disorder,[15] while 45 per cent of young women and 36 per cent of young men are worried about their mental health.[16] Pervasive technology use, increasing levels of poverty and the prevalence of abusive behaviour in young people's relationships are all contributing factors.

Another aspect of youth culture that parents and other adults struggle to understand is diversifying gender identities. Many young people are highly literate about trans people, queer culture and non-binary and gender-fluid identities. There is such a huge generational chasm between the under-30s and those over 40 that I have developed a training day to enable people to understand more. There is not enough space to cover that here, but suffice to say it is another huge element of youth culture that most parents and other adults are ill equipped to deal with.

NSPCC research with vulnerable young people found that over half 'stated that their social worker was interested only in issues about their family, and unconcerned about wider aspects of their lives'.[17] Prioritizing the historical abuse of young women and ignoring their current relationship with an abuser is not only an issue for social workers, it is reflective of wider society. As adults, we rarely take young people's relationships seriously, yet over half of all sex offences are perpetrated against women under 25 years old.[18] The implications of this were particularly stark for dozens of girls in Rochdale in the late 2000s. Professionals including police officers and social workers viewed the systematic rape, drugging and exploitation of girls by gangs of men as girls making lifestyle choices.

Young people are inherently vulnerable. Their lack of experience and their developing bodies, brains and identities leave them less equipped to identify abusive behaviour or assert their needs and rights. Many parents, carers, teachers and other professionals assume young people's own intimate relationships are immature and have little impact on their lives. There can be an assumption that boys and young men are not abusive, while girls (and boys) with older boyfriends are presumed to be making consensual choices, particularly if they appear to have finished puberty. The power differential between an older male and a young person is rarely recognized.

There are few differences between adult abusers' usage of the Biderman tactics and that perpetrated by or towards a young person. Parents may wish for a list of warning signs to identify their daughter as a likely victim of abuse or their son as a potential perpetrator, but there simply isn't an exhaustive list. Building awareness about abuse, as you are doing in reading this book, will give you some of the knowledge needed. The first step is to acknowledge that your daughter could be subjected to abuse or that your son could be abusive. If we resolutely refuse to accept this possibility we will never notice that abusive behaviour could be taking place.

When I first met Craig, my parents were pleased that he was working and seemed polite. When I began to resist their rules and principles, they presumed it was a rebellious teen stage. Craig deliberately pushed me to miss my curfew and at 17, when my parents had a night away requiring me to be responsible for my 15-year-old brother, Craig convinced me to sneak out and stay overnight with him. If teenage rebellion coincides with a new relationship, it is worth considering that your teenager may not have as much control as you might assume.

The ideas provided in Chapter 10 can be utilized with a teenager who is being subjected to abuse. Seeking to keep communication open and remaining present with your teenager can make a huge difference. Showing her the Biderman behaviours and seeing whether she is able to identify them in her partner may be a positive strategy.

If you already have rules around technology use, this may prevent her partner controlling her via her phone and you may be able to keep an eye on her communications. It can be infuriating and may involve accepting behaviour that would be otherwise challenged but, just as if she had a serious illness, allowances can be made to prioritize the more pressing issues. Avoid giving ultimatums and be aware that her partner will seek to undermine her relationship with you. It is a brutal and painful situation. Ensure that you have emotional support and safe places to process your frustration, anger and grief. As hard as it can be, please be encouraged that things can change and there is hope. I am proof of that!

If you have a teenager who seems to be behaving in a controlling or abusive manner towards his partner (or you), it is important to acknowledge this and challenge him. It is painful to accept that our child is not who we want him to be, but our love for him is not dependent on him making good choices. Providing consequences for him and reporting his behaviour to the police are both important. It may seem an extreme step, but without intervention and consequences why would he change his behaviour? You can seek further advice from the Respect phoneline.[19]

Throughout previous chapters we've considered the issues with Christian teaching about sex and relationships. It is really important that your children have a more holistic understanding of sex than just 'Don't do it'. As children grow, our attitudes to sex and bodies will influence how they experience their bodies. Expressing disgust at their genitals will not help them, but telling them their genitals are private and belong to them will help. God made the whole of them, including their genitals, and they need to know that. Using the correct terminology for their genitals is important. If someone sexually abuses them and they try to tell an adult using a nickname for their genitals, it might be missed. 'My uncle touched my vagina' will definitely cause a nursery teacher to take action, whereas 'My uncle touched my minnie/fluff/squidgy/mary/flower/stuff/hoohoo/

coocoo/nunni' may not (these are all actual names adults use to describe girls' genitals). If your teenagers are part of a Christian youth group, get a sense from their youth leader of what teaching they will receive about sex and relationships. As parents, we are the primary disciplers of our children and we must not abdicate responsibility for teaching them about this subject. Yes, it can be awkward, but creating an open culture, particularly with younger children, will make it easier. Lindsey and Justin Holcomb have written the Christian children's book *God Made All of Me* to help parents protect their children from sexually abusive people. It includes nine principles.

1   Explain to your child that God made his or her body.
2   Teach proper names of private body parts.
3   Invite your child's communications.
4   Talk about touches.
5   Don't ask your child to maintain your emotions (so children don't feel responsible for keeping you happy).
6   Throw out the word 'secret'.
7   Clarify rules for playing 'doctor'.
8   Identify whom to trust.
9   Report suspected abuse immediately.[20]

I have created a short video and resource pack to help parents talk with their pre-adolescent children about pornography.[21] By having proactive conversations with our children about sex, relationships, pornography and abusive and controlling behaviour, we enable them to have a language to talk with us about these difficult subjects. We cannot guarantee that children will remain abuse-free, but we can do everything within our power to increase the possibility.

It is horrid to entertain the idea that our children may be subjected to or may perpetrate abuse. My children are 16 and 13. There are moments when I feel utterly incapacitated by my inability to protect them from harm. After these moments pass I am even more motivated to make the world a better place for them. When I first took my daughter to buy a razor to shave her armpits, she rolled her eyes at my diatribe about the lies patriarchy tells women about hairlessness. When my son told me that girls always have long hair, he did not really welcome my speech about gender stereotypes. When his bad behaviour was explained away as 'boys will be boys', I responded by stating that my son's ownership of a penis does not give him a free pass. In parenting, work, friendships, marriage and faith, I am driven to challenge sexism and misogyny and to make patriarchal oppression visible to others.

For the non-Christians among you, when praying Christians may hear God giving them a message for another person this is referred to as a 'word', but is usually at least a sentence and maybe even a paragraph. In a prayer meeting my friend Peter Grant shared with me a word God had given him that 'God sets me on fire and people come to watch me burn'. Wrongly attributed to John Wesley,[22] this resonated with me so deeply. God has set me on fire. Within me the Holy Spirit burns to see women and girls freed from patriarchal oppression and boys and men liberated from patriarchal expectations.

Years before, I hadn't felt that God was even with me. On one occasion, I really had wanted to die. Craig had convinced me the world would be better off if I was dead. I locked myself in the bathroom and began taking tablets. Craig banged on the door until I came out. He was on the phone to someone he had been having sex with and saw the tablets. 'Take another one,' he goaded. I did. He laughed down the phone, telling her I was taking an overdose. I took another tablet. And another. And another. It is estimated that around three women a week die by suicide as a result of domestic violence.[23]

I didn't die that night. And months later I found myself in a hospital choosing to be obedient to God no matter what. Jesus saved my life. I would be dead without him. Yet it was feminism that made sense of my life. Feminism has had a bad rap within Christian culture. One female pastor told me of casting the spirit of feminism out of women. Feminism is usually associated with abortion, destroying 'family values' and man-hating, but feminism is when women realize there is something wrong with the way they are being treated. Throughout history and on every continent, women (many of them Christians) have begun to name the injustice they face. Feminism is the liberation of women through the abolishing of patriarchy. Just as Christianity is as varied as the number of people who love Jesus, so feminism has countless forms and ideologies. If the f-word has put you off what I have to say, that is unfortunate. God is moving and feminism is part of the truth he is outworking in the world. Hallelujah!

Professor Robert Jensen, an anti-pornography academic, writes:

> We live in a time of sexual crisis. That makes life difficult, but it also creates a space for invention and creativity. The possibility of a different way of understanding the world and myself is what drew me to feminism. I was drawn to the possibility of escaping the masculinity trap set for me, and the chance to become something more than a man, more than just a john. I was drawn by the possibilities of becoming a human being.[24]

Chimamanda Ngozi Adichie, author of the book *We Should All Be Feminists*, says:

> Some people ask: 'Why the word feminist? Why not just say you are a believer in human rights, or something like that?' Because that would be dishonest. Feminism is, of course, part of human rights in general – but to choose to use the vague expression human rights is to deny the specific and particular problem of gender. It would be a way of pretending that it was not women who have, for centuries, been excluded. It would be a way of denying that the problem of gender targets women.[25]

We come to the end of this chapter. Hopefully it has given you food for thought, which admittedly isn't as tasty as cake. There may be bits that offend you and bits that disturb you. In 1997, gang violence prevention advocate Dr Cesar A. Cruz wrote a poem entitled 'To Comfort the Disturbed and Disturb the Comfortable'.[26] My writing may disturb, but consider whether that is because you are comfortable and unwilling to recognize the truth. It may also be that I am wrong! Please take time to reflect on your feelings and consider the potential for truth. If praying is helpful, here's one I made earlier (I'm still awaiting the *Blue Peter* badge for it).

Dear God, I don't want to live in a world where we need to prepare children to understand abuse. I don't want girls and boys to be damaged by technology, media or pornography. Please show me how to be part of the solution. Guide me in your ways and show me your truth as I reflect on the messages within this chapter. Amen.

As long as the people don't fear the truth, there is hope. For once they fear it, the one who tells it doesn't stand a chance. And today, truth is still beautiful . . . but so frightening.

Alice Walker (2011)[27]

12 What does freedom look like? (Things can get better)

Now the Lord is the Spirit, and where the Spirit of the Lord is, there is freedom.[1]

Leaving an abusive partner rarely feels like freedom. He will often begin to stalk or harass his partner, threatening her or those she cares about, demanding she take him back. Fighting against a traumatic attachment that seeks to drag her back to him and her stress hormones being out of balance, she feels depressed and anxious. Her single status leaves her ignored by their couple friends (many single women tell stories of being rejected by couples, seen as an 'infidelity threat' by wives), while the children are upset about losing their dad and probably blame their mum for leaving. It might be the first time they feel safe enough to be naughty, and so she is left with out-of-control children. She might be utterly petrified about what her partner is going to do; at least while she was with him she knew where he was most of the time. Her single-parent status leaves her feeling ashamed; she's become one of *those* women that papers like the *Daily Mail* castigate. Financially she has no security and she might be living in a refuge or other temporary accommodation. The house she loved and worked hard to furnish is put up for sale, and her ex-partner tells her that he burned all the photos filled with precious memories. She is unable to continue working, as the refuge is far from her workplace and anyway she couldn't afford to continue paying childcare. The children have had to move out of school and they're waiting for another school place to become available. They spend weeks living all together in one small room, with no money. At church, people avoid making eye-contact, she is unable to even think about the abuse, and she certainly doesn't want to tell them about it. He's been at church every week crying. He's convinced them all that she's totally unreasonable. Supposedly close friends tell her how upset he is, recommending marriage counsellors and Christian books about forgiveness. The church leader preaches on divorce and she's sure it is directed at her. Her partner takes her to court, he hires expensive legal support, he wins sole custody of the children. She can't stop crying. She feels totally alone, and she is.

When delivering training I do an exercise where I draw a line on flipchart paper. On one side of the line we list all the things a woman may lose when she leaves an abusive partner. The list is long: home, friends, secure accommodation, status, family, childcare provision, financial stability, car, job, children, pets, possessions, a legal right to remain in the country, known quantities, holidays, her partner, marriage, hope that her partner will change, her moral position on divorce or separation, church, her life. On the other side of the line we write the things a woman may gain by leaving an abusive partner: friends, family, freedom, self-esteem, confidence, her life, children, choices, stability, a new career. Most of what she loses is immediate and definite. Most of what she gains is possible, eventual and intangible. As valuable as self-esteem is, it feels pointless if she doesn't have a home to love herself in. Freedom is powerful, but it is incremental and utterly intangible.

We need to make freedom tangible. One of the ways we can do this is by enabling women to 'feel their freedom' by recognizing what they can do as a result of leaving – all the things their partner prevented them from doing. We can ask women to make a list (either in their head or on paper) of what they can now do that their partner prevented them from doing.

- Eat what I want.
- Spend more than 20 minutes in the supermarket.
- Meet up with friends.
- Wear make-up/be make-up free.
- Cuddle my children.
- Choose my own clothes.
- Sleep all night.
- Make eye-contact with strangers.
- Go for a walk.
- Leave the house messy.
- Talk about his behaviour.
- Decide when to end a phone call.
- Have privacy.
- Leave my legs unshaved/shave my legs.
- Sit quietly.
- Have control of the TV remote.
- Leave the house.

Each woman will have a unique list. Only by identifying how our freedom has been curtailed can we rebuild it. The practical implications of leaving an abuser can be earth-shattering. We need to make the benefits of leaving as visible as possible. Particularly when social care, police, and criminal, civil or family courts are involved, it can often feel like swapping one abuser for a collection of them: the social worker who patronizes us, the police officer who demeans us, the court system that is so alien to us. As important as the principle of 'innocent until proven guilty' is for a functioning society, it definitely left me feeling that I was guilty of lying about rape until proven innocent by the courts. As it was, that didn't happen. It took a long time to come to terms with that. The criminal justice system is designed to convict and punish offenders, not to support victims. The criminal justice system rarely brings healing and transformation to women subjected to abuse by a partner.

Post-separation harassment can be very difficult to deal with. The presumption that the end of the relationship will end the abuse is held by many, with 'stalking' perceived as something perpetrated by strangers (usually towards celebrity victims). US research found that strangers account for 14 per cent of those who stalk women and 24 per cent of those who stalk men.[2] In the UK, one in five women and one in ten men will be subjected to stalking.[3] Paladin, the National Stalking Advocacy Service, defines stalking as

> a pattern of repeated and persistent unwanted behaviour that is intrusive and engenders fear. It is when one person becomes fixated or obsessed with another and the attention is unwanted. Threats may not be made but victims may feel scared. Even if there is no threat this is still stalking and it is a crime.[4]

When supporting someone whose ex-partner is stalking her, we might be inclined to encourage her to change her phone number. Although this may work for some, many abusers will escalate their behaviour if phone contact becomes impossible, turning up at their ex-partner's workplace or home. Rather than her changing her number, a better option is often to buy a second phone, making the number available only to trusted friends and family. The abuser can continue to text and harass her on the other number, but she has the freedom to choose when to engage with his communications. She can set boundaries without him even knowing. Social media is more difficult to control. Women may have to curtail Facebook and Instagram use; currently Twitter is more suited for pseudonymous use.

I sat across from the counsellor. It was our first session together. 'How do you feel?' she asked in that way only a counsellor can. *How do I feel?!* a voice inside my brain screamed. *If I knew how I felt, I wouldn't be here asking you, would I?!* But no words came out of my mouth. I shrugged and then a quiet 'Dunno' made its way out as I stared at the floor. Identifying how we're feeling can be extremely difficult. Having spent a long time squashing our feelings down, making space for them can feel very unsafe. It usually was unsafe while we were with the abuser.

It can be much easier to identify our feelings if we have a set of words to work with. You can find a 'feeling words' resource in Appendix 4. We can quite easily move through the ones we definitely are *not* feeling, which itself can be a really helpful exercise. Regularly using a sheet of feeling words can provide evidence of our progress. Memories of feelings will often fade as life changes, and changes are often so incremental that they are hard to see in the microcosm of day-to-day life. Keeping a record of our feelings can help us see progress, while only in the macrocosm of weeks and months can we see how our lives have changed.

Measuring progress through journalling can also help. Writing about stressful events improves the clinical health evaluations of those with asthma, rheumatoid arthritis and HIV/AIDS.[5] Creativity guru Julia Cameron created 'Morning Pages', where people write three sides of A4 paper first thing every morning. Many say that doing this exercise regularly improves their mental health and creativity.[6] Writing about stressful events and feelings can be cathartic and gives a sense of control over the feelings and the overwhelming nature of the abuser's behaviour, particularly if we have left and it is safe to keep a journal. I have found it transformative to then review my journals at the beginning of each month and annually. Being able to review the past month (and year) provides perspective. If we are exhausted, reviewing the previous month can help make sense of why, and seeing progress from month to month can be so encouraging. After leaving an abuser, it feels as if the world has stopped and we can continue to feel totally out of control. Taking time to write in a journal and then review it can be a huge step towards feeling more in control of life. We build literacy about ourselves and become conscious of patterns of behaviour and feelings that are negatively affecting us.

Another important aspect of freedom is gaining understanding about abusive behaviour. Until we understand the abuser's behaviour we will be constantly blindsided by it. He may seem to be totally irrational and erratic, but understanding that an abuser's entire communication is based on a different 'currency' from ours can enable us to navigate his post-separation abuse more successfully. We may assume that he has similar intentions to us: caring for the children, learning to be civil, finding ways to move forward. But an abuser's intention is always related to power and control. He operates in a currency of power. Instead of asking ourselves, 'Why is he doing this?' we need to begin asking ourselves, 'How is he gaining power in this?' That shift can make such a difference. His erratic behaviour suddenly takes on another shape: he is trying to keep us confused so that he always has the upper hand. His constant shifting of contact arrangements is not about unreliability but instead is a way of monopolizing our time. His threats are designed to keep us fearful and give him power over us. It can take a lot of emotional and psychological processing to accept that he is motivated by power and not love, but it is only by identifying his intentions that we can 'play him at his own game'. Our good intentions and kindness are a defunct currency within an abuser's economy. They count for nothing. As distressing as it is to realize this, it enables us to take steps to regain ownership of our lives.

Previously child contact had been stressful for Abbie and her daughter Holly. Every time, her ex-husband Gary would turn up 20 minutes early, revving his engine and beeping the horn until Holly came out. Now Abbie and Holly go out for breakfast on contact days. They have a special time together and arrive back just in time for contact. Gary can no longer control contact days.

Eric spent months threatening to send naked images of his ex-girlfriend Zoe to her parents and employer. Utterly petrified for months, Zoe concluded that she couldn't continue to live in fear. She spoke to her parents and employer, explaining that Eric was threatening her. They were all very supportive. When Eric next threatened her, she calmly told him that they already knew about the images and it made no difference to them. Eric had lost his power over her.

Zaffi's church didn't understand what her husband David had done to her and fully supported him. She felt totally alone. It had been her home church for 20 years and she was so hurt by the way they were behaving. She had spent the last year refusing to move church. Why should she leave when he was the cause of the problems? After realizing how much control he was still exerting over her through the church community, she decided to leave. It was a heartbreaking decision. She visited other churches locally and found one that fitted her theology and worship style. A few weeks after moving she felt so much lighter, no longer surrounded by people telling her she needed to restart the relationship. She had to grieve the loss, but she felt so much freer.

There is often a cost to moving outside the abuser's control. We might have to end relationships with friends or family members; we may need to move to a new town or find a new job. Choosing not to seek child support payments, our financial capacity might be greatly reduced. Regaining control of our lives may require us to act in ways that are contrary to what comes naturally to us, acting counter-intuitively. We might have to cease responding quickly to his communications. Where we would normally be amenable and polite, we may have to be cold and uncommunicative to assert effective boundaries. We may have to give up our desire for him to face consequences for his behaviour. It is not fair, but if we want to become free it will often be necessary.

During the early days of separation, my friend Andy saw Craig manipulating me through my mobile and he marched me to purchase a new sim card. I created a new email address and asked a friend to change my password for the old account so that I couldn't re-access it, knowing that the more difficult it was to get communications from Craig, the more likely I would be not to seek to reconnect with him when the traumatic attachment told me I must. We are in the very blessed position that my children have no contact with Craig. When we moved to the south of England, even the letters he had committed to writing to the children every month never were monthly and tailed off within less than a year. Many women are ordered by courts to stay in the same locality as the abuser, with their children forced to have contact with him. Some insist on contact between the abuser and their children, believing it is in the children's best interests. Others are chased and harassed; no matter where they flee, the abuser is never far behind.

What does freedom look like? For me, freedom is being able to make my own choices and knowing I am worth loving. It means being able to make mistakes without fear of reprisals. I can trust myself and trust others. It means choosing if and when to have sex. Protecting my children from harm, I can help them make sense of their history with honesty, and comfort them in the complicated bits. I can live with integrity and in full obedience to the God who saved me. Because my life belongs to me, I can choose to give it up to follow Jesus. My heart is open, and though brokenness is part of me, it is not all of me. There is no second-guessing the important people in my life and I can set healthy boundaries. I live with hope, joy and peace. I have friends. My feelings matter and I can feel them and not squash them. I can be angry, frustrated, cry and laugh. I enjoy food, and cooking no longer scares me. My finances are stable and my family can live within our means. I can work hard and play hard and learn hard. Life can be beautiful, and most of the time it is.[7]

Freedom will be different for every woman. But seeing that freedom exists is crucial after leaving an abuser. With so much loss, damage and pain, we must celebrate the enormous freedoms of days free of violence or nights free of rape, and the small freedoms of laughing freely, taking time to shop or choosing to leave the washing-up until the next day. Our life becomes more our own with each small freedom.

At last, a chapter that doesn't need a spoonful of sugar to lighten the taste! There is hope! Freedom is possible, but some of the battle is in making freedom visible. Take a moment to pause. What thoughts did this chapter raise for you? How can you make freedom visible for women with abusive ex-partners? How can you help us feel our freedom? Let's pray!

God, thank you that freedom is possible. Please help me to contribute positively to the lives of those who need to feel their freedom. Give me your wisdom in being part of their freedom. Show me where I need to shift my perspective. Guide me into more of your purposes. Amen.

> The young generation does not accept the doctrine that woman's only destiny is wifehood and motherhood . . . nor that her only place is in the home . . . why should a woman be confined to home and denied her rightful place in society? . . . Women of to-day desire, without fear or inhibitions, all round self-development.
>
> Kamini Roy (1924)[8]

13 Do real men hit women? (Well, do they?)

> Real men do not hit women. I call for men to join me in
> standing up to the violence directed at women and girls.
>
> Antonio Banderas (actor)

What makes a man real? On hitting a woman, will a man's penis
fall off? Is his masculinity invalidated when he chooses to abuse
and violate women? Is he a non-man? A fake man? A grown-up
Pinocchio man? Where exactly does his manhood go? What is a man
anyway? I'm unlikely to have the opportunity to ask Mr Banderas
these questions. Made in his role as UNDP Goodwill Ambassador
for the 'He For She' campaign, his statement is part of the increased
efforts to encourage men to address male violence. Interestingly, as
his quote indicates, rarely are men mentioned as the agents within
these campaigns; the more general phrase of 'violence against women
and girls' is used. Running since 1991 has been the global White
Ribbon Campaign, while more recently we've seen the launch of
First Man Standing by UK-based Christian charity Restored.[1]

The good intentions of campaigns mobilizing men to be part of
the solution to male violence against women are not always matched
by their impact. Male violence prevention specialist Michael Salter
has analysed the impact of campaigns to mobilize men:

> primary prevention efforts [around male violence towards
> women] should be reorientated away from decontextualised

and quasi-transcendental accounts of masculinity and towards non-violence as a suppressed possibility within the existing social order, and one that requires economic and political as well as cultural change if it is to be realised.[2]

The 'real men don't abuse' narrative rarely considers deeply what exactly makes a man. Is a man more than biology? If so, what is he? Author and masculinity theorist Joseph Gelfer points out:

> Masculinity is a complex issue: you might think some of the popular writers are writing about it with 'clarity', but they are simply stripping it of all subtlety and nuance. It's certainly desirable to aim for clarity, but at some point compromise becomes fatal . . . Complex issues require appropriately complex handling.[3]

'Real men don't hit women' is a simple enough slogan; it sounds *right*. Yet masculinity isn't simple or sloganifiable. Boys are socialized into identities that exclude any perceived feminine characteristics: being told not to cry, not to be a girl, encouraged to play at war and killing, they are taught to stay in the man box, to be strong, powerful and virile. They mustn't admit weakness or feel anything but anger. Stepping outside this man box leads to being called names associated with women or gay men. The brutality of this leaves men's identity much more closely aligned to their masculinity than that of women to femininity. Women will be abused or called names regardless of whether or not they stay in the woman box. While women generally have less power than men, they benefit from having access to a much broader spectrum of human characteristics. Questioning masculinity is likely to threaten men's identity much more than the questioning of femininity threatens women. When you're brought up in a small box, that restriction soon becomes the basis of your identity.

Men's abuse of women is not extraneous to masculinity; it is a consequence of masculinity. Men are socialized to see women as alien creatures, totally different from them; no wonder their empathy towards women can be low. Ron Clark is a church planter (if you're a non-Christian, this describes a sort of 'Christian entrepreneur' who starts new churches instead of new businesses; we Christians love a good buzzword). His book *Am I Sleeping with the Enemy?* reflects on men's perception of women as the enemy:

> When a boy cries, his father trains him in the way of the ancients. He is taught to 'man up', and rejects anything feminine in his life. Thus he begins the process of becoming a man in the image of his culture. This transformation comes at the expense of his own calling to reflect the image of God. Men and women, however, were both created in this divine image and were meant to live in harmony rather than enmity.[4]

The 'real man' ideal props up abusive behaviour, and trying to use 'the devil's tool to dismantle the devil's house' isn't going to work. Masculine norms contribute to a culture where men choose to abuse women and other men. Masculinity presents itself as devoid of anything feminine: strong, powerful and virile. Women are so different, so 'other', that men don't have to treat them equally. Appealing to 'real manhood' insists that there is something innate to men that is not in women. The idea that men and women sit at opposite poles is tackled by Joseph Gelfer:

> because polarity is a 'fact' of nature in *some* circumstances, it does not mean it is a fact of nature in *all* circumstances . . . Magnetism as a *metaphor* has historically been applied to sexual attraction, but somewhere along the line its metaphorical truth has been confused with its literal truth.[5]

Men and women are not polar opposites; we are human beings and designed to be in continuing relationship with one another. Efforts to define male or female identity inevitably exclude more men or women than they include, and though there can be a broad acknowledgement that biological differences lead to some differences between them more generally, the minute we try to articulate those differences we reduce men and women to less than God intended.

The 'real man' trope also allows abusive men to falsely see themselves as non-abusive. The man who never hits his partner but demeans and devalues her every day gets to claim he's a good guy, as does the man who masturbates to images of women being sexually degraded. The man who hits his partner also perceives himself as one of the good guys: 'I only did it because she made me.' An abuser manipulates not only his partner but also himself into believing he isn't the bad one.

When do efforts to engage men in ending male violence start reinforcing problematic stereotypes? Does an event's use of a chocolate brand whose slogan is 'No girls allowed' perpetuate men's alienation from women? (That's without raising the issue about how such a brand might be owned by a company that exploits many in the majority world.) Is it helpful for a campaign to focus on men protecting women? Appealing to men's paternalistic ideals of protecting women, where women are fragile creatures unable to manage without male intervention, seems to perpetuate an abuser's narrative: 'She's irrational and needs me to help her make good decisions, because she's weak and can't cope without me.' Men are protecting women from other men. Maybe it would be better for them to focus on building a society in which men no longer choose to abuse women. In an assembly for 300 Year 10 students,[6] one boy informed us all that girls need boys to help them 'because girls are emotionally weaker than boys'. He was confounded when I asked how much emotional strength it had taken for his mother to give birth to him and bring him up. He had forgotten that his mother was female.

Christian masculinity has had a few reincarnations in recent years, from the muscular Christianity preached by disgraced pastor Mark Driscoll to the excessively confident David Murrow, who wrote a whole book on why men hate going to church. Mark Driscoll wrote pseudonymously on his church's online forum,

> We live in a completely pussified (*sic*) nation . . . As a result,
> [Adam] was cursed for listening to his wife and every man since
> has been pussified [sitting] quietly by and watch a nation of
> men be raised by bitter penis envying burned feministed single
> mothers who make sure that Johnny grows up to be a very nice
> woman who sits down to pee.[7]

David Murrow acknowledges that male socialization is a 'precarious and artificial state' but he also tells us: '"Being manly" is a universal obsession among men . . . Without man laws, civilization would crumble.'[8] His version of Jesus seems closer to *Mission Impossible* than the Gospels:

> Christ came to earth as a dangerous man – skilled, knowledge-
> able, and in control. He held the power of life and death in his
> hands. He was given an impossible assignment – to overcome a
> ruthless enemy single-handedly . . . He was betrayed by an ally
> and handed over to his enemy, whose henchmen beat him almost
> beyond recognition. Yet he miraculously escaped his captors and
> completed his mission in the most unexpected fashion . . . In the
> end, he will receive a radiant bride.[9]

David Murrow's book remains the go-to guide for getting more men into church, but his analysis squashes men into an ever-smaller man box. Joseph Gelfer offers an alternative perspective: 'instead of assuming spirituality is the changeable variable that can be shifted into line with men, why not consider that men are the changeable variable that can be shifted into line with spirituality?'[10] As Christians, surely we believe that God can transform and change people; that manhood is not fixed?

Masculinity is defined by its opposition to the feminine, operating in war, violence and aggression. Where Murrow and others bemoan a feminized Church that is alienating men, Stan Goff's story offers another possibility:

> I decided to look into Christianity for a while thinking it was
> something I ought to know more about. At some point while I

was gazing into the Jordan River, a Jew from ancient Nazareth with rough hands and a loving heart reached up and pulled me in. For the first time in my life, death did not have the last word. That's a pretty big deal for anyone. For me, it meant everything I'd thought I'd known about being a man had changed, because as a man my life had always been determined by death; I had always operated on the assumption that death had the last word. Had I not been prepared by feminism and its insights into my life (and sins) as a man – had feminism not prepared me to relinquish the control that I'd needed to be 'a man' – I might have rejected the vulnerability that Jesus demands before I ever got to the good parts. God does indeed work in mysterious ways.[11]

For those who don't know him, John Piper is a conservative theologian who believes that there are profound differences between men and women that 'go to the root of our personhood'.[12] Practically, this means men can lead in church and women can't. A Christian youth worker once pointed out to me that no feminist seems able to effectively answer John Piper's question of how to respond to a six-year-old boy who asks, 'What does it mean to be a boy?' I'm always thrilled to be asked to offer a response to John Piper (I'm not). At the time my six-year-old son was much more interested in watching TV than deep ontological questions. However, hypothetically my response to him would have involved explaining that there are as many ways to be a boy as there are boys in the world, and asking my son what it means to be him. What are his gifts, talents and challenges? That is the important question. Why is it so important to explain what it means to be a boy, a girl, a man or a woman? Do men want their infallibility validated? Is men's sexual objectification justifiable because men are supposedly more visual, even though women have eyes too? I know, this is a big surprise to many people. Why are we seeking validation through rather flimsy ideas of masculinity and femininity, which need significantly more maintenance than John Piper, Mark Driscoll and David Murrow seem willing to admit? A restrictive model of masculinity is not only unrealistic, it is simply one option among many.

When Baggy and I got married, various Christian men praised him for taking on another man's children, one man informing him, 'I couldn't do it!' Jesus' dad was a stepfather, yet Christian culture seems wedded to the nuclear family, almost as if our views of family are based on Western ideals rather than the Bible. When Baggy left the church football team after we became a couple, one man asked, 'Is that a thumbprint on your head?' By choosing me and our relationship over playing football with other men in the church, Baggy had stepped out of the man box and needed challenging. Heaven forbid that men would be more interested in their wives and children than football! What would that mean for the sexist man's own priorities? He might have to re-evaluate them, and we can't have that, can we? Best to mock him back into his box. It didn't work. Baggy didn't laugh along and he didn't start re-attending football either.

When Baggy and I first met, my expectations of him were shaped by Craig's behaviour. Early on he rang me to ask whether he could go out socially after work. Perplexed, I wanted to know why he was asking me. His answer has stuck with me: 'I will never assume that you are available to look after the children. They are my responsibility too and I will never presume that you have not made plans.' I was stunned. I didn't even realize that I had believed myself to be solely responsible for the children. Men often simply accept the benefits of their partner holding greater responsibility; however, Baggy has often helped me to see where I am operating out of gendered socialization.

For years Baggy has been the primary carer of the children. As my workload increased, he took on the childcare and household responsibilities. When informed that Baggy is a stay-at-home dad, most non-Christians normally simply smile and nod, yet Christians are often dubious. One particular Christian man would interrogate Baggy about whether he had found a 'proper' job yet, leaving Baggy to patiently explain yet again that looking after his children *was* a proper job.[13]

I asked Baggy what role he thinks men have in ending male violence. He said:

> It's about being a role model to other men and to children; by living it, and showing people that it can work and what the advantages are. It is important to speak up if someone tells a sexist joke or resorts to gender stereotyping. I don't laugh along or agree, instead I challenge it and offer a different perspective. I view our marriage as a partnership and always see any decisions as being made together, whether regarding finances, parenting or holiday destinations. I see Natalie as a competent human being who is equal to me and I feel no pressure to be 'in charge'. I never assume that anything is all Natalie's responsibility; instead we decide stuff together. We have a lot of fun together, particularly as neither of us is coming to the relationship with any hidden agendas. We work through stuff together and if we can't agree and it takes us a while to make a decision, then so be it. No decision is more important than ensuring we're both on board with it.

It is not fake men who hit women. Real men hit women. Real men control, demean and isolate women, frightening and violating them and their children. It is not some other species. All anti-violence work must recognize that men are the majority agents of violence, acknowledging that masculinity is part of the problem, not part of the solution.

In a meeting with a men's ministry leader, he told me his wife was the rose and he was the thorns. He wanted to know why I wouldn't let him be the thorns. He can be the thorns if he wants, but he doesn't have to be the thorns. It doesn't seem like a particularly good deal for either of them. We are made in the image of God, not roses. And God made us interdependent. As one author puts it, 'in the Lord woman is not independent of man, nor is man independent of woman. For as woman came from man, so also man is born from woman. But everything comes from God.'[14] As a full person I am not merely a collection of delicate petals, just as Baggy is not simply a set of spiky thorns. Healthy relationships are not calculated as 'you + me = us'. Instead it is 'you + me = you + me + us'.[15] Baggy is not my other half or my better half and God did not make me deficient until marriage; I was enough (Baggy would probably say I was *more* than enough . . .) and I was whole. And so was Baggy.

As Joseph Gelfer explains, the Bible offers diverse representations of men:

> Indeed, contemporary scholarship of masculinity across all Christian sacred texts (and historical periods) demonstrates one big counter-conspiratorial claim: Biblical masculinity is wildly diverse, encompassing almost every point you can imagine (including eunuchs and men who may or may not even be human!). So ironically, the contemporary Christian claim about there being some kind of singular and authentic Biblical masculinity does nothing [but] expose a fundamental lack of understanding when it comes to reading the Bible.[16]

God did not create men and women to be restricted by the human constructs of masculinity and femininity. They may have served a useful purpose, but in Jesus we are told of a better way: we are 'neither . . . male and female, for [we] are all one in Christ Jesus'.[17] As we grow in the way of Jesus we should become more loving, joyful, peaceful, patient, kind, generous, faithful, gentle and able to control ourselves.[18] If we were to give a gender to those characteristics, we would probably see them as 'feminine', yet these are the fruits of a relationship with Jesus, for both women *and* men. Isn't that interesting?

Male identity need no longer be established in opposition to women. In Jesus there is neither male nor female; we are identified as those who have the Spirit of the living God within us. By choosing to accept our incapacity and through becoming obedient to God, our identity is in Jesus. We are told this should lead us to abundant life. For men that path will often be harder to follow. A lifetime of being told that weakness is to be avoided leaves men resistant to the gospel of Jesus Christ. Each of us (both women and men) must humble ourselves before Jesus and say, 'I cannot do this alone. I am a failure and I am weak.' Masculinity will make those words hard to say. But liberation cannot be achieved independently of that. Male socialization is one of the biggest barriers to men accepting the gospel of Jesus Christ. On realizing that he would have to give up his riches, the rich man walked away,[19] and many men will do likewise upon realizing that they have to give up their strength, self-sufficiency and perceived competence. A gospel that is a less bitter pill to swallow is not worth having. It is only in dying to ourselves[20] (including dying to masculinity) and denying ourselves[21] that we can be raised into the new life that Jesus offers.

Real men do hit women. But they don't have to and they can make different choices. As can all men. We are all part of the problem and we can all be part of the solution. We begin by recognizing the nature of abuse and through being sensitized to the areas of our lives where we have previously colluded with narratives that prop up abuse. Continuing by no longer needing identities that stem from our genitals, we take responsibility and choose to live differently. Then we keep on keeping on, remembering during the painful times Jesus' promise, 'In this world you will have trouble. But take heart! I have overcome the world.'[22]

You may have spent this chapter infuriated with me. Hold on to that fury and ask God to show you its roots. If you are not a Christian, perhaps simply ponder why, rather than asking for help from an entity you don't believe in. You may be right. I may be wrong. I am not invested in being right. I merely want to see men no longer abusing women. It's a huge goal, and if you have a better way then by all means take it. But please take time to understand whether your resistance is rooted in my wrongness or your discomfort with the truth. Thankfully, if we can't agree, on the other side of eternity there is a Saviour who can welcome us both and gently guide each of us into the whole truth, which shines brightest of all. Let us pray . . .

O God, there is much to think about. Some of this stuff shatters many of life's foundations. I am thankful that I can trust in you even when everything else is shaken. Please help me to know your truth in the midst of all this information. Enable me to know you more and show me your ways. Amen.

Govern everything by your wisdom, O Lord,
so that my soul may always be serving you
in the way you will
and not as I choose.
Let me die to myself so that I may serve you;
let me live to you who are life itself.
Amen.

St Teresa of Avila (1515–82)

14 Can we end domestic abuse? (There is hope)

Dear reader, we have come to the end of our time together! This is the last chapter. Fear not, though: if you would like us to have more time together you can always re-read this book. Such is the magic of reading!

There is much to learn. When embarking on this magical mystery journey filled with misery, awfulness and at least some hope, you were probably in a different headspace. You may be surer than ever in your position or perhaps you have been challenged and come to new conclusions about gender, relationships, abuse, theology and life more generally. I hope for the latter, but am not fazed by the former.

My next statement is rather contentious, which you will probably be unsurprised about by now. None of us can end male violence, and the campaigns that claim this are well-meaning nonsense. Male violence will only end when men stop being violent. But do not lose all hope! We cannot end male violence, but we are able to reduce the space in which men can abuse. We must build a society in which men find that their abuse is no longer tolerated and where women find they are believed. And although we cannot stop men being violent, we can help women recover.

My journey to recovery started when I left Craig. It was not deep inner strength which enabled me to escape. When I was forced to move into a hospital with my son, circumstances beyond my control were the catalyst for recovery. My parents would visit us in hospital each week, occasionally taking my daughter for a few nights. Andy and Alice Smith, two friends who had previously been my church youth workers, would visit me most weeks. Before I escaped Craig, they had occasionally welcomed me and my daughter into their home when I attempted to leave him. I always went back to him and they never judged me. Andy was the first person I told about Craig raping me. They drove me to the police station and looked after my daughter while I made a statement. It took three hours and required me to detail every second of the assault. Alice organized a flat for us to move into when my son recovered.

At three months old, my son was deemed well enough to be released from hospital. Sitting between my son and daughter in the back seat of my parents' car, I realized my son had turned blue. I was attempting to resuscitate my tiny son on my lap while my daughter cried hysterically and my mum panicked, all the while on the phone to the emergency services trying to identify our location. Once we arrived back at the hospital, I sat on the floor colouring in with my toddler daughter, watching out of the corner of my eye as my tiny son's body was hidden from view by a big group of doctors and anaesthetists.

A month later they released my son again. Days after settling into the flat I was breastfeeding him and looked down. He was no longer breathing and his skin was grey. I carried his apparently lifeless form around the flat, desperately trying to find my mobile phone. I breathed air into his mouth and nose, and the air came back out with a sound like an accordion. Eventually he coughed and started breathing again. After stabilizing him, the emergency doctors decided that this time he couldn't leave hospital for a while.

Weeks later, along with another tiny baby on the ward, my son was diagnosed with bronchiolitis. He was transferred to intensive care, and on visiting him I found he had an IV line in a vein in his head, all his other veins having collapsed from overuse. The consultant explained that my son needed a lung bypass and told me there was a 70 per cent chance that the procedure would lead to mental or physical disability. 'You'll only do it if it's desperate?' I asked. 'It is desperate,' came the doctor's bleak response. My son was transferred to a specialist lung hospital, but on the way he miraculously improved, no longer needing the bypass. Months later I saw the parents of the other tiny baby in the supermarket. I asked them how she was. They explained that she had died on the way to the bypass treatment. At home I wept. Those parents were walking around the supermarket without their baby. Mine had survived. Why did I get a miracle while they did not?

Eventually my son was allowed home on low-flow oxygen, with tubes in his nose and a heavy canister to take everywhere with us. He also had a night-time oxygen monitor. Andy and Alice moved away and mostly it was just me and the two children. This was a healing time. We would paint, go to the park and make use of libraries (libraries are such important, life-enriching resources, particularly for poorer families!). We took advantage of many of the free sessions offered by our wonderful local children's centres. I was allocated a support worker through local Christian charity the Aquila project,[1] while another local charity, Homestart,[2] assigned me a volunteer befriender. I was living in a new town with few friends and the visits from the support worker and befriender restored my sanity and were so precious to me.

We started attending a large local church. It was a hard church to be part of, despite some lovely people who became my friends. I was one of very few single parents in a congregation of 600. Six months into my time there, I began chatting with a woman. 'Oh!' she exclaimed. 'You're the lady with the sick baby.' That was the first and last time she spoke to me.

When I told my children's health visitor about the court case, she referred me to a local domestic abuse service. They invited me on to a 12-week domestic abuse recovery programme and, though I didn't think it really applied to me, I attended because of free childcare provision which gave me a break from the kids. The first session shocked me: Craig was actually abusive. It was the first time I had realized it. Julia, one of the facilitators, was a Christian, and the fact that she shared my culture and beliefs was so important in processing Craig's abuse.

I learned so much. Craig's treatment of me wasn't because of his bad childhood; I discovered it was his choice. I found out that his sexual demands were abusive, not his right as my husband. His love was actually manipulation and mind games. Everything he did was intentional, not accidental or inevitable. Realizing that I had struggled to change myself, I began to understand that I would never be able to change Craig. My belief about forgiveness was that I should forgive and forget, but I learned that forgiveness does not mean nullifying the consequences. Forgiveness made me stronger, not weaker.

Towards the end of the course I felt called to move to the south of England, where Baggy and I miraculously decided to get married. Our church supported us immensely. They made themselves available and loved us, becoming our second family. After we had been married a while and I had moved out of the most severe PTSD episodes, God spoke to me very clearly during a women's conference, telling me I would work nationally on domestic abuse issues. After a bit of back and forth with God, he said to me, 'If I call you, I will resource you.' At 24 years old, with two small children, I had no idea how this would happen, but while living in hospital with my children I had committed to being obedient to God.

Soon after this I contacted the woman who had created the recovery course. Offering me a free training space, she invited me to speak at a conference. The first time I shared my testimony was at a non-Christian conference for professionals working on domestic abuse issues. After hearing my story and learning that I was trained to run the course, a local authority commissioner offered me a role supporting the delivery of training events and running recovery courses. In this role I connected with many Christian professionals who suggested the Church needed to address domestic abuse issues. On investigating the available resources, I discovered very little provision and began a project to support church leaders dealing with disclosures about abuse, and it was while doing this that I ended up connecting to the International Director and the Gender Advisor for the large Christian charity Tearfund. God had called them to address male violence towards women and I offered to help them. Over the next two years the charity Restored emerged, an international alliance of Christians working to end violence against women.[3] Alongside this I created and began delivering the DAY Programme and developed a campaign to raise awareness of abuse within the Fifty Shades book series. I organized the first large UK Christian domestic abuse conference, where Restored was launched. The legendary theologian and anti-violence advocate Dr Catherine Clark Kroeger travelled from the USA to speak, and I praise God for the opportunity to meet her, as she sadly died less than a year later. I stand on the shoulders of giants like Cathy Kroeger, Elaine Storkey, Marie Fortune and Nancy Nason-Clarke; they are the foremothers of this work and they deserve great honour. At 25, as I arrived at a conference in Canada, one of the conference participants presumed I was a child and asked me, 'Are you here with your mum?' I didn't have the heart to tell her that although I only looked 14, I was actually one of the keynote speakers.

After four years, I moved on from Restored and my work broadened. I organized protests at the premieres of the *Fifty Shades* films and began to work on Project 3:28,[4] seeking to increase the representation of women in Christian culture. Releasing statistics of how many men and women have spoken at different Christian events, we developed an online database of women who can speak at such events.[5] Through social media I connected with some awesome Christian women and, with some great women, co-founded the UK Christian Feminist Network.[6] I built relationships with some incredible radical feminists who didn't see my Christian faith as a barrier to friendship.[7] They continue to teach me a lot.

Over the years wonderful women and men have walked alongside me (and Baggy), cheering us on and loving us deeply. Some financially support my work, while others pray regularly for us; others remain available for coffees and talks long into the night. My precious friend Vicky Walker describes her first meeting with me as 'the day the sky turned dark' as we talked for hours. Recently I secured funding to develop a new programme for adult women called the Own My Life course and I won *Preach* magazine's inaugural sermon competition.[8] The prize was free study at the London School of Theology[9] and so I found myself studying for a Master's in Integrative Theology without any previous academic experience.

Unsurprisingly, what God called me to do has come to pass. Working both nationally and internationally on domestic abuse issues, I am also addressing gender injustice more broadly. Baggy and I had our wedding rings engraved with Ephesians 3.20, a reference to the Bible verse which tells us that, with his power working in us, God can do more than we could ever ask or imagine. God continues to do more than we could ever ask or imagine.

Dear reader, you may find this book leaves you feeling overwhelmed by your lack of knowledge and the fear of making someone's life worse. On my darkest days, people's most important gift to me has been remaining present. There is much to learn and do, but remaining present with people can make all the difference. In 1999, American children's TV host Mister Rogers said:

> When I was a boy and I would see scary things in the news, my mother would say to me, 'Look for the helpers. You will always find people who are helping.' To this day, especially in times of disaster, I remember my mother's words, and I am always comforted by realizing that there are still so many helpers — so many caring people in this world.[10]

If you are reading this and you are already a helper, be encouraged! I made it through the most painful years of my life because people like you were present with me. My parents and some friends remained present even when it was deeply unpleasant. My youth workers became dear friends who opened their home to me and my children. The woman who volunteered as a befriender and the woman who was employed as a support worker interrupted the intense loneliness of my single parenthood with their presence. The facilitators of the recovery course were an integral part of my journey. The church family who loved me, the woman who gave me free training, the commissioner who employed me, and the others who gave me opportunities to begin working on these issues, were all part of my recovery. Those who continue to financially support my work are my partners in making a difference. If you are a helper, even when you feel discouraged, take heart: your presence, your action and your support is making a difference, even when you don't feel that it is.

For those not yet helping, know that you can make a difference! Do not feel disabled by the sheer enormity of the issues. Each time you smile at someone, each time you remain present with someone in her pain, you can be part of the solution. Invite single parents into your lives, support domestic abuse services with your time or money, be a good friend, remain present in the lives of those with toxic or abusive partners. You may not realize it, but you could help save her life.

Some of you are reading this while still in the midst of the pain. Moving forward seems impossible. However difficult it all feels right now, know that this isn't all there is. Hope is possible. I have walked a similar path to you. It is brutal, but there is the potential for light and for life.

The world has changed since I was a single parent. Thankfully my son was born in a country with free healthcare – his treatments would have cost hundreds of thousands of pounds and I took it for granted that his care would remain free and that accommodation would be available to my daughter and me while he was being treated. Many of the resources I had access to are no longer available. The welfare system provided me with enough money to survive and I could afford to rent a flat with a bedroom each for my children. I took my children to Sure Start children's centres where we could access high-quality activities, and the domestic abuse services had secure funding, enabling them to even provide free childcare. The voluntary services I benefited from were supported. I received counselling from a well-funded youth service. Most of these services either no longer exist or are filled with permanently exhausted staff and volunteers seeking to stay above water, their funding so insecure that there is a permanent threat of redundancy. The welfare system has been stripped away. Since 2010, the number of people using food banks has increased from 41,000 to more than 1.2 million. In the current climate I would not have been able to find secure housing and I would have struggled to feed my children (never mind myself!). A horrific situation would have been made even more unbearable.

Christians are often reluctant to get political, believing in a God who is supreme above all earthly authority. The earthly authorities are making decisions that affect the most vulnerable in society. Jesus was anointed by God to bring good news to just these people; they are the ones he came to liberate.[11] 'Politics' is a fancy word to describe how a society organizes itself, involving everything from bin collection and street lighting to the decision to take a country to war. Regardless of where we sit on the political spectrum, we have a responsibility as Christians to build a system that enables the most vulnerable to flourish.

Each year, the poorest people in the world become poorer. Natural disasters, war and political decisions leave many more destitute. Even within the relative wealth of Britain, doctors are treating children with rickets (a condition that is usually a result of poverty and children not having nutritious food), while schools wash children's clothing as poverty increases dramatically.[12] Yet we find that the wealthiest grow ever wealthier, with the richest people in the world growing $1 trillion richer in the space of one year.[13]

While each of us can make a difference by ensuring we are helpers in the lives of those subjected to abuse, we must not neglect the systemic and political spheres in which women's and children's lives are often the collateral damage. Some of us may feel called to work in politics; others can write letters to their MP, attend protests or sign petitions calling for change; yet others will vote to ensure the government prioritizes the most vulnerable in society. Journalist Stephen Bush, who was brought up by a single mother, wrote about seeing the father he never knew on a London tube:

> I don't want to absolve [my father]. He couldn't know, close to 30 years ago, that the child he was walking out on would have the good fortune to be born into a country about to experience close to two decades of uninterrupted, low-inflation growth . . . My father couldn't know that I would benefit from investment in schools, museums and fantastic teachers, and the world's best mother. But I did, which means that while a number of people – the taxpayer, society, my mum – have a legitimate grievance against my father, I don't, not really. It worked out OK. The dispiriting truth is that it might be different today: child poverty has increased every year for the past three years, even during periods of economic growth. Changes to the child maintenance regime have made it even harder to force absent parents to pay up, while the botched introduction of Universal Credit makes it more difficult for single parents in work to stay out of poverty. And so I walked away from the man who was – or might have been – my father thinking this: I need to spend less time writing about an imaginary, lost parent, and more time writing about how much harder it is to be a kid like me today.[14]

In understanding that we cannot end domestic abuse, we can become deeply depressed. Everything seems so bleak. If we can't stop men abusing women then what's the point? If we can effect change, that is enough. As a Christian, I know that things will not be fully transformed until Jesus returns. (I can almost see non-Christian eyebrows rise as I admit to such craziness.) I do not believe that this lifetime is the end. We are promised a new heaven and a new earth, where a loud voice will proclaim,

> Look! God's dwelling-place is now among the people, and he will dwell with them. They will be his people, and God himself will be with them and be their God. 'He will wipe every tear from their eyes. There will be no more death' or mourning or crying or pain, for the old order of things has passed away.[15]

I am in awe of secular feminists who see the world as it is and do not remain collapsed in a heap of pain. My hope is found in the belief that there is more than just this life. Women's suffering is not the end; there is hope for a redeemed reality. I don't know exactly what this looks like or how it will be worked out but, as they say, 'It will be OK in the end, and if it's not OK, it's not the end.'

We can't end domestic abuse, but we can be present in women's lives. We can build a society where women and children benefit from secure welfare and have the services and support they need to move forward. We can reduce the space in which men can perpetrate violence and abuse with impunity. We can bring up children to know their value and the value of others. We cannot do everything, but we can all do something.

Let us finish by praying.

God, there is much to process and think through. Please show me your purposes for me as this book comes to an end. Teach me to be obedient to you and to choose you no matter what. Bring hope to those who are subjected to abuse and show me how to be part of that hope. Help me to be present in women's pain. Guide me in holding abusers to account and show me how to be part of that process. Show me what it means to be part of a politics that brings hope to the vulnerable. Lead me further into your truth and love. Amen.

My soul glorifies the Lord,
and my spirit rejoices in God my Saviour,
for he has been mindful of the humble state of his servant.
From now on all generations will call me blessed,
for the Mighty One has done great things for me –
holy is his name.
His mercy extends to those who fear him
from generation to generation.

He has performed mighty deeds with his arm;
he has scattered those who are proud in their inmost thoughts.
He has brought down rulers from their thrones
but has lifted up the humble;

He has filled the hungry with good things
but has sent the rich away empty.

Mary's Magnificat[16]

Appendix 1
Signposting

DOMESTIC ABUSE HELPLINES

Emergency services (999): when someone is in immediate danger.

National Domestic Violence Helpline (0808 2000 247; <http://nationaldomesticviolencehelpline.org.uk>): advice for women (and their supporters) who are being subjected to abuse by a partner or ex-partner.

Men's Advice Line (0808 801 0327; <http://mensadviceline.org.uk>): advice for men (and their supporters) who are being subjected to abuse by a partner or ex-partner.

National LGBT+ Domestic Abuse Helpline (0800 999 5428; <www.galop.org.uk/domesticabuse/>): advice for lesbian women, gay men and bisexual and transgender people who are being subjected to abuse by a partner.

Rape Crisis (0808 802 9999; <rapecrisis.org.uk>): for those who have been subjected to sexual harm, including but not limited to rape (whether recent or historical).

National Stalking Helpline (0808 802 0300; <www.stalkinghelpline.org>): advice for anyone being subjected to stalking or harassment (and those who want to support them).

Revenge Porn Helpline (0345 6000 459; <http://revengepornhelpline.org.uk>): for those who have had intimate photographs or videos posted online without their consent.

Rights of Women Family Law (020 7251 6577; <http://rightsof women.org.uk>): for women who need help with family law.

Rights of Women Immigration and Asylum Law (020 7490 7689): for women who need help with immigration and asylum law.

Respect Phoneline (0808 802 4040; <http://respectphoneline.org. uk>): for perpetrators of abuse who want help to stop, and those who want to help them change their abusive behaviour.

RELATED HELPLINES

Childline (0800 1111; <http://childline.org.uk>): for children who need support and help.

NSPCC (0808 800 5000; <http://nspcc.org.uk>): for adults worried about a child.

Karma Nirvana (0800 5999 247; <http://karmanirvana.org.uk>): for those at risk of so-called 'honour-based violence' or forced marriage (and their supporters).

NSPCC Female Genital Mutilation Protection Line (0800 028 3550): if you are worried a female child is at risk of (or has been subjected to) genital mutilation.

Say Something (116 000; <http://faceup2it.org>): a text helpline for children and young people to report sexual exploitation.

Lifecentre (0808 802 0808; <https://lifecentre.uk.com>): for children and young people who have been subjected to sexual harm.

Samaritans (116 123; <www.samaritans.org>): for anyone who needs a safe person to talk to.

SANEline (0300 304 7000; <www.sane.org.uk>): for those needing help with mental health issues.

Beat (0808 801 0677; <www.beateatingdisorders.org.uk>): for people struggling with disordered eating.

Missing People (116 000; <www.missingpeople.org.uk>: for those who have gone missing or are considering running away.

Talk to Frank (0300 123 6600; <http://talktofrank.com>): for those who need help with substance misuse.

DENOMINATIONAL SAFEGUARDING PROCESSES

These can be found by using an online search engine (e.g. Google). Type in 'safeguarding' and the denomination name, and their safeguarding web page will be at the top of the search results. For the main denominations the current weblinks are:

Baptist: <www.baptist.org.uk/Groups/220754/Safeguarding_ Policy_and.aspx>

Catholic: <www.csasprocedures.uk.net>

Church of England: <www.churchofengland.org/more/safe guarding>

Church of Ireland: <www.ireland.anglican.org/about/safeguarding>

Church of Scotland: <www.churchofscotland.org.uk/about_us/ safeguarding_service>

Church in Wales: <www.churchinwales.org.uk/structure/ representative-body/hr/safeguarding/>

Methodist: <www.methodist.org.uk/for-ministers-and-office-holders/safeguarding/>

Quakers: <www.quaker.org.uk/our-organisation/quaker-roles/ safeguarding-coordinators>

URC: <https://urc.org.uk/good-practice-policy-and-procedures. html>

CHURCH-WIDE RESOURCE

Thirtyone:eight (previously CCPAS) offer advice, consultancy and training to churches: <www.ccpas.co.uk>.

Appendix 2
Resources

DOMESTIC ABUSE

Details of your local domestic abuse service can be found by using an online search engine (e.g. Google). Type in 'domestic abuse' and your local area, and your local resources will be found in the first five or ten search results.

Women's Aid are the federations supporting member organizations who run refuges and domestic abuse services nationally:

Women's Aid (England): <www.womensaid.org.uk>

Welsh Women's Aid: <www.welshwomensaid.org.uk>

Scottish Women's Aid: <https://womensaid.scot>

Women's Aid Northern Ireland: <www.womensaidni.org>

Women's Aid Ireland: <www.womensaid.ie>

Refuge (<www.refuge.org.uk>): the largest single provider of refuges and domestic abuse services in England.

Southall Black Sisters (<www.southallblacksisters.org.uk>): help for black and minority ethnic women with resources available in English, Hindi, Punjabi, Gujarati and Urdu, with interpretation available in Somali.

OTHER

Holes in the Wall (<https://holesinthewall.co.uk>): support and resources for those dealing with child to parent violence.

Disrespect Nobody (<http://disrespectnobody.co.uk>): UK government resource for young people about abusive behaviour, consent and other issues.

Oii My Size (<www.oiimysize.com>): helping young people make good choices in relationships.

Creepy Naked Stuff (<www.dayprogramme.org/creepy-naked-stuff>): free resource for under 11s, parents and educators about pornographies.

Urban Dictionary (<http://urbandictionary.com>): for adults to understand the language children and young people may be using.

BOOKS

ABUSE

Lundy Bancroft, *Why Does He Do That? Inside the minds of angry and controlling men* (New York: Berkley Publishing Group, 2002)

Elaine Storkey, *Scars Across Humanity: Understanding and overcoming violence against women* (London: SPCK, 2015)

Phyllis Trible, *Texts of Terror: Literary–feminist readings of biblical literature* (London: SCM Press, 1992)

Leslie Vernick, *The Emotionally Destructive Marriage: How to find your voice and reclaim your hope* (Colorado Springs, Colorado: WaterBrook, 2013)

Delores Williams, *Sisters in the Wilderness: The challenge of womanist God-talk* (Maryknoll, New York: Orbis, 1993)

TRAUMA

Judith Herman, *Trauma and Recovery: The aftermath of violence – from domestic abuse to political terror* (New York: Basic Books, 1992)

Bessel van der Kolk, *The Body Keeps the Score: Mind, brain and body in the transformation of trauma* (London: Penguin, 2014)

Bruce Perry, *The Boy Who Was Raised as a Dog: And Other Stories from a Child Psychiatrist's Notebook: What traumatised children can teach us about loss, love, and healing* (Philadelphia, Pennsylvania: Basic Books, 2006)

PORNOGRAPHY

Heather Brunskell-Evans (ed.), *The Sexualized Body and the Medical Authority of Pornography: Performing sexual liberation* (Newcastle: Cambridge Scholars Publishing, 2016)

Gail Dines, *Pornland: How porn has hijacked our sexuality* (Boston, Massachusetts: Beacon Press, 2010)

Robert Jensen, *Getting Off: Pornography and the end of masculinity* (Boston, Massachusetts: South End Press, 2007)

SEX

Emily Nagoski, *Come As You Are: The surprising new science that will transform your sex life* (London: Scribe UK, 2015)

GENDER

Sarah Bessey, *Jesus Feminist: God's radical notion that women are people too* (London: Darton, Longman and Todd, 2013)

Natalie Collins, *Gender-Aware Youth Practice: Confronting gender-based injustice with young people* (Cambridge: Grove, 2017)

Cordelia Fine, *Delusions of Gender: The real science behind sex differences* (London: Icon Books, 2010)

MASCULINITY

Ron Clark, *Am I Sleeping With the Enemy? Males and females in the image of God* (Eugene, Oregon: Cascade, 2010)

Joseph Gelfer, *The Masculinity Conspiracy* (London: Createspace, 2011)

Stan Goff, *Borderline: Reflections on War, Sex and Church* (Eugene, Oregon: Cascade Books, 2015)

FOR CHILDREN

Justin and Lindsey Holcomb, *God Made All of Me: A book to help children protect their bodies* (Greensboro, North Carolina: New Growth Press, 2015)

Kristen A. Jenson and Debbie Fox, *Good Pictures Bad Pictures: Pornproofing today's young kids* (Richland, Washington: Glen Cove, 2014)

ABOUT CHILDREN

Marianne Hester, Chris Pearson and Nicola Harwin, *Making an Impact: Children and domestic violence* (Philadelphia, Pennsylvania: Jessica Kingsley, 2006)

Bex Lewis, *Raising Children in a Digital Age: Enjoying the best and avoiding the worst* (Oxford: Lion, 2014)

Thomas W. Phelan, *1–2–3 Magic: Effective Discipline for Children 2–12* (Naperville, Illinois: Sourcebooks, 2016)

Nicky Stanley and Cathy Humphreys (eds), *Domestic Violence and Protecting Children: New thinking and approaches* (Philadelphia, Pennsylvania: Jessica Kingsley, 2015)

Appendix 3
Safety plan

This safety plan has been developed from <www.lawc.on.ca/ResourceSafetyWomen.htm>, which was originally developed by the Domestic Abuse Intervention Project, Duluth, Minnesota, USA.

SAFETY DURING A VIOLENT INCIDENT

In order to increase safety during a violent incident, you may use a variety of strategies. Here are some strategies for you to consider.

1   What are the possible escape routes from my home? What doors, windows, lifts, stairwells or fire escapes could I use? ....
    ....
    ....
    I will take the time to practise how to get out safely.

2   I can keep my purse/wallet and keys handy, and always keep them in the same place (..
    ....
    ....),
    so that I can locate them easily if I need to leave in a hurry. I can also have a second set of keys made in case my partner/ex takes the first set.

3   If it is safe for me, I could tell the following people about the violence, and request that they call the police if they suspect I am

in danger: ....

....

and ....

4 Children's safety in abuse situations is central to a safety plan. I may be able to teach my children a safety plan specifically for them in these circumstances.

5 It may be helpful to have a code word to use with my children or other family members if I should need them to call for help. My code word is ....

6 Safe places that I can go to if I need to leave my home:

(a) A place to use the phone: ....

....

(b) A place I could stay for a couple of hours: ....

....

(c) A place I could stay for a couple of days: ....

....

7 During an abusive incident it is best to try to avoid places in the house where I may be trapped or where weapons are readily available, e.g. the bathroom or kitchen. Bigger rooms with more than one exit may be safer.

(a) The places I would try to avoid would be ....

....

....

(b) The places I would try to move to/stay in are ....

....

....

8 With an abusive partner, women sometimes say or do things that in an equal non-abusive partnership they would not. For some women this involves survival skills such as claiming to agree with the abuser even when something is not true in order to increase safety. On other occasions, women may retaliate against the abuser with violence; however, I need to be aware that such actions could lead me to be charged with a criminal offence.

9   Calling the police is always an option.

10 Given my past experience, other protective actions that I have considered or employed are:

(a) ....
....

(b) ....
....

SAFETY PLANNING IF YOU ARE PREPARING TO LEAVE

Some women leave the home they share with the abusive partner. These are protective actions you may wish to consider if you are in this situation. Even if you are not planning to leave your partner, it is important to review a safety plan regarding leaving in case the violence escalates and you need to leave quickly.

1   It may not be safe to inform my partner that I am leaving.

2   Should I need to leave quickly, it would be helpful for me to keep some emergency cash, an extra set of house and car keys and extra clothes with some people who I can go to for help: ....
....
....
and ....
....
....

3   I can keep copies of important documents such as immigration papers or birth certificates at someone's house.

4   I can open a savings account to increase my freedom to leave. I should make sure to alert the bank not to send any correspondence to my home address.

5   I can get legal advice from a solicitor who understands domestic abuse. But, as with the bank, I should make certain the solicitor knows not to send any correspondence to my home address. (It is critical to consult a family solicitor if you have children. Your

local domestic abuse service may be able to recommend a suitable solicitor.)

6   The local domestic abuse helpline number is ....
....
I can seek safe shelter and support by calling this helpline.

7   I can keep change for phone calls on me at all times. I must be careful if I am using my mobile or home number because my partner or ex could see the numbers I have called on the next telephone bill. To keep telephone communications confidential, I can use a pay phone, a friend's phone or a pay-as-you-go mobile phone that my partner or ex is unaware of.

8   These are people I could ask for assistance with:
(a) money: ....
....
(b) childcare: ....
....
(c) support attending appointments: ....
....
(d) transportation: ....
....
(e) other: ....
....

9   If I need to return home to get personal belongings, I can call the police for an escort to stand by and keep the peace. To do this, I call 999 and ask the police to meet me somewhere close to my home. They will stay while I pick up my personal belongings and those of my children.

10 Other protective actions I have considered are: ....
....
....
....
....
....

11 When leaving an abusive partner, it is important I take certain items with me. Items with asterisks in the following list are the most important, but if there is time the other items might be taken, or stored outside the home. Keeping them all together in one location makes it much easier if I need to leave in a hurry.

(a) Identification for myself ★

(b) Children's birth certificates★

(c) Any papers relating to injunctions or other legal proceedings★

(d) My birth certificate★

(e) Immigration papers★

(f) School and vaccination records★

(g) Money★

(h) Cheque book, bank book/cards★

(i) Credit cards★

(j) Keys – house/car/office★

(k) Driver's licence and car ownership details★

(l) Medication★

(m) Passport(s)★

(n) Any medical records★

(o) Divorce/separation papers★

(p) House lease/mortgage/insurance documents★

(q) Address book★

(r) Pictures/photos

(s) Children's favourite toys/blankets

(t) Jewellery

(u) Items of special sentimental value.

12 Telephone numbers I need to know (for safety reasons I may need to keep these telephone numbers hidden (but accessible!) and/or memorize them).

Police: ....

Domestic abuse helpline (24 hours): ....

....

Solicitor: ....

Work: ....

Religious leader (minister/rabbi/priest/imam): ....

....

Other: ....

....

....

SAFETY IN MY OWN HOME

The following are some suggestions regarding safety measures in your own home that you may wish to consider (most of these safety measures cost money).

1   If financially possible I could:

(a) change the locks on my doors and windows (it may be necessary to inform the landlord (for rental properties) or a solicitor (for homeowners) before taking this action);

(b) install a peep-hole in the door;

(c) replace wooden doors with steel/metal doors;

(d) install window bars and poles to wedge against doors;

(e) install an electronic alarm system;

(f) purchase rope ladders to be used for escape from second-floor windows;

(g) install smoke and carbon monoxide detectors and purchase fire extinguishers for each floor in my house/apartment;

(h) install a motion-sensitive lighting system outside that lights up when a person is coming close to my home;

(i) leave the lights on at night and when I am away from home;

(j) install CCTV.

2   If I have custody and access issues, I can inform all the people who provide childcare about who has permission to pick up my children and who does not. I can give these people copies of the custody and access order to keep with them and a picture of the abuser. The people I will inform about pick-up permission include:

(a) school: ....

....

(b) teacher: ....

....

(c) nursery staff: ....

....

(d) before/after-school club: ....

....

(e) babysitters: ....

....

(f) childminder: ....

....

(g) Sunday school teacher: ....

....

(h) relatives: ....

....

(i) other: ....

....

3 I could inform the following people that I am separated and ask
   that they call the police if my ex-partner is seen near my home:
   (a) Neighbour: ....

....

   (b) Landlord: ....

....

   (c) Friend: ....

....

   (d) Other: ....

....

4 Other strategies that I am already using or that I might use
   include: ....

....

....

....

SAFETY WITH AN INJUNCTION

Injunctions are protection orders that a person can apply for in the court (magistrates' court, family court, county court).

If granted by the court an injunction is not active until it is served to the respondent. An applicant can apply for an emergency order without notice to the respondent – but this is dependent on specific factors inclusive of the timeline of the last incident; however, the respondent (perpetrator) will be given notice of another hearing whereby he will have the right to 'respond'/'object' to the order.

Injunctions come under civil law. It *only* becomes a criminal matter if the perpetrator breaks an injunction. It is important that applicants request that the court attach a 'power of arrest' to the order.

DIFFERENT TYPES OF INJUNCTION

1 **Non-molestation order** These can have varying characteristics attached to them, but all would stipulate that the perpetrator is not to threaten or cause physical harm or to incite a third party to cause or threaten harm. The perpetrator is not to pester, harass or contact the applicant. (Sometimes courts will stipulate that the perpetrator is not to enter the street or the property if he doesn't have a legal right to reside there.) These orders are usually granted for six months, although they can go up to 12 months. Once an order has expired, an applicant can reapply if there is still risk of harm to her.

2 **Occupation order** This deals with the property, if the perpetrator has a legal right to reside there. These orders can be difficult to obtain as the court does not like to intentionally make a party homeless. If the perpetrator has another place to reside (for instance, with family or friends) ensure the court is aware of this.

The order can prohibit the perpetrator from attending the entire property or can make restrictions to how the two parties live in the dwelling, dividing up the rooms and/or times of access. For example, 'A' can go into rooms 1, 2 and 3 between the hours of 9.00 and 5.00 but is restricted from entering these rooms outside these hours, or 'A' can dwell in rooms 1 and 2 and 'B' can dwell in rooms 3 and 4.

3   **Prohibited steps order** This involves children and may be appropriate where the perpetrator has parental responsibility. These orders are primarily granted if there is a risk that the perpetrator will attempt to remove the child or children from the home, area or country. There are residency orders and child contact orders that can also be obtained from the courts to offer protection regarding the children. Without one of these specific orders it is not possible for a school to avoid giving the children to the perpetrator, as he has a legal right to take them; one exception would be if children's social care have a child protection plan open.

4   **Undertaking** This is essentially a 'promise' to the court by the perpetrator that he won't do anything bad. It is used when either there is not enough evidence to grant a non-molestation order or the perpetrator objects to such an order. There is no power of arrest with this; however, if the perpetrator breaks his promise to the court he is held to be in contempt of court. If this happens the applicant must inform the court and a non-molestation order is then likely to be granted.

STEPS I CAN TAKE TO HELP SUPPORT THE ENFORCEMENT OF MY PROTECTION ORDER

1   It is important to know the specifics and limitations of the injunction. I will find out the conditions and what they mean for my safety.
2   I can call the police station to ensure that the protection order is registered on the police computer system (PNC).

3　If my ex violates the protection order, I can call the police and report the violation. Depending on the type of protection order, I can also contact my ex's probation officer or contact my solicitor and/or my advocate. (It is important that every violation of the order is reported to the police.)

4　If the police do not help, I can immediately call the duty sergeant at the police station and express my concern. I can also contact my advocate (if I have one), my ex's probation officer or my solicitor, as well as filing a complaint with the police.

5　I will keep my injunction document(s) (originals, if possible) in this location:

(a) ....
....
....

(b) It is beneficial to keep the document(s) on or near me. It may also be helpful to keep a copy in a second safe location.

6　If my partner destroys the injunction paperwork, I can get another copy from the court, my lawyer or:

(a) ....
....
....

7　If it is safe to do so, I can inform the following people that I have an injunction in effect:

(a) my employer: ....
....

(b) my friend: ....
....

(c) my family: ....
....

(d) other: ....
....
....
....

SAFETY AT WORK AND IN PUBLIC

Each woman must decide if and when she will tell others that her partner has abused her and that she may be at continued risk. Friends, family and co-workers may be able to help protect her. Each woman should consider carefully which people to recruit to help secure her safety.

1 If I feel comfortable doing so, I can inform the following people at work of my situation:

(a) my boss: ....

(b) the security supervisor: ....

(c) other: ....

2 According to how comfortable and safe I feel, I can ask the following person to help screen my telephone calls at work:

(a) ....

(b) It may be of assistance to me if these calls are documented.

3 If I feel comfortable doing so and I feel it would be supportive to me and my situation, I could discuss the possibility of having my employer call the police if I am in danger from my partner or ex.

4 Some safety suggestions regarding arriving or leaving work:

(a) I could let someone know when I'll be home.

(b) I could walk with someone to my car.

(c) I could scan the car park.

(d) If I think my partner is following me, I could drive to a place where there are people to support me, e.g. a friend's home, the police station.

(e) If I am walking, I could take a route that is likely to be busier.

(f) I could vary my route home.

(g) If I see my partner on the street, I could try to get to a public place, e.g. a shop.

(h) I can also call attention to myself and request help.

(i) I could purchase a personal alarm device.

5   I can use different supermarkets/shopping centres and shop at different times from those I previously used to reduce the risk of contact with my partner or ex.

SAFETY AND DRUG OR ALCOHOL CONSUMPTION

Many people consume alcohol or mood-altering drugs. Much of this consumption is legal but some is not. The disclosure of the use of illegal or legal drugs can put a woman at a disadvantage in legal actions with her abusive partner. Women should carefully consider the potential cost of the use of legal and illegal drugs. Beyond this, the use of any alcohol or other drugs can reduce a woman's awareness and ability to act quickly to protect herself from the abusive partner. Furthermore, the use of alcohol or other drugs by the abuser may be used as an excuse for violence.

SAFETY AND MY EMOTIONAL HEALTH

Being subjected to abuse by a partner is exhausting and emotionally draining. Survival requires much courage and incredible energy. To conserve my emotional energy and resources, and to support myself in hard emotional times, I can do some of the following:

1   If I have left the relationship and I am experiencing loneliness or manipulative tactics from my abusive partner, I can take care of myself by:

(a) ....

....

(b) ....

....

2   When I have to communicate with my partner in person or by telephone, I can emotionally prepare by:

(a) ....

....

(b) ....

....

3   When I face potentially difficult times like court cases, meetings with solicitors and so on, I can prepare by doing the following:

(a) ....

....

(b) ....

....

4   The people I can call for support are:

(a) ....

....

(b) ....

....

(c) ....

....

5   I can find out about and attend workshops and support groups in the community by calling my local domestic abuse service on:

....

....

Appendix 4
Feeling words sheet

Open	Confident	Kind	Interested	Amazed	Satisfied	Cheerful	Joyful	Cared for
Happy	Lucky	Overjoyed	Important	Glad	Alive	Liberated	Proud	Pleased
Courageous	Free	Energetic	Wonderful	Good	Calm	Secure	Excited	Delighted
Peaceful	Comfortable	Encouraged	Surprised	Content	Certain	Rebellious	Self-compassionate	Rested
Relaxed	Bright	Blessed	Reassured	Loving	Considerate	Unique	Trusting	Caring
Devoted	Passionate	Warm	Sympathetic	Loved	Comforted	Sure	Receptive	Safe
Inspired	Amused	Intrigued	Curious	Positive	Eager	Optimistic	Elated	Absorbed
Determined	Enthusiastic	Brave	Challenged	Hopeful	Strong	Playful	Liked	Relieved
Angry	Irritated	Enraged	Sore	Upset	Bitter	Afraid	Overwhelmed	Shocked
Resentful	Provoked	Hostile	Indignant	Depressed	Disappointed	Worried	Sensitive	Numb
Ashamed	Powerless	Guilty	Dissatisfied	Disgusting	Despairing	Crushed	Outraged	Cautious
Bad	Grieving	Confused	Doubtful	Indecisive	Embarrassed	Victimized	Distrusting	Spiteful
Shy	Lost	Unsure	Tense	Helpless	Incapable	Tearful	Disillusioned	Disturbed
Alone	Vulnerable	Empty	Forced	Desperate	Dominated	Alarmed	Suspicious	Uncomfortable
Concerned	Affected	Anxious	Isolated	Indifferent	Weary	Tortured	Inferior	Regretful
Neutral	Bored	Alienated	Lifeless	Cold	Terrified	Humiliated	Hateful	Ambivalent
Anxious	Alarmed	Aching	Nervous	Panic	Restless	Mournful	Disliked	Exhausted
Threatened	Wary	Weary	Aching	Cowardly	Tormented	Appalled	Dreading	Insecure
Deprived	Rejected	Sad	Hurt	Injured	Heartbroken	Unhappy	Defeated	Hopeless

Notes

1 PRETENDING I'M A TRAFFIC WARDEN

1 <www.finedictionary.com/domestic%20violence.html>; <www.etymonline.com/index.php?term=domestic>.
2 <hansard.millbanksystems.com/commons/1973/jul/16/battered-wives>.
3 <www.collinsdictionary.com/dictionary/english/domestic-abuse>.
4 You can find out more at <www.dayprogramme.org>.
5 <www.stmungos.org/malcolms-blog/a-rumble-of-clergy/>; <https://en.oxforddictionaries.com/explore/what-do-you-call-a-group-of>.
6 <www.nytimes.com/1991/12/12/nyregion/excerpts-from-rushdie-s-address-1000-days-trapped-inside-a-metaphor.html>.
7 Julia Wilkins and Amy Janel Eisenbraun, 'Humor theories and the physiological benefits of laughter, *Holistic Nurse Practice* 23, 6 (2009): 349–54; <www.psychologytoday.com/us/blog/the-heart/201401/laughter-improves-overall-health-0>.
8 <www.linkedin.com/pulse/why-laugh-scott-burton/>.
9 Proverbs 31.25.
10 Crown Prosecution Service, *Violence against Women and Girls: Crime report 2015–16* (London: CPS, 2016), p. 5.
11 South East Wales Women's Aid Consortium, *Domestic Abuse and Equality; Gypsy and Traveller women briefing* (Cardiff: South East Wales Women's Aid Consortium, 2010).
12 Marianne Hester, *Who Does What to Whom? Gender and domestic violence perpetrators* (Bristol: University of Bristol in association with the Northern Rock Foundation, 2009), p. 9.

13 <www.ons.gov.uk/peoplepopulationandcommunity/crimeandjustice/
compendium/focusonviolentcrimeandsexualoffences/yearending
march2015/chapter2homicide>.

14 <www.theguardian.com/society/2015/feb/08/killing-of-women-by-
men-record-database-femicide>.

15 <http://itspronouncedmetrosexual.com/2012/05/what-does-the-
asterisk-in-trans-stand-for/#sthash.DsBsJGvl.dpbs)>.

16 Emily Nagoski, *Come as You Are: The surprising new science that will transform your sex life* (London: Scribe UK, 2015), Kindle edition, loc. 2146.

17 Priscilla J. Owens, hymn, 'We Have an Anchor'(1882).

2 BULLDOZING SAFETY

1 <www.gov.uk/guidance/domestic-violence-and-abuse#domestic-
violence-and-abuse-new-definition>.

2 Scottish Partnership on Domestic Abuse, *National Strategy to Address
Domestic Abuse in Scotland* (Edinburgh: Scottish Government, 2003).

3 <www.cps.gov.uk/legal-guidance/controlling-or-coercive-behaviour-
intimate-or-family-relationship>.

4 A. D. Biderman, *Communist Attempts to Elicit False Confessions from Air
Force Prisoners of War* (Alabama: Office for Social Science Programs,
Air Force Personnel and Training Research Center, Air Research and
Development Command, Maxwell Air Force Base, 1957).

5 <www.leslievernick.com/is-marital-indifference-emotionally-abusive/>.

6 <https://news.vice.com/en_us/article/eva5zk/kevin-spacey-concedes-
he-may-have-assaulted-a-child-but-cant-remember>.

7 <http://stageagent.com/shows/play/2044/angel-street-gaslight>.

8 <www.bbc.co.uk/news/stories-42460315>.

9 <http://metro.co.uk/2017/04/04/police-confronted-with-horrific-
scene-at-domestic-violence-call-out-6554341/>.

10 <www.cps.gov.uk/legal/l_to_o/obscene_publications/#a10b>.

11 <www.telegraph.co.uk/news/uknews/law-and-order/11531954/
What-is-the-law-on-revenge-porn.html>; <www.bbc.co.uk/news/
uk-37278264>.

12 <www.christiandomesticdiscipline.com/how_to_discipline.html>.

13 <www.psychologytoday.com/blog/dreaming-in-the-digital-age/ 201412/why-sleep-deprivation-is-torture>.

14 <www.amazon.co.uk/Cults-Our-Midst-Continuing-Against/dp/ 0787967416>.

15 <www.psychologytoday.com/blog/reading-between-the-headlines/ 201703/love-bombing-have-you-ever-been-the-target>.

16 <www.hup.harvard.edu/catalog.php?isbn=9780674808157>.

17 Genesis 2.18.

18 <www.powerandcontrolfilm.com/the-topics/academics/evan-stark/>.

19 Office for National Statistics, *Intimate Personal Violence and Partner Abuse* (London: ONS, 2014), p. 1.

20 Christine Barter, Melanie McCarry, David Berridge and Kathy Evans, *Partner Exploitation and Violence in Teenage Intimate Relationships* (London: NSPCC, 2009), pp. 54, 64, 72.

21 Vicky Campbell-Hall, Sue Clegg, Vanessa de Guzman and Keith Bolling, *British Crime Survey – Interpersonal Violence Question Development* (London: TNS, 2010), pp. 35–9.

22 The Church of England, *Responding Well to Domestic Abuse: Policy and practice guidance* (Canterbury: Church House Publishing, 2017), p. 2.

23 Church of England, *Responding Well to Domestic Abuse*.

24 John 8.32.

25 Sojourner Truth, 'Ain't I a woman?' (letter, 1851), <https://sourcebooks. fordham.edu/mod/sojtruth-woman.asp>.

3 IT'S NOT HIS DIABETES

1 <www.telegraph.co.uk/journalists/sarah-knapton/10679238/ Educated-and-well-paid-women-more-likely-to-suffer-domestic- abuse.html>.

2 Lundy Bancroft, *Why Does He Do That? Inside the minds of angry and controlling men* (New York: Berkley Publishing Group, 2002), p. 351

3 Liz Kelly, *Moving in the Shadows: Violence in the lives of minority women and children* (Abingdon: Routledge, 2012), p. 17.

4 <www.dashriskchecklist.co.uk/wp-content/uploads/2016/09/ Findings-from-the-Domestic-Homicide-Reviews.pdf>, p. 17.

5 John 10.10.

6 <www.nhs.uk/news/mental-health/mentally-ill-often-victims-of-violence/>.

7 <https://thepsychologist.bps.org.uk/volume-22/edition-10/looking-back-making-and-breaking-attachment-theory>.

8 Anita Ilta Garey and Terry Arendell, 'Children, work and family: some thoughts on "mother blame"', Berkeley Collection of Working and Occasional Papers, Working Paper 4 (1998), p. 1.

9 <https://workfamily.sas.upenn.edu/sites/workfamily.sas.upenn.edu/files/imported/new/berkeley/papers/4.pdf>, p. 4.

10 Bancroft, *Why Does He Do That?*, p. 25.

11 <http://womenandpolicing.com/violenceFS.asp#notes>.

12 Alexis Jay, *Independent Inquiry into Child Sexual Exploitation in Rotherham, 1997–2013* (Rotherham: Rotherham MBC, 2014).

13 Bancroft, *Why Does He Do That?*, p. 47.

14 Respect UK, *Evidence Base for Interventions with Domestic Violence Perpetrators* (London: Respect UK, 2015); <www.senedd.assembly.wales/documents/s30731/GBV%2090a%20-%20Respect.pdf>.

15 <www.telegraph.co.uk/news/uknews/law-and-order/6448201/Moves-to-stop-infidelity-as-defence-for-murder-defeated.html>.

16 <www.myspectrumsuite.com/meet-judy-singer/>.

17 <http://metro.co.uk/2017/09/12/piano-man-ends-bid-to-win-back-girlfriend-after-being-punched-in-the-head-6920857/>.

18 <www.washingtonpost.com/news/morning-mix/wp/2016/10/13/turkish-man-22-fatally-shoots-himself-on-facebook-live/?utm_term=.742a392967fc>.

19 <www.theguardian.com/uk-news/2017/feb/27/man-andrew-saunders-kills-ex-zoe-morgan-and-her-new-partner-after-looking-up-jail-terms-for-murder#img-1>.

20 <https://mrsglw.wordpress.com/2014/07/25/guest-blog-dr-kate-middleton-on-gender/>.

21 <www.oxfordbibliographies.com/view/document/obo-9780199756841/obo-9780199756841-0030.xml>.

22 <www.thoughtco.com/private-and-public-spheres-3026464>.

23 Stephanie Coontz, *Marriage, a History: How love conquered marriage* (New York: Penguin, 2005), p. 121.

24 <www.huffingtonpost.com/2014/03/08/countries-no-domestic-violence-law_n_4918784.html>.

25 <www.theguardian.com/world/2017/feb/07/putin-approves-change-to-law-decriminalising-domestic-violence>.

26 <www.sciencedaily.com/releases/2013/09/130919112709.htm>.

27 <www.manchestereveningnews.co.uk/news/greater-manchester-news/jilted-husband-jailed-life-after-12883990>.

28 <www.news.com.au/world/north-america/did-a-broken-heart-lead-colin-kingston-to-kill-two-people/news-story/688f10d82af5244d808
5f17762b1c3a6>.

29 <www.tampabay.com/news/publicsafety/crime/counselors-memorial-greet-students-and-staff-at-lakeland-school-rocked-by/
2314638>.

30 <www.telegraph.co.uk/news/2017/04/04/husband-stabbed-wife-death-discovered-having-affair-joiner-court/>.

31 <www.dailymail.co.uk/news/article-2563518/Husband-murdered-wife-told-leaving-start-relationship-waiter-Tunisia.html>.

32 <www.dailymail.co.uk/news/article-129800/Girls-frantic-999-father-kills-cheating-wife.html>.

33 <www.dailymail.co.uk/news/article-129800/Girls-frantic-999-father-kills-cheating-wife.html>.

34 Elaine Storkey, *Scars Across Humanity: Understanding and overcoming violence against women* (London: SPCK, 2015), pp. 156, 158, 159.

35 Storkey, *Scars Across Humanity*, pp. 160, 161, 167.

36 <https://namimc.org/untangling-gun-violence-mental-illness/>.

37 Bancroft, *Why Does He Do That?*, p. 75.

38 <https://theconversation.com/leopards-cant-change-their-spots-but-domestic-violence-programmes-do-change-lives-36157>.

39 <https://theconversation.com/leopards-cant-change-their-spots-but-domestic-violence-programmes-do-change-lives-36157>.

40 Sarah Grimké, 'On the equality of the sexes and the condition of woman' (letter, 1837), <www.worldculture.org/articles/12-Grimke%20
Letters,%201-3.pdf>.

4 WHAT IN THE WORLD IS GOING ON?

1 Marilyn French, *The War Against Women* (London: Ballantine, 1992), p. 18.

2 Speech, 'I want a twenty-four-hour truce during which there is no rape', 1983; <www.nostatusquo.com/ACLU/dworkin/WarZoneChaptIIIE.html>.

3 <www.theguardian.com/science/2015/may/14/early-men-women-equal-scientists>.

4 <www.theguardian.com/science/2015/may/14/early-men-women-equal-scientists>.

5 <news.bbc.co.uk/1/hi/world/africa/8107039.stm>.

6 <www.independent.co.uk/news/world/africa/crisis-in-south-africa-the-shocking-practice-of-corrective-rape-aimed-at-curing-lesbians-9033224.html>.

7 <https://rapecrisis.org.za/rape-in-south-africa/>.

8 <www.pri.org/interactive/2017/08/awl-hiv/>.

9 <www.independent.co.uk/news/world/africa/crisis-in-south-africa-the-shocking-practice-of-corrective-rape-aimed-at-curing-lesbians-9033224.html>.

10 <www.news24.com/SouthAfrica/News/Outcry-at-Xingwanas-Afrikaner-comments-20130227>.

11 <www.news24.com/SouthAfrica/News/Outcry-at-Xingwanas-Afrikaner-comments-20130227>.

12 Jostein Gaarder, *Sophie's World* (London: Dolphin Paperback, 1995), p. 107.

13 <www.un.org/en/women/endviolence/situation.shtml>.

14 <www.theatlantic.com/politics/archive/2016/10/trumps-black-voter-dilemma/505586/>.

15 <https://timeline.com/nell-mccafferty-ireland-b9b972ca2696>.

16 Scotland's Muirfield Golf Club only changed its position on this in 2017.

17 <http://news.bbc.co.uk/1/hi/uk/7244701.stm>.

18 <www.fawcettsociety.org.uk/close-gender-pay-gap>.

19 <https://rapecrisis.org.uk/statistics.php>.

20 <www.theguardian.com/world/2017/mar/09/women-bearing-86-of-austerity-burden-labour-research-reveals>.

21 <https://sjinsights.net/2014/09/29/new-research-sheds-light-on-daily-ad-exposures/>.

22 Cordelia Fine, *Delusions of Gender: The real science behind sex differences* (New York: W. W. Norton, 2010), pp. 236, 264.

23 Fine, *Delusions of Gender*, p. 159.

24 <www.ncbi.nlm.nih.gov/pubmed/19002678>.

25 Stan Goff, *Borderline: Reflections on war, sex and church* (Eugene, Oregon: Cascade Books, 2015), p. 31.

26 BBC, *No More Boys or Girls: Can our kids go gender free?*, July 2018.

27 <http://onlineslangdictionary.com/thesaurus/words+meaning+sex,+sexual+intercourse.html>.

28 <www.thecalmzone.net/help/get-help/suicide/>.

29 <www.aquinasonline.com/Questions/women.html>.

30 Elaine Storkey, *Scars Across Humanity: Understanding and overcoming violence against women* (London: SPCK, 2015), p. 205.

31 Storkey, *Scars Across Humanity*, p. 205.

32 Storkey, *Scars Across Humanity*, p. 205.

33 <www.telegraph.co.uk/news/earth/earthnews/3338519/Stupid-and-unimaginative...-the-curse-of-the-Brummie-accent.html>.

34 <www.washingtonpost.com/local/education/study-black-girls-viewed-as-less-innocent-than-white-girls/2017/06/27/3fbedc32-5ae1-11e7-a9f6-7c3296387341_story.html?utm_term=.8664a861d07c>.

35 Galatians 5.22–23.

36 1 Corinthians 5.12.

37 <www.cbeinternational.org/resources/article/mutuality/ancient-israel's-queen-hearts>.

38 Romans 16.7.

39 <https://juniaproject.com/who-was-junia/>.

40 <http://bidisha-online.blogspot.com/2011/12/do-you-like-women-today-today.html>.

41 This is a great cartoon exploring the reality of emotional labour: <www.theguardian.com/world/2017/may/26/gender-wars-household-chores-comic>.

42 <http://news.bbc.co.uk/1/hi/uk/7244701.stm>.

43 Riet Bons Storm, *The Incredible Woman: Listening to women's silences in pastoral care and counseling* (Nashville, Tennessee: Abingdon Press, 1996), p. 71.

44 Adrienne Rich, *Sources* (Woodside, California: Hayeck Press, 1983), quoted in Bons Storm, *The Incredible Woman*, p. 153.

5 WHAT WOULD JESUS DO?

1 <https://growrag.wordpress.com/2012/01/02/a-critique-of-the-what-would-jesus-do-society/>.

2 <www.affcrit.com/pdfs/1998/02/98_02_sd.pdf>.

3 Romans 3.23.

4 Carol L. Meyers, 'Gender roles and Genesis 3.16 revisited', in Athalya Brenner (ed.), *A Feminist Companion to Genesis* (Sheffield: Sheffield Academic Press, 1993), p. 130.

5 Romans 8.2.

6 Ephesians 6.12.

7 Walter Wink, *Engaging the Powers: Discernment and resistance in a world of domination* (Minneapolis: Fortress Press, 1992).

8 <www.gq.com/story/health-myth-does-the-average-man-really-think-about-sex-every-7-seconds>.

9 Dave Murrow, *Why Men Hate Going to Church* (Nashville, Tennessee: Thomas Nelson, 2005), p. 38.

10 Although the historical context of the text and the reception history of the text should be separated out; hopefully proper exegetes will forgive my lack of detail here.

11 Leviticus 11.12.

12 Matthew 20.25–30.

13 Philippians 2.5–8.

14 A good book to start with if you'd like to read more is Phyllis Trible, *Texts of Terror: Literary–feminist readings of biblical literature* (London: SCM Press, 1992).

15 Debi Pearl, *Created to Be His Help Meet: Discover how God can make your marriage glorious* (Pleasantville, Tennessee: No Greater Joy Ministries, 1994), cited in <www.challies.com/book-reviews/created-to-be-his-help-meet/>.

16 <http://academic.udayton.edu/michaelbarnes/E-Rel103/RG4-Trible.htm#N_9_>. Stan Goff notes that it's interesting that despite Thomas Aquinas's problematic views, he did agree to some degree with feminist biblical scholar Phyllis Trible; Stan Goff, *Borderline: Reflections on war, sex and church* (Eugene, Oregon: Cascade Books, 2015), p. 66.

17 Since 1792 the traditional view that Ephesians was written by the Apostle Paul has been questioned and scholars have concluded it was probably not written by him.

18 <http://margmowczko.com/lsj-definitions-of-kephale/>.

19 Elaine said this at an event we were both speaking at.

20 Matthew 6.14–15; Mark 11.26.

21 Psalm 51.7.

22 <www.bibleshark.com/bible/AMP/Luke/15/10/>.

23 Matthew 19.9.

24 Mark 10.11–12.

25 <www.instonebrewer.com/divorceremarriage/index.htm>.

26 <https://nogreaterjoy.org/articles/39260/>.

27 <www.opendoorsusa.org/christian-persecution/world-watch-list/>.

28 Matthew 4.1–11; Mark 1.12–13; Luke 4.1–3.

29 Matthew 4.6 and Psalm 91.11–12.

30 Matthew 4.7 and Deuteronomy 6.16.

31 Matthew 7.7.

32 John 14.14.

33 Mark 11.24.

34 Luke 18.1–18.

35 Luke 11.8.

36 1 Samuel 18—24.

37 Numbers 15.37–39.

38 1 Chronicles 10.4.

39 *Strong's Exhaustive Concordance*, quoted at <www.gotquestions.org/Shalom-meaning.html>.

40 John 4.1–42.

41 John 7.53—8.11.

42 Matthew 9.20–22; Mark 5.25–34; Luke 8.43–48.

43 Luke 10.38–42.

44 <www.biblestudytools.com/dictionary/apostle/>.

45 Walter Wink, *Engaging the Powers: Discernment and resistance in a world of domination* (Minneapolis: Fortress Press, 1992), Loc. 1737.

46 Luke 10.1.

47 Luke 8.3.

48 Hebrews 12.25–29.

49 Josephine Butler, 'Some Thoughts on the Present Aspect of the Crusade' (speech, 1874), <http://webapp1.dlib.indiana.edu/vwwp/view?docId= VAB7174>.

6 WHY DOESN'T SHE JUST LEAVE?

1 <www.independent.co.uk/life-style/love-sex/stealthing-man-take-off-condom-sex-no-consent-rape-sexual-assault-a7740611.html>.

2 <www.theguardian.com/lifeandstyle/2017/jan/16/removing-condom-without-permission-rape-swiss-court-definition-non-consensual-sex>.

3 Marsha Wood, Christine Barter and David Berridge, *'Standing on My Own Two Feet': Disadvantaged teenagers, intimate partner violence and coercive control* (London: NSPCC, 2011), p. 66.

4 Cynthia Hess and Alona Del Rosario, *Dreams Deferred: A survey on the impact of intimate partner violence on survivors' education, careers, and economic security* (Washington, DC: Institute for Women's Policy Research, 2018), p. 30.

5 <https://jezebel.com/philosopher-kate-manne-on-himpathy-donald-trump-and-r-1822639677>.

6 <www.fbi.gov/history/famous-cases/patty-hearst>.

7 <www.dailymail.co.uk/news/article-2320628/Inside-mind-kidnap-victim-How-Stockholm-Syndrome-leaves-scars-lifetime.html>.

8 <www.zoelodrick.co.uk/services/expert-testimony/sample-statement>.

9 <www.zoelodrick.co.uk/training/article-1>.

10 Zoe Lodrick, *Sexualized and Relational Trauma*, <https://docs.google.com/viewer?a=v&pid=sites&srcid=ZGVmYXVsdGRvbWFpbnx6b2V sb2RyaWNrNrfGd4OjE4MmYyN2ZjZTkyYWJlMA>, p. 19.

11 Zoe explained this at a conference we were both speaking at a few years ago.

12 This is the quinquelateral of filters through which we make theological conclusions: <www.lstonline.ac.uk/sites/default/files/MAITH_Prospectus.pdf>.

13 This is based on the work of Pat Craven, a social worker and probation officer who created the Freedom Programme for survivors of domestic abuse.

14 Calgary Women's Aid have created an excellent resource on honouring women's resistance, *Honouring Resistance: How women resist abuse in intimate relationships*: <www.calgarywomensshelter.com/images/pdf/cwes Resistancebookletfinalweb.pdf>.

15 <www.dashriskchecklist.co.uk/wp-content/uploads/2016/09/DASH-Practice-Guidance-2016.pdf>, p. 10.

16 <www.refuge.org.uk/our-work/forms-of-violence-and-abuse/domestic-violence/domestic-violence-the-facts/>.

17 Nicholas Wall, *A Report to the President of the Family Division on the Publication by the Women's Aid Federation of England Entitled Twenty-nine Child Homicides: Lessons Still to be Learnt on Domestic Violence and Child Protection with Particular Reference to the Five Cases in which There Was Judicial Involvement* (London: Judiciary UK, 2006).

18 <www.womensaid.org.uk/what-we-do/campaigning-and-influencing/campaign-with-us/sos/>.

7 LIFE CAN BE BEAUTIFUL

1 Emily Nagoski, *Come As You Are: The surprising new science that will transform your sex life* (New York: Simon and Schuster, 2015), p. 38.

2 Nagoski, *Come As You Are*, pp. 16–17.

3 <www.christianpost.com/news/churchtoo-women-share-stories-of-rape-sexual-abuse-leaving-church.html>.

4 Matthew 18.9.

5 <https://vimeo.com/222111805>.

6 Nagoski, *Come As You Are*, p. 277.

7 <www.newhealthadvisor.com/how-many-times-can-a-guy-come.html>.

8 This TED Talk from Jean Kilbourne is brilliant on this point: <https://youtu.be/Uy8yLaoWybk>.

9 <www.pornhub.com/insights/2016-year-in-review>.

10 Hentai is Japanese for 'pervert' and is a form of animated Japanese pornography. The characters often have exaggerated genitals and breasts.

11 This is an acronym for 'Mum I'd Like to Fuck'.

12 <www.pornhub.com/insights/2017-year-in-review>.

13 Legally the girl depicted will be over 18, even though she looks much younger.

14 Search took place on 19 December 2017.

15 <www.nspcc.org.uk/services-and-resources/research-and-resources/2016/i-wasnt-sure-it-was-normal-to-watch-it/>.

16 Moschino: <http://photos1.blogger.com/blogger/2485/1843/1600/moschino%20perfume.0.jpg>.

17 <http://bechdeltest.com>.

18 <www.indiewire.com/2016/12/top-movies-2016-passed-bechdel-test-bad-moms-ghostbusters-1201756648/>.

19 1 Kings 11.3.

20 Song of Solomon 4.5, 5.2.

21 Genesis 38, 19.32–35.

22 1 Corinthians 7.9, 7.5. It does also say the wife shouldn't deprive her husband, but I think this verse often misses that husbands shouldn't deprive their wives, so I thought I'd focus on that . . .

23 Genesis 16.2, 19, 20.2, 34; Numbers 31.15–18; Judges 19; 2 Samuel 11, 13.1–14; Isaiah 3.16–17; Jeremiah 13.22; Ezekiel 16, 23; Revelation 17.16.

24 Deuteronomy 22.25–29.

25 Judges 21.25.

26 A helpful analysis of this brutal passage is found in Phyllis Trible's book *Texts of Terror: Literary–feminist readings of biblical literature* (London: SCM Press, 1992).

27 <https://rapecrisis.org.uk/statistics.php>.

28 Stan Goff, *Borderline: Reflections on war, sex and church* (Eugene, Oregon: Cascade Books, 2015), p. 21.

29 Goff, *Borderline*, pp. 23–24.

30 <www.d.umn.edu/~bmork/2306/readings/scullyandmarollis.htm>.

31 It emerged that I was Craig's 18th sexual partner when he was 17 years old.

32 Stormie Omartian, *The Power of a Praying Wife* (Eugene, Oregon: Harvest House, 2014), p. 63.

33 <www.challies.com/book-reviews/created-to-be-his-help-meet/>.

34 <www.tandfonline.com/doi/full/10.1080/14753634.2013.778485>.

35 <www.tandfonline.com/doi/full/10.1080/14753634.2013.778485>.

36 <http://alfredadler.edu/sites/default/files/Tyree%20MP%202012. pdf>.

37 Erica Garza, *Getting Off: One woman's journey through sex and porn addiction* (New York: Simon and Schuster, 2018), p. 184.

38 Delores S. Williams, *Sisters in the Wilderness: The challenge of womanist God-talk* (Maryknoll, New York: Orbis Books, 1993), p. 65.

39 British Psychological Society, *The Power Threat Meaning Framework* (Leicester: BPS, 2018), p. 84.

40 <https://brenebrown.com/blog/2013/01/14/shame-v-guilt/>.

41 <http://makechurchsafe.com/2018/01/07/transcript-of-chris-conlee-and-andy-savage-live-statement-to-highpoint/>.

42 <http://watchkeep.blogspot.co.uk/2018/01/silent-no-more-survivor-of-sexual.html>.

43 <http://makechurchsafe.com/2018/01/07/transcript-of-chris-conlee-and-andy-savage-live-statement-to-highpoint/>.

44 <https://heleo.com/conversation-embrace-the-uncool-brene-brown-on-overcoming-shame/12402/>.

45 Rana Awdish, *In Shock: My journey from death to recovery and the redemptive power of hope* (New York: St Martin's Press, 2017), p. 169.

46 Sadly, Jill Saward died on 5 January 2017 at 52 years old. Her legacy lives on as we continue to fight for transformation in the treatment of women and girls in the judicial system.

47 <www.inbrief.co.uk/media-law/media-identification-of-suspects/>.

48 <www.rapecrisisscotland.org.uk/false-allegations/>.

49 <www.telegraph.co.uk/news/2016/09/05/violent-crimes-against-women-in-england-and-wales-rise-by-10-in/>.

50 <www.cps.gov.uk/sites/default/files/documents/publications/cps_vawg_report_2016.pdf>.

51 Marianne Williamson, *A Return to Love: Reflections on the principles of 'A Course in Miracles'* (New York: HarperCollins, 1992), Ch. 7, Section 3 (1992), p. 190.

8 WE DID THE BEST WE COULD

1 <www.nhs.uk/Conditions/pregnancy-and-baby/pages/domestic-abuse-pregnant.aspx>.

2 W. M. Harris, A. F. Lieberman and S. Marans, 'In the best interests of society', *Journal of Child Psychology and Psychiatry*, 48, 3/4 (2007), pp. 392–411.

3 <http://lundybancroft.com/articles/the-batterer-as-parent/>.

4 I have chosen unusual names to avoid them being familiar to anyone reading the book.

5 <www.theguardian.com/society/2017/jun/17/we-didnt-recognise-that-he-was-dangerous-our-father-killed-our-mother-and-sister>. You can read Luke and Ryan Hart's story in their book *Operation Lighthouse: Reflections on our family's devastating story of coercive control and domestic homicide* (London: Seven Dials, 2018).

6 <www.theguardian.com/society/2017/jun/17/we-didnt-recognise-that-he-was-dangerous-our-father-killed-our-mother-and-sister>.

7 <www.endingviolence.com/about/princips.php>.

8 <www.legislation.gov.uk/ukpga/1989/41/section/31>.

9 My dear friends Andy and Alice Smith paid the lovely Liz to teach me how to cook.

10 If you're in the USA, a duvet is known as a comforter.

11 Anne Steele, 'Dear Refuge of My Weary Soul' (hymn, 1791).

9 IT'S ALL IN YOUR HEAD

1 He tried to demonstrate that at death the human body becomes lighter, proving that the soul had left it.

2 <www.snopes.com/religion/soulweight.asp>.

3 Paula Gooder, *Body: Biblical spirituality for the whole person* (London: SPCK, 2016), p. 54.

4 C. S. Lewis, *Mere Christianity*, Kindle edition, loc. 933.

5 James 2.17.

6 <https://aeon.co/amp/essays/your-brain-does-not-process-information-and-it-is-not-a-computer?__twitter_impression=true>.

7 Although I am using a number of information processing analogies within this chapter, I recognize the flaws in this, as articulated here by Robert Epstein: <https://aeon.co/amp/essays/your-brain-does-not-process-information-and-it-is-not-a-computer>.

8 <www.zoelodrick.co.uk/training/article-1>.

9 This excellent video from Rape Crisis Scotland explains the nature of the Freeze response: <www.youtube.com/watch?v=O5h-N0N8DaY>.

10 Robert Scaer, *The Body Bears the Burden: Trauma, dissociation, and disease* (London: Taylor & Francis, 2001), p. 124.

11 <www.apa.org/monitor/2012/06/shell-shocked.aspx>.

12 Bessel van der Kolk, *The Body Keeps the Score: Mind, brain and body in the transformation of trauma* (London: Penguin, 2014), Kindle edition, loc. 176.

13 Judith Herman, *Trauma and Recovery: The aftermath of violence – from domestic abuse to political terror* (New York: Basic Books, 1992), p. 21.

14 Van der Kolk, *The Body Keeps the Score*, Kindle edition, loc. 333.

15 <www.ptsd.va.gov/professional/PTSD-overview/ptsd-overview.asp>.

16 <www.huffingtonpost.co.uk/entry/piers-morgan-lady-gaga-ptsd_us_58514b8de4b0e411bfd47582>.

17 <www.nhs.uk/conditions/post-traumatic-stress-disorder-ptsd/causes/>.

18 <www.dictionary.com/browse/disorder>.

19 <www.ptsd.ne.gov/what-is-ptsd.html>.

20 <www.mind.org.uk/information-support/types-of-mental-health-problems/post-traumatic-stress-disorder-ptsd/complex-ptsd/#.WkaUOSOcZmA>.

21 <www.cdc.gov/violenceprevention/acestudy/>.

22 Van der Kolk, *The Body Keeps the Score*, loc. 2596.

23 Van der Kolk, *The Body Keeps the Score*, loc. 907.

24 Van der Kolk, *The Body Keeps the Score*, loc. 3627.

25 Van der Kolk, *The Body Keeps the Score*, loc. 1185.

26 Van der Kolk, *The Body Keeps the Score*, loc. 1232.

27 Van der Kolk, *The Body Keeps the Score*, loc. 843.

28 Van der Kolk, *The Body Keeps the Score*, loc. 826.

29 Van der Kolk, *The Body Keeps the Score*, loc. 800.

30 Van der Kolk, *The Body Keeps the Score*, loc. 3938.

31 Van der Kolk, *The Body Keeps the Score*, loc. 1244.

32 Van der Kolk, *The Body Keeps the Score*, loc. 1789.
33 Van der Kolk, *The Body Keeps the Score*, loc. 4553.
34 <https://traumahealing.org/about-us/>.
35 <http://bethelsozo.com>.
36 Check out their website: <http://rightuseofpower.org>.
37 Thank you to the youth counsellor in Newcastle, Tina Holland, SERICC and Lynne Ford. You have helped me immensely!
38 Herman, *Trauma and Recovery*, p. 13.
39 Herman, *Trauma and Recovery*, p. 14.
40 Bons-Storm, *The Incredible Woman*, p. 76.
41 Emily Nagoski, *Come As You Are: The surprising new science that will transform your sex life* (New York: Simon and Schuster, 2015), Kindle edition, loc. 5411.

10 HELP! I DON'T KNOW HOW TO HELP

1 Debra Parkinson, *Raped by a Partner: A research report* (Victoria, Australia: Women's Health Goulburn North East, 2000), p. 50.
2 Parkinson, *Raped by a Partner*, p. 50.
3 <www.mdpi.com/2076-0760/6/3/71/htm>.
4 Luke 6.45.
5 Sylvia Walby, *The Cost of Domestic Violence: Update 2009* (Lancaster: Lancaster University, 2009), p. 9.
6 This description of Jesus comes from a children's hymn by Charles Wesley. While it may be a helpful hymn for children, it's perhaps not something to base adult faith on.
7 Matthew 9.10–12, 12.1–7, 16.1–12; Mark 7.1–16, 12.18–27; Luke 5.30–32, 20; John 5.10–18.
8 James 1.27.
9 A helpful website for learning more about this is <www.compassion fatigue.org>.
10 This concept comes from Joan Laird, 'Women and stories: re-storying women's self-constructions' (1991), cited in Riet Bons-Storm, *The Incredible Woman: Listening to women's silences in pastoral care and counseling* (Nashville, Tennessee: Abingdon Press, 1996), p. 57.

11 Bons-Storm, *The Incredible Woman*, p. 57.

12 <http://criminologyinpublic.blogspot.co.uk/2014/03/how-many-times-women-assaulted-before.html>.

13 Safelives, *Getting It Right First Time* (Bristol: Safelives, 2015), p. 18.

14 The Church of England, *Responding Well to Domestic Abuse: Policy and practice guidelines* (Canterbury: Church House Publishing, 2017), p. 11.

15 <www.reducingtherisk.org.uk/cms/content/identifying-risk-indicators>.

16 My husband Baggy is 13 years older than me, so please don't think I am stating that all age gaps are wrong in a relationship, merely that a significant age gap between an abuser and his partner is an indicator of increased risk.

17 Lundy Bancroft, *Why Does He Do That? Inside the minds of angry and controlling men* (New York: Berkley Publishing Group, 2002), p. 372.

18 All churches should have clear safeguarding procedures. If they don't, you can contact <www.ccpas.co.uk> for further guidance.

19 The NSPCC helpline is 0808 800 5000.

20 Liz Kelly, Nicola Sharp and Renata Klein, *Finding the Costs of Freedom: How women and children rebuild their lives after domestic violence* (London: Child and Woman Abuse Studies Unit and Solace Women's Aid, 2015), p. 4.

21 Scottish Women's Aid, Women's Aid Federation Northern Ireland and Welsh Women's Aid.

22 For further details on injunctions, see Appendix 3.

23 <www.theguardian.com/money/2008/apr/23/charitablegiving.childprotection>.

24 The Respect phoneline is 0808 802 4040.

25 <www.respect.uk.net>.

26 Cynthia Go, 'Forest Fire', <http://cynthiatingo.com/2016/11/06/forest-fire/>, used with permission.

11 THERE IS NO CHRYSALIS SEASON

1 Christine Barter, Melanie McCarry, David Berridge and Kathy Evans, *Partner Exploitation and Violence in Teenage Intimate Relationships* (London: NSPCC, 2009), p. 64.

2 1 Corinthians 6.19.

3 Thomas W. Phelan, *1–2–3 Magic: Effective Discipline for Children 2–12* (Naperville, Illinois: Sourcebooks, 2016), p. 19.

4 Phelan, *1–2–3 Magic*, p. 17.

5 <http://uk.businessinsider.com/facebook-google-information-nsa-iphone-android-data-personal-2016-2>.

6 <www.psychologytoday.com/blog/raising-grieving-children/200903/being-honest-children>.

7 <http://nottinghamshirechildcare.proceduresonline.com/chapters/p_life_story_prep.html#why_life_imp>.

8 <www.urmc.rochester.edu/encyclopedia/content.aspx?ContentTypeI D=1&ContentID=3051>.

9 <www.theguardian.com/lifeandstyle/2015/jan/25/secrets-of-the-teenage-brain>.

10 Daniel Romer, 'Adolescent risk taking, impulsivity and brain development: implications for prevention', *Developmental Psychobiology* 52, 3 (2010): 263–76.

11 <www.theguardian.com/culture/2014/mar/20/youth-subcultures-where-have-they-gone>.

12 <www.independent.co.uk/life-style/health-and-families/health-news/bigorexia-what-is-muscle-dysmorphia-and-how-many-people-does-it-affect-10511964.html>.

13 Elena Martellozzo, Andy Monaghan, Joanna R. Adler, Julia Davidson, Rodolfo Leyva and Miranda A. H. Horvath, *I Wasn't Sure It Was Normal to Watch It* (London: NSPCC, 2016).

14 <www.bbc.co.uk/news/health-40410459>.

15 <www.telegraph.co.uk/news/2016/09/29/one-in-four-young-women-suffering-from-mental-health-problems-as/amp/>.

16 <https://amp.theguardian.com/commentisfree/2017/sep/29/young-women-poverty-mental-health-pay-jobs-debt>.

17 Marsha Wood, Christine Barter and David Berridge, *'Standing on My Own Two Feet': Disadvantaged teenagers, intimate partner violence and coercive control* (London: NSPCC, 2011).

18 <www.buzzfeed.com/hannahalothman/women-under-25-account-for-more-than-half-of-all-female-sex?utm_term=.pyO3Rk9Dw#.qgYmwzV5p>.

19 The helpline is 0808 802 4040.

20 Justin and Lindsey Holcomb, *God Made All of Me: A book to help children protect their bodies* (Greensboro, North Carolina: New Growth Press, 2015).

21 You can access it at <www.dayprogramme.org/creepynakedstuff. htm>.

22 <https://vitalpiety.com/2010/09/06/wesley-didnt-say-it-set-myself-on-fire-watch-me-burn/>.

23 Professor Sylvia Walby, *The Cost of Domestic Violence* (London: Women and Equality Unit, DTI, 2004), <http://www.leeds.ac.uk/sociology/people/swdocs/researchsummarycosstdomesticviolence.pdf>.

24 Robert Jensen, in Shira Tarrant (ed.), *Men Speak Out: Views on gender, sex, and power* (Abingdon: Routledge, 2013), p. 79.

25 <www.theguardian.com/books/2014/oct/17/chimamanda-ngozi-adichie-extract-we-should-all-be-feminists>; Chimamanda Ngozi Adichie, *We Should All Be Feminists* (London: Fourth Estate, 2014).

26 <www.hartford-hwp.com/archives/41/335.html>.

27 Alice Walker, *The Temple of My Familiar* (New York: Weidenfeld & Nicolson, 2004), p. 162.

12 WHAT DOES FREEDOM LOOK LIKE?

1 2 Corinthians 3.17.

2 <http://victimsofcrime.org/docs/default-source/src/stalking-fact-sheet-2015_eng.pdf?status=Temp&sfvrsn=0.994206007104367>.

3 <www.bbc.co.uk/news/uk-38226264>.

4 <https://paladinservice.co.uk/key-facts-and-figures/>.

5 <www.apa.org/monitor/jun02/writing.aspx>.

6 <www.theguardian.com/lifeandstyle/2014/oct/03/morning-pages-change-your-life-oliver-burkeman>.

7 The psychological name for this is 'post-traumatic growth'.

8 Kamini Roy, 'Thakurmar Chithi', <https://feminisminindia.com/2017/07/07/kamini-roy-essay/>.

13 DO REAL MEN HIT WOMEN?

1 <www.firstmanstanding.com/about/>. I worked with Restored for four years, helping to set it up and as part of the team that launched First Man Standing.

2 Michael Salter, '"Real men don't hit women": constructing masculinity in the prevention of violence against women', *Australian and New Zealand Journal of Criminology* 49, 4 (2016): 463–79.

3 Joseph Gelfer, *The Masculinity Conspiracy* (London: Createspace, 2011), p. 133.

4 <www.amazon.co.uk/Am-Sleeping-Enemy-Males-Females-ebook/dp/B005S5IJ8M/ref=sr_1_1?ie=UTF8&qid=1539800520&sr=8-1&keywords=ron+clark+am+i+sleeping+with+the+enemy>.

5 Gelfer, *The Masculinity Conspiracy*, p. 44.

6 This is 14- and 15-year-olds (fourth year in old money).

7 <http://matthewpaulturner.com/2014/07/29/mark-driscolls-pussified-nation/>.

8 David Murrow, *Why Men Hate Going to Church* (Nashville, Tennessee: Thomas Nelson, 2005), pp. 39, 38.

9 Murrow, *Why Men Hate Going to Church,* p. 164.

10 Gelfer, *The Masculinity Conspiracy*, p. 123.

11 Stan Goff, *Borderline: Reflections on war, sex and church* (Eugene, Oregon: Cascade Books, 2015), Kindle edition loc. 221.

12 <www.desiringgod.org/articles/women-teaching-men-how-far-is-too-far>.

13 US celebrity Christian Mark Driscoll has stated that stay-at-home dads should be disciplined by their church; <http://marccortez.com/2010/10/28/stay-at-home-dads-should-be-disciplined-by-the-church/>.

14 1 Corinthians 11.11–12.

15 This comes from the work of Sue Penna, a psychotherapist specializing in trauma and recovery from abuse.

16 Gelfer, *The Masculine Conspiracy*, p. 116.

17 Galatians 3.28.

18 Galatians 5.22–23.

19 Matthew 19.22.

20 Romans 6.6–7.

21 Luke 9.23.

22 John 16.33.

14 CAN WE END DOMESTIC ABUSE?

1 <https://oasisaquilahousing.org>.
2 <www.home-start.org.uk>.
3 <www.restoredrelationships.org>.
4 <www.project328.info>.
5 <www.speaker328.info>.
6 <www.christianfeministnetwork.com>.
7 Dear Jo and Cath Planet, I'm talking about you!
8 <www.preachweb.org/sermon-of-the-year/>.
9 <https://lst.ac.uk>.
10 <www.youtube.com/watch?v=-LGHtc_D328>; <www.emmytv legends.org/interviews/people/fred-rogers>.
11 Luke 4.18–19.
12 <www.itv.com/news/granada/update/2017-12-12/the-frightening-truth-about-child-poverty-in-working-families/>.
13 <www.independent.co.uk/news/business/news/world-richest-welath-increase-1-trillion-2017-economy-success-business-shares-a8129576.html>.
14 <www.newstatesman.com/politics/uk/2018/01/commons-confidential-miserly-mr-davis>.
15 Revelation 21.3–4.
16 Luke 1.46–53.

Index